ADVANCE PRAISE FOR "THE NEW YO SCIENCE AND TECHNOLOGY"

"This book is so smart and such an illuminating look at how to do good science writing that I cannot wait to use it in the classroom. It's really the perfect combination: work by some of the best science journalists in the world analyzed by one of the most respected experts in the field of science communication. There are how-to tips here, there's useful background on putting stories together, and there's the pleasure of reading some gloriously good writing. I wish the book had been available earlier—we need more good tools in teaching science writing—but I'm delighted to find it now."

—Deborah Blum, Helen Firstbrook Franklin Professor of
Journalism, University of Wisconsin, and Co-editor of
"A Field Guide for Science Writers"

"Economic restructuring and the failure of the traditional business model to transfer to the world of the Web have taken their toll on journalism, especially on science writing, which seems suddenly defined as an expendable luxury rather than a vital dimension of news in our postmodern, postindustrial society. This collection—created by one of the most thoughtful and insightful journalism academics around—reminds us of what we stand to lose if we lose track of the importance of connecting science to society."

—Susanna Hornig Priest, Professor of Journalism and
Media Studies, University of Nevada, Las Vegas, and
Editor, "Science Communication"

"There is only one problem with this book: You and your students might have trouble putting it down. We have needed a book like this for a long time. The stories Holly Stocking has selected are wonderfully written and will enrich and inform courses on science writing, science journalism and feature writing."

—Katherine Rowan, Professor of
Communication, George Mason University

"Master journalism professor and media scholar Holly Stocking has given to readers, would-be science writers, and even the most accomplished science communicators an invaluable primer on how to tell the most consequential stories of our times. She does so in a book that is simultaneously an ode to the scientific way of knowing, revealing, thinking and engaging the world."

—Ivan Amato, Author of "Super Vision: A New View of Nature"

"Holly Stocking has compiled a practical, entertaining volume for teachers and students of science journalism. Her comments on the well-chosen articles will help new writers enrich their stories for readers who, more than ever, need informed reporters. Throughout, Stocking and her interview subjects also convey the challenges and deep rewards of our profession."

—Robert Irion, Director, Science Communication
Program, University of California, Santa Cruz

The New York Times Reader

science
AND
technology

S. Holly Stocking
and the Writers of
The New York Times

CQ PRESS

A Division of SAGE
Washington, D.C.

CQ Press
2300 N Street, NW, Suite 800
Washington, DC 20037

Phone: 202-729-1900; toll-free, 1-866-4CQ-PRESS (1-866-427-7737)

Web: www.cqpress.com

Cover design: Matthew Simmons, www.myselfincluded.com
Cover photo: ©iStockphoto.com/Rafael Pacheco
Composition: C&M Digitals (P) Ltd.

⊚ The paper used in this publication exceeds the requirements of the
American National Standard for Information Sciences—Permanence of
Paper for Printed Library Materials, ANSI Z39.48-1992.

Printed and bound in the United States of America

14   13   12   11   10   1   2   3   4   5

Library of Congress Cataloging-in-Publication Data

The New York Times reader : science and technology / written and edited
by S. Holly Stocking and the writers of The New York Times.
    p. cm.
Includes bibliographical references.
ISBN 978-1-60426-481-4 (pbk. : alk. paper)
   1. Journalism, Scientific. 2. Science news. I. Stocking, S. Holly.
II. New York times. III. Title.

PN4784.T3N48 2010
070.4'495—dc22

                                                            2010002819

For all who seek to tell
the tales of science
. . . and for all who stand to benefit.

about S. Holly Stocking

Carol Posgrove

S. Holly Stocking taught science writing at Indiana University for more than two decades until her retirement in 2009. Before earning her PhD in mass communications, she worked as a staff writer for the Minneapolis Tribune, the Los Angeles Times, and the Associated Press, and as a science writer for the Boys Town Center for the Study of Youth Development. As an educator, she won numerous teaching awards at her university, and in 2007 she was named a fellow of the American Association for the Advancement of Science (AAAS) for outstanding teaching in science writing and journalism ethics, influential research on media coverage of scientific ignorance and uncertainty, and work that has enhanced the scientist/journalist interaction and the public's understanding of science-related issues.

contents

foreword

LAURA CHANG

science editor

© The New York Times

SOME YEARS AGO I FOUND MYSELF on a pre-med track at the University of Washington, staring at solvents for hours on end and doing my best to find the humor in organic chemistry. Then it sunk in that I didn't really want to live any of the possible lives I was preparing for. I hated being stuck in the lab. Nor did I wish to be stuck in the field: the prospect of 40 years' work on, say, schistosomiasis, made my skin itch. As for becoming a doctor, which is what my hardworking parents must have hoped, I simply didn't have the stomach for it.

Next thing I knew, I was a communications major with a sideline in psychology, and then a copyediting intern at The San Diego Tribune. It all felt so natural that it was as if journalism had chosen me, instead of the other way 'round.

The funny thing was that the farther my days as a science major receded, the greater my fascination with the sciences became—sort of the way the "strong force" binds quarks. I tried to read anything aimed at science amateurs: Lewis Thomas's "Lives of a Cell," David Quammen on barnacles and other neat creatures, Isaac Asimov's fiction and non-, Omni magazine, Scientific American and, of course, the Science Times section in The New York Times. When, after many wayward orbits, I landed in the Science Department of The Times, it seemed both improbable and inevitable.

This is about the most I can offer in response to the question that students, writers and scientists ask me more than any other: How did you get into science journalism?

The answer to the broader question—how does anyone get into science journalism—can be summed up in three words: every which way.

The reporters whose work lights up these pages come from backgrounds in biology, physics and chaos theory, but also English, architecture and law. Some dreamed of being science writers from an early age; others did a backflip into the field. What they all have in common is the essential formula for success: infinite curiosity and a love of good writing.

If your own interest in science writing has brought you this far, then you will know that these men and women are not only uncommonly talented, but also lucky to be thriving in a sadly diminished newspaper job market. So if your goal is a science reporting slot at a big newspaper, keep in mind, as the prescription-drug ads say in the fine print, that your results may vary.

But sure as nature abhors a vacuum, new forms and venues for science writing arise weekly. And just as you don't need a particular background to learn science writing, you needn't be bound for a career in journalism to benefit from absorbing the principles and techniques of the trade. Beyond providing a uniquely practical guide for journalism students, Holly Stocking's collection of articles exemplifies values of straight thinking and creative expression that would serve any writer well.

Of course, it's the challenge of explaining science that helps to bring out the creativity: genetic riddles that multiply, interlocking forces affecting climate change, spaces so vast and bits of matter so small that most minds can only begin to grasp them indirectly, through metaphor and something akin to poetry.

Politics or finance, for all their importance and complexity as beats, seldom test the writer's powers of description in quite this way. Science also offers more chances to mix factual reporting with pure fun. This book includes talk of teleportation, brain-controlled prosthetics, manatees and life beyond Earth.

So you see that good science writing can be a legitimate form of entertainment. But if there were nothing more to it than that, most science reporters around here would go plug their brains into some other line of work.

They would blush to be described as people who have a calling or a mission. But they are deeply aware of a responsibility to bridge a worrisome gap—between science, on the one side, with its ever-growing power to change the world for better or worse, and a distracted public that may be, in general, only vaguely aware that science is at the heart of virtually every issue facing modern society.

A big part of their job is to make science comprehensible to the public. At least equally important is to hold science accountable to that public. This is because science is not done by something called "science," but rather by human beings, universities, corporations and governments. In other words, it isn't immune to the egomania, arrogance, greed and incompetence that are intrinsic to life in the real world. If for no other reason, we keep a close eye on this enterprise because our money is usually involved—it's our tax dollars at work.

This line of thought leads to places beyond the scope of this book. It's important to understand that science reporting as a profession is evolving, becoming more integral to "mainstream" issues in response to the pervasive influence of science in politics, business, international relations, the environment and public health.

This means we will have to be fluent in areas outside the traditional specialties. At The Times, for example, science staffers have become intimately involved in covering cyber warfare and nuclear proliferation, as breaking-news reporters of Page 1 stories as well as analysts.

I believe this is a positive trend, both for people grounded in science and for the quality of news coverage in general. In addition to their love for science and good writing, science writers tend to approach their work with something much healthier than hard-boiled cynicism: a point of view that manages to combine idealism about the possibilities of progress with a dispassionate skepticism toward the motives and methods of those who claim to have made the next great step forward.

No less a master than my colleague Dennis Overbye, who has seen the best and worst of it, strongly believes in a "historic connection between science and democracy," as the potential of both depends ultimately on the same values, including respect for evidence and the free flow of information. I can think of nothing more professionally rewarding than helping to keep that great idea alive.

preface

The best writers, it is said, are good readers.

Most teachers of writing believe this. So we try to give our students plenty to read even as we're giving them their own assignments to write. But it can be a daunting task to find model science stories that inspire students without intimidating them. Existing anthologies of science writing contain the kind of long and often elegant stories that our students aspire to write *one* day, but few of the kinds of stories that can help them learn to write *today*. None contain discovery stories, meeting covers, narrative interviews, Q&As, reviews or many other conventional stories of the sort most of us actually assign to our students.

This collection of science writing from The New York Times does. It does not ignore the kinds of long, insightful pieces that entice students in other anthologies and inspire them to aim high. Indeed, many of the stories here pass the "linger" test that one editor used in selecting pieces for one volume in the "Best American Science Writing" series.[1] But it was not flashiness or even the quality of the writing that led to the selection of these stories so much as it was what they reveal about matters important for aspiring science writers to learn—the elements that belong in discovery stories or trend and issue features, for example, or the various techniques of explaining science. In the end, the collection emphasizes news stories, features and commentary that students are likely to believe they can emulate. As such, it is a reader that should be of immediate help to our students as they work to transform themselves into writers.

SCOPE

The scientific disciplines that these stories cover include everything from astronomy and physics to environmental science, medical science, evolutionary biology, neuroscience, sociology and psychology—disciplines as diverse as the interests of students who usually sign up for a course in science writing. Technology stories are in the volume, too, though they are not pieces about computers, GPS systems and other gizmos regularly covered and reviewed by business or technology writers. Rather, they are about technology as science writers encounter it in their work—in scientific studies of people's uses of cellphones, for example, or in research on the functioning of artificial limbs, or in unmanned space probes, in vitro fertilization and genetic testing.

No anthology of science and technology stories can include every kind of story that might be written about these fascinating subjects. So not surprisingly, there are absences in this collection. It does not include break-ing news that erupts outside of the routines of monitoring scientific journals and meetings—for example, news of oil spills, volcanic eruptions or a politi-cian's diagnosis of cancer. This is because the more predictable stories offer more manageable opportunities to discuss the finer points of science writing. In addition, there are no investigative pieces, business-and-science stories or stories that dissect the politics and economics of science (as important as they are), because much of what is required to report these stories can be taught in other classes. Health columns containing "news you can use" are also missing, as they are in a companion volume on health and medical reporting.

But, all in all, these are models students can analyze and learn from.

ORGANIZATION

The collection is organized into three parts: News, Features and Commen-tary. The boundaries between these categories have blurred in recent years, with more and more news infused with the elements of both features and commentaries. Still, these categories continue to appear on working maps of the journalistic world, so I've used them, too, in the hopes that they will help students navigate from one end of the vast terrain of science writing to the other.

Each story is preceded by a *headnote,* or abstract, which highlights mat-ters of reporting, writing and multimedia extras that are worth your students' notice. In addition, several other features have been added to assist students to read analytically and glean from these stories concepts and techniques that will help their own work.

So You Want to Write? Then Read!

A brief essay at the front of the book introduces students to the importance of reading a lot and well and shows them some of the most general things to look for when evaluating their own or others' work: story focus, information, organization, writing and editing.[2]

Annotated Stories

Four stories in the collection are annotated. They highlight elements that belong in discovery stories, explanatory techniques that can help the public to better understand science and elements to consider when writing trend or issue stories and reviews. These pieces appear under the name "StoryScan," a name chosen to suggest the kind of reading that, like a medical scan, reveals the inner workings of a piece.

Making Connections

Following most selections are study questions for students to think about ("Consider This") and various reporting, writing and editing tasks to try ("Try This").

Read Like a Writer: Checklist for Discovery Stories

The first chapter also contains a checklist of elements students would do well to consider when writing discovery stories, which are all too easy to do poorly. In addition, this reader includes the following:

Conversations With Writers

Original interviews with writers whose work appears in the collection—Natalie Angier, Denise Grady, Amy Harmon, Dennis Overbye and Andrew Revkin—are interspersed throughout the book. Not all of these individuals (or others in the volume, for that matter) call themselves "science writers." Harmon writes for the national desk, for example, and until December 2009 Revkin wrote news and features stories for the environment desk, where the concerns range well beyond the science beat. However, each writes frequently about science and technology and offers inspiration and advice to those who aspire to do the same.

Suggested Resources

At the back of the book is an annotated list of suggested resources for science writers. The list includes Times stories on science hype, peer review, research methods, risk and other issues of interest to science writers; an online site where you can find discussions between Times staffers and their readers; associations for science writing professionals; and a few books and articles on science writing by science writing professionals and academics.

Online Access to Multimedia Features and Additional Stories

In addition to these features of the print collection, a special Web site has been established to provide links to interactive graphics and other multimedia efforts that accompanied the online versions of the stories in this reader. That Web site—college.cqpress.com/nytimes—also offers an annotated list of additional stories that could easily have been included in this reader had there been the space. An effort has been made to ensure that many of these extra stories provide added instructional value. There are stories about risk, for example. In addition, two stories discuss the implications of animal research for humans, and one problematic profile (written for The New York Times Magazine) is of a scientist who, while not an expert on global warming, blasts the science.

Tips for Using This in Your Course

There are many ways to use this book. But it's probably a good idea to begin, as the book does, with discovery stories.

Part I: News

Before students even write a word, the short discovery stories or briefs at the start of Chapter 1 can be used as prompts for an accompanying exercise in news selection. The exercise itself can help launch discussions of what counts as newsworthy in science and what counts as credible science, two aspects of science writing that often are in tension.

The longer discovery stories that follow can be used to initiate discussions of the basics of science writing. Good science writing professionals know that if you want the public to understand cutting-edge science as something other than the accepted "facts" in textbooks, there are certain elements that belong in science news. These include (but are not limited to) information about context, methods and caveats. Longer discovery stories offer some of the easiest ways to convey these points. The concluding conversation with Times writer Denise Grady, who has worked not only as a science writer but also as an editor at a medical journal, offers invaluable insights into the challenges associated with writing these pieces.[3]

Meeting stories, which are offered in Chapter 2, can be introduced at any time, depending on when a scientific conference or symposium is scheduled to meet on your campus. It's useful to send students to such gatherings, if only because meetings are an important part of scientific culture and offer hunting grounds not just for news but for less time-sensitive features. It's important to notice that while these stories are in the News section of this collection, they often appear a few days after the meeting has ended and contain many elements of less time-bound feature stories.

Part II: Features

The stories in Chapter 3 ("Explanatory Features") are especially good to present early on, as they will move students to think about definitions, comparisons, visuals and other explanatory tools that are good no matter what kind of science story they produce. The conversation with Times writer Natalie Angier will be particularly useful to students seeking guidance and inspiration for explaining science in ways that both engage and inform.

A good first *feature* to assign is a Q&A with a newsworthy scientist (see Chapter 4). This will give students a chance to do background research on a scientist, come up with interview questions and a meaningful order for those questions and conduct an interview. The actual writing of these pieces is fairly straightforward, with fewer things to think about than with full-blown features, though students are likely to have questions about how to edit the stories (without ellipses, and informing readers that they've been edited for length and flow).[4] A conversation with Dennis Overbye, which concludes this chapter, talks about his love of physics writing, but also offers some useful tips for interviewing experts, especially if one feels unfamiliar with a subject.

Narrative interviews with scientists in the field are slightly more complex, for they require students to attend not only to what scientists are saying, but also to what they are doing, making them one step more ambitious. But they too can make good first feature assignments. Traditional profiles and trend and issue stories, which usually are even more ambitious in terms of reporting and organization, can come next, and for the really ambitious and more experienced, extended narratives.

An excerpt from one story, a long piece on toxic shock, is included in the chapter on extended narratives as an exercise in editing for the Web. Written for The New York Times Magazine before the Age of the Internet, this Pulitzer Prize–winning story contains lots of information that today would be edited out and put on the Web as online sidebars. If students read it after they have had a chance to examine and discuss online options for other stories, including those by writer Amy Harmon in the same chapter, they ought to immediately see ways to streamline the narrative and create their own sidebars, including multimedia possibilities. The conversation with Harmon at the end of this chapter reveals her as a technologically savvy member of the younger generation, who nevertheless appreciates a genre many associate with writers many decades her senior.

Part III: Commentary

A terrific way to wind up the course is with a review of a book by a professional science writer. It will not only give students a little more education in science, it will also plant the seed for book-length forms of science writing. After many weeks of hewing to traditional forms in which the writer takes a back seat to sources and subjects, students should also find it a welcome change to air some of their own thoughts and opinions.[5] A review of a recent book on decision making provides a great model for what to include and how to order a review that is primarily positive. The two additional reviews, both shorter, offer models for reviews that are more critical. If you don't like the idea of a review, ask students to write an editorial, op-ed piece or blog about a subject they've reported on earlier. Freelancers often have to revisit their reporting to produce different kinds of pieces, and this is one way to practice that skill. Personal essays are simply a nice change of pace for those students who have something to say. A conversation with writer Andy Revkin in the final chapter talks about the challenges of reporting on the environment, and offers insights into the unique value of blogging for covering this complex topic.

ACKNOWLEDGMENTS

This collection would not have come together without the kind assistance of several Times science writers, editors and staff, including Laura Chang, science editor of The Times; deputy science editor James Gorman; and Times writers Natalie Angier, Cornelia Dean, Claudia Dreifus, Denise Grady, Amy Harmon, Dennis Overbye and Andy Revkin. Each took time out of a hectic schedule to explain The Times's ways of doing things, offer suggestions and feedback or talk about science writing for future generations. Alex Ward, too, helped greatly, a patient go-between in the delicate stages of bringing this book to fruition.

Independent journalists also helped, including science blogger Bora Zivkovic, who at the last minute helped me track down information on science bloggers and an annual conference about science on the Web.

Nor could this reader have come together without the staff of CQ Press, a company that works hard to do the right thing. CQ Press is one of those rare publishing houses that still hires development editors, immensely talented ones like Aron Keesbury and Jane Harrigan, who know how to elevate both the prose and the spirits of writers like me. To Charisse Kiino, who hired these two—along with Christina Mueller, who oversaw every phase; Judy Myers, who created the book's design; Allyson Rudolph, who managed production; Talia Greenberg and Sarah Bright, who edited and proofed the manuscript before it went to press; and the marketing department's Erin Snow, who worked to get the book into the right hands—thank you, thank you. Finally, to Jane, who as development editor sweated the longest and hardest and recommended changes that made this an infinitely better book for teaching: I bow before you. You are the best.

I am also indebted to the School of Journalism and the Women in Science Program of Indiana University–Bloomington for much-needed funding and staff support, to Indiana University librarians Sarah Mitchell and Roger Beckman for help gathering needed statistics and reference information and to Jennifer Bass of the Kinsey Institute at Indiana University for story suggestions. Journalism educators David Boeyink, Sharon Dunwoody, Bruce Lewenstein, Kathy Rowan and JoAnn Valenti, and fellow New York Times Reader editors Tom Linden and Don McLeese also offered helpful information, ideas or suggestions along the way.

I am grateful, too, to former Indiana University science writing students Jennifer Akst, Leigh Krietsch Boerner, Sarah Schrock and Lauren Younis. They helped me sort stories and offered opinions on the graphics for the series Web site, and when I grew overwhelmed with printouts and decisions, they jumped in to assist and kept me going. I never forgot that it was for them, and for other eager and talented students like them, that I was doing this. They were—and continue to be—an inspiration.

Finally, I want to say a special "thank you" to Bill Timberlake for his many acts of kindness throughout our 30-year marriage, including too many times during this project when I stayed up into the wee hours of the morning. And I want to express deep gratitude to my teachers, who never let me lose sight of why I am here.

I have done my best to honor you all.

introduction

To New York Times science writer Natalie Angier, science is "good news for the forebrain." If you listen to all the bad news in the media, she says, you can get pretty glum. "It's the human race getting things wrong," she explains. But with science, "It's the human race getting things right."

That is one reason Angier, winner of the Pulitzer Prize, loves what she does. Put simply, science gives her hope for the future.

THE ATTRACTION OF SCIENCE WRITING

Not every science writer is going to take this kind of personal sustenance from science. However, all are hooked on some aspect of this enterprise—the way it sorts truth from superstition or explores and reveals realities that would be impossible to fathom using our ordinary senses. Or the way it shakes up our understandings of the world and our place in it and launches treatments and technologies that extend our comfort and reach in ways that would have astounded our ancestors. Not that science is stainless. It has its dark and troubling sides. But few science writers are likely to argue with the statement that science is one of the most powerful ways of knowing ever devised.

Not only are most science writers hooked on science, but most are hooked, too, on writing, and they have been, many for as long as they can remember. Still, it's not unusual for many professionals in the field to have felt a little adrift while in college—part science geek, part creative writer, without the drive to make careers in either lab or loft. It was only on discovering science writing that they realized they'd suddenly, irrevocably come "home." Science writing offered a way to unite these sometimes warring aspects of themselves. It was a way to use their writing skills to capture a subject that invigorated them, but that in science textbooks, and the minds of those who read them, too often appeared as dull, lifeless facts.

Nor is it unheard of for journalists with broader interests to have stumbled into science writing, only to wind up smitten. Cornelia Dean, for example, got into the field only after someone saw her carrying a copy of Scientific American in The Times newsroom. Apparently on the strength of that, her editors shifted her to the science desk. Dean had a degree in American Civilization and no training in science beyond high school, but she loved the work and went on to become science editor, a position she held for more than half a dozen years.

Frankly, it's not all that hard to get hooked on a career in science writing. After all, in what other jobs could you:

- Tag along with an evolutionary biologist who speaks "firefly" as she translates flirty blinks on a summer evening?
- Hang out with astrophysicists who have spent their entire careers in search of other planets that sustain life?
- Get paid to attend a conference on neuroscience and art?

It's not just science writers for the news media who have all the fun, either. Science writers who work for scientific journals, scientific societies, universities and other scientific institutions also get the chance to mingle with world-class scientists whose discoveries alter the way we do things and think about our worlds. They produce profiles of researchers for in-house magazines. They write press releases about new discoveries to feed the voracious appetites of journalists. And they package science news for a growing number of Web sites that are aimed directly at the public.[1] Many also help to organize conferences and meetings for the scientists they serve. Few days are the same, and with new discoveries always cascading through the pipeline, there is little chance for boredom.

SCIENCE WRITING AT THE TIMES

Still, there's little doubt that those who work for the news media and finally make it to the science desk at The New York Times have snagged one of the plumb jobs in science writing. Mere mention of their association with this venerable newspaper offers these writers unprecedented access to scientists in the highest reaches of the academy and industry. This is because, despite a rapidly changing media environment, publicists for universities, scientific societies and industry continue to think of landing a science story in The Times as a major coup. The Times may have more competition these days, but it still has the capacity to set the science news agenda for other journalists and the agenda for public policymakers too.

Times staffers also tend to get more time to write their stories than many other journalists, though that's also changing. With the unending addition of new networking tools, and the need to attract an audience using all the bells and whistles of the Internet, the work just gets busier and busier. The compensations, though, are more and different ways to tell a story, a challenge that technology-savvy staffers like Amy Harmon relish. Andrew Revkin, who blogs about the environment for The Times, appreciates the challenge, too, for it enables him to tell the urgent story about humans adjusting to the limitations of their habitat in ways traditional journalism has only rarely allowed.

There's a push at The Times these days, as elsewhere, to make science more user-friendly. Stories are shorter than they once were, and there's more "news you can use." And increasingly, one signal of a story's value is the number of clicks it receives on The Times Web site. That said, all the writers I've talked to for this collection cleave to traditional standards of responsible science writing—to write about science in ways that help the public to understand this amazingly complex human enterprise. They thus seek not only to *engage* readers in science, but also to responsibly *explain* it.

The interpretive challenges faced by those who explain science to the public are many. They include, but are not limited to, identifying credible research, avoiding hype, explaining scientific concepts and research methods clearly and concisely, positioning individual studies in a larger scientific context and evaluating and conveying interests that could bias the research findings.

It sounds daunting, and it can be, at least initially. But science writers don't rise to these challenges without assistance. Most consult trusted experts to help them decipher the strengths and weaknesses of research findings. The best seek out multiple independent assessments of the science they're writing about. And they learn as they go: Science writing is one long, independent study for those who sign up.

THIS COLLECTION OF SCIENCE WRITING

Speaking of study: The Reader you hold in your hands is not a textbook. It's a collection of stories that I hope will serve as models as you learn by doing. An underlying assumption, supported by writers over the centuries, is that good readers make good writers. If you read these stories well, you ought to be able to learn from them in ways that enhance your own work. (And if you aren't clear about what it means to read well, check out the short essay on reading that follows. It should get your started.)

As you soon will see, not all these stories are flashy. Some are simply direct and clear. But spanning a range of writers and disciplines, each offers something that will help you learn. Many I hope will also be of interest, for as often as I could, I selected stories about people and topics that I thought would interest those younger than the primary audience of The New York Times; in this, I received help from a few young science writers who only last year sat where you do now. In the end there were many stories I wish I could have included, but I had to choose. When it was a toss-up, I consulted my gut: Was there something in the piece I especially liked—a turn of phrase, perhaps, or a kicker of an ending? And did the story linger?

The resulting collection ranges widely, from stories on robotics and cell phones to pieces on ice melts and endangered species. The pieces are ordered in a way that will help you read and study the basics of science writing first. Early chapters offer models and tips for choosing credible studies that are newsworthy, for writing stories that cover most of the elements needed for the public to understand emerging science and for explaining strange concepts and processes with familiar comparisons, clear definitions, illuminating graphics and other explanatory tools. Pay particular attention to the annotated stories and to "Consider This," which follows individual stories or related sets of stories; they will help you read these stories in ways that will inform your own work. "Try This" at the end of many of the selections will give you things to do to apply what you learn.

On the premise that you'll have some of the basics in hand, Chapters 4–6 offer features of graduated complexity for you to read and learn from, everything from Q&As through extended narratives. These features show different aspects of science: the passions of the scientists who delight in work many of the rest of us would deem a slog, trends in scientific thinking, the sometimes dicey involvement of science and technology in the lives of ordinary people and a whole lot more. The final chapters (7–10) offer various models of stories in which writers say what is on their own minds, including editorials about technology, reviews of books and films about science and personal essays and blogs.

Along the way as you read this collection, you will meet a number of Times science writers who have produced these pieces. In interviews conducted with you in mind, they discuss their own fascinations with science and technology, and the challenges they face as professional science writers. Like me, they hope you will take inspiration from their stories to write your own and garner a few "clips."

Clips, if you haven't heard, are critical to securing the internships that will launch you as a science writing professional. In fact, if you want to even be considered for the Science Writing Club, there are two rules you must swear to. The first is: *Get lots of clips.* The second is: *Get lots of clips.* So read these stories with care, learn what it takes to write a story that both engages and informs and then get out there and write your own. With any luck, you too will get hooked on science writing.

Oh, and if you do get hooked, take the lead of some of my former students at Indiana University. Juicing up what had became the running theme of the course, they printed the following advice on T-shirts at the end of the term:

SCIENCE IS SEXY

. . . so practice safe science writing

SO YOU WANT TO WRITE? THEN READ!

If you want to be a good writer you need to read, read, read, read and to always be looking as you read for how other people do things and how they accomplished something that you admire. I used to tell my students you have to read a lot, but they would say, "We don't have time." What do you mean you don't have time? It's your job! Do you have time for your job? You do! You just have to make time for it and read promiscuously.

—Natalie Angier

So here's the drill: Good readers make good writers.

But what exactly is a good reader? It depends on whom you ask. Some journalists claim to read a lot and simply absorb what they need. Others say they don't get anywhere until they take a piece apart to see what makes it go.

In my experience, it's good to read both ways: If you read a lot of excellent writing without pausing to take it apart, you will pick up things that help you in your work. And if you read fine writing with an analytical mind—paying attention to topic, focus, informational and emotional details, organization and other essentials—you will pick up even more.

Reading *a lot* is all about motivation. Reading *well* is knowing what to look for. So if you have the motivation and you want to know what to read for, press on.

What to Read For

☐ **The Gut Test**. O.K., so you thought this was going to be about reading with an analytical eye. Well, it is. But first, it's a good idea to read a piece of writing to the end without thinking. When you are done, pause and ask yourself if you liked it. If you liked it, great. If you hated it, great. Now go back and try to figure out why. To puzzle out the why, check for the following things (in this order):

☐ **The Topic**. Some readers love physics. Others spy a physics story and can't click to a new page fast enough. Maybe you like a piece of writing simply because of the subject matter. Nothing wrong with that. Just notice. The more you notice, the easier it will be to figure out what topics turn you on as a writer.

☐ **The Focus**. Focus is what the writer says about the topic—or, in the case of commentary, the arguments the writer makes about it. Is the focus fresh? Is it interesting or important? And most critical, is it clear? If the focus is clear, you ought to be able to write a short statement that clearly summarizes what the writer is trying to say. In fact, you ought to be able to write a focus statement of six words or less: *Biologists fear growing bat die-off*, or *Teacher faces challenges teaching evolution*. As you gain experience in recognizing the focus of other writers' work, it will get easier and easier to realize the focus of your own.

☐ **Information**. Good journalism is rich with information and insights that support the focus at every turn: Facts. Numbers. Quotes. People. Anecdotes. Scenes. Explanatory material. Context. History. Speculation. Abstract information and concrete information. The whole, steamy compost. Notice the informational richness of fine writers' efforts, and try to figure out where and how they got those bits that sparkle. The more you do this, the clearer you will be about the information and insights you need to gather to enrich your own writing efforts.

☐ **Organization**. Fine journalism reels you in and keeps you reading. The lede engages. Early on, the piece conveys why you should care and signals what's to come, using a nut graf (which summarizes the story's focus or theme), foreshadowing or some other signaling device. The body of the story flows, one paragraph to the next, using related concepts, ideas, words or phrases (conceptual transitions), or connecting words like so, then and however (mechanical transitions). And if at all possible, the ending satisfies. The best pieces appear seamless. If you pay attention to how writers make the writing look easy, you can learn techniques that will help you structure your own seamless prose.

☐ **Writing**. Good science writing captures the vibrant qualities of a carefully observed reality. It makes use of vivid nouns and strong, active verbs, and where appropriate, language and images that are drawn with the senses. The prose is lean, not bloated; conversational, not stiff. And if the subject calls for it, it may contain a writer's own insights or asides, even humor. Watch how writers breathe life into their prose, so you can enliven yours.

☐ **Editing**. The pieces in this collection have been edited for grammar, accuracy, spelling, punctuation and journalistic style (GASPS).[2] The information has also been vetted for credibility, completeness and fairness to the weight of the evidence. But even at The Times, lapses get through.[3] If they do, notice how they affect you. Certainly with your own work, it's critical to edit for these essentials. Audiences will trust you more if you do.

☐ **Extras.** Links, photos, graphics, slideshows, videos and other "extras" on the Web should provide added value. Do they? If they don't, how could they?

news

Ask New York Times science writer Dennis Overbye what it's like to decide what's news in science, and he'll tell you "it's hard." As he once put it in a conversation with readers on The Times Web site:

> Everybody at the newspaper sits at the bottom of a gigantic funnel, into which press agents, information officers at public and private institutions, journals, the climbers who keep going up the side of our new building here, politicians and anybody with a grievance pour in material every day.[1]

Some of this material alerts writers to new findings in science. Some announces upcoming conferences and symposia. Some describes new books or movies in the hopes of initiating a story or review.

Science writers often complain about this deluge, but at least much of it is predictable: Releases from journals create a rhythm of sorting and selecting that can easily be worked into a journalist's routines. Schedules for scientific meetings, too, can be posted on a smart phone months in advance, with the presentations, press conferences and noisy rooms of vendors offering a comforting familiarity.

But clearly not all the news that science writers produce is tied to the work of scientists, public information officers and others jockeying for media attention: Terrorists may ram airplanes into two buildings in a major American city. Ice may collapse in the Antarctic. A hurricane may drown a coastline. When science is a part of breaking stories like these, science writers often swoop in to provide knowledge, context and insight.

This section of "The New York Times Reader" could easily contain news stories based on these less predictable events. But a decision has been made to limit the stories to ones that science writers produce in the course of sorting through e-mail alerts and monitoring normal channels of communication in science—articles in research journals and presentations at scientific conferences and symposia. This is not because stories based on events outside of science are unimportant. It is because the more routine stories clearly and reliably prompt attention to basic issues that all science writers need to understand.

Discovery stories, in particular, are the kinds of stories that you are going to need to learn to produce, whether you end up taking a public information job in science or you become a science writer for news media. If you don't know what to include, you can create a lot of public confusion. On the other hand, if you do these stories well, in a way that both engages and responsibly informs, you will not only gain respect as a science writer, you will perform a public service. People depend on stories about new discoveries, whether it's to learn about the risks of drugs or climate change, or the benefits of meditation or chocolate, and it is important to get them right.

Chris Gash

discoveries

IT'S AN UNUSUAL DAY when you don't learn about a new discovery in science. Wildly popular with editors and producers, stories that announce new findings in science pop up with regularity in newspapers, on television and in magazines, newsletters and blogs. Even at The Times, which contains an uncommon variety of science stories, they remain the No. 1 category of science news, according to research.[1] A few of the stories are judged of sufficient social or scientific significance to land on Page 1, with lengthy jumps. But most are shorter, some just a few paragraphs scattered throughout the Tuesday Science Times. Many are intended to entertain as much as to inform.

Choosing which studies to cover from among the more than 6,000 peer-reviewed journals in the English-speaking world[2] is daunting for any science writer—"more an art than a science," according to Times science editor Laura Chang. On the science desk, a number of factors go into deciding what's newsworthy, she says. In the case of discovery stories: Is the particular study "important, interesting, contentious, irresistibly quirky, novel or a noteworthy update on a long-running issue?" Space and time also play a role. So does the notion of mix, particularly in selecting the short discovery reports for the weekly health column "Vital Signs" and the general science column "Observatory."

Whether long or short, most discovery stories are "pegged" to the publication of studies in peer-reviewed scientific journals or their online equivalents—at The Times, usually highly prestigious journals like Science, Nature, The New England Journal of Medicine, The Journal of the American Medical Association and The Lancet. Peer-reviewed means the study has been sent to outside reviewers for vetting before it was published. It's a rough indicator that the scientists didn't do anything stupid.

Underline the word *rough*.

Seasoned science writers know that the peer-review system in science is imperfect. They understand that even when articles by top scientists are published in top journals, bad science can slip through. They understand, too, that "frontier science" is not "textbook science."[3] The studies reported in today's issue of Science or Nature are not the accepted understandings in your biology or physics book, and what looks as solid as ice this month may—in the heat of fresh studies, using new, improved methods—be all but melted in the next.[4]

So experienced science writers cast a skeptical eye on claims for new discoveries. Especially for the longer, more important stories, they consult trusted scientists concerning the quality and significance of the findings, whether and how the research fits with other studies in the field, the uncertainties of the conclusions and other matters.

At The Times, as at other media, journalists receive advance lists of articles to be published in many of the major scientific journals. They are sent these lists usually a week ahead on the understanding that they will not write about them until the release date. News embargoes, which expect journalists to delay their accounts until a study is published, are controversial.[5] This is especially true when they keep from the public findings that could significantly affect public policy or individuals' course of treatment. But they do give reporters a chance to do more than rewrite the news release—to read the actual article, consult independent experts, talk to the principal investigator and write their story without the frenzy of a looming deadline.

The discovery stories in this chapter are of different lengths, from briefs to full-length stories. Briefs, which summarize the findings of scientific studies in 100–350 words, usually lack the voices of independent observers and other elements of longer stories. But they say a lot in a short space—and, like popcorn, they are tasty, and to a regular reader, addictive. At least two of these news bites are ones that would work for a campus newspaper; the exercise at the end of these briefs invites you to find studies that might work for other specialized news media.

Of the longer selections in this chapter, the first is a straightforward summary of research in which scientists claimed monkeys could control a mechanical arm with just their thoughts. This story, which runs more than 900 words, covers most of the elements a science writer should consider when reporting on discoveries of potential social or scientific significance, and it has been annotated to highlight those elements.

The next two stories are an account of a neuroscience study revealing benefits of meditation and a physics story about basic research on teleportation. They provide much of the same information, but by virtue of their subjects, offer more room for creative play. The two stories that follow these, about a cell phone–tracking study and a survey of patients who had used in vitro fertilization, are included because they do what these stories seldom do: One incorporates a discussion of research ethics, and the other frames the new findings around real people, turning a conventional news story about new findings into an involving news feature. The final story is one of those pieces science writers sometimes feel compelled to write, even if their reporting suggests that there may be less to the findings than meets the investigator's eye; it is included here to show the skeptical eye that the best science writers develop with experience.

On The Times Web site, most discovery stories link to the scientific study on which the story is based, but in addition, the longer stories are often accompanied by photos, videos, graphics and other multimedia features.

Embedded links also appear in many of the pieces, connecting readers to Times pages that list related stories.

Selection 1.1

Sleep-deprived as we all are, this study on napping and its relationship to performance is a natural candidate for a campus news bite. In writing this 180-word brief for "Vital Signs," a weekly compilation of news briefs about health, Nicholas Bakalar makes a direct appeal to readers, all of whom have problems. But a nap as solution to those problems? Sometimes it's the unexpected that reels you in.

VITAL SIGNS
Behavior: Better Performance After a Dreaming Nap
By NICHOLAS BAKALAR

Have to solve a problem? Try taking a nap.

But it has to be the right kind of nap—one that includes rapid eye movement, or REM, sleep, the kind that includes dreams.

Researchers led by Sara C. Mednick, an assistant professor of psychiatry at the University of California, San Diego, gave 77 volunteers word-association tests under three before-and-after conditions: spending a day without a nap, napping without REM sleep and napping with REM sleep.

Just spending the day away from the problem improved performance; people who stayed awake did a little better on the 5 p.m. session than they had done on the 9 a.m. test. Taking a nap without REM sleep also led to slightly better results. But a nap that included REM sleep resulted in nearly a 40 percent improvement over the pre-nap performance.

The study, published June 8 in The Proceedings of the National Academy of Sciences, found that those who had REM sleep took longer naps than those who napped without REM, but there was no correlation between total sleep time and improved performance. Only REM sleep helped.

Published: June 22, 2009.

Selection 1.2

This little story on the sexual attractiveness of a woman's voice is another natural for campus media. In 250 words, "Vital Signs" writer Eric Nagourney conveys a lot of information: the study's findings, the methods scientists used, and (check out the ending) a research context to die for.

VITAL SIGNS
Patterns: Serious Message in a Seductive Voice
By ERIC NAGOURNEY

A come-hither sound in a woman's voice may carry a message about her readiness to conceive.

A new study finds that women who are at the peak time of fertility in their menstrual cycle may have changes in their voices that make them sound more attractive.

The study, which appears online in Evolution and Human Behavior, was done by R. Nathan Pipitone and Gordon G. Gallup Jr. of the State University of New York at Albany.

The researchers recorded voice samples from about 50 undergraduate women at four times in their menstrual cycle. Then they asked 34 men and 32 women to listen to the recordings and rate them in terms of attractiveness.

On the surface, the recordings were not terribly sexy. The women were asked to count from 1 to 10. But they must have been doing something different when they were closest to ovulating, because that was when they received the highest ratings, the researchers said.

Part of the explanation may lie in the fact that the larynx changes both its shape and size in response to hormones related to reproduction.

The findings are in keeping with earlier research showing that the voice can convey a good amount of information about sexual desirability. Sexual encounters do tend to occur in the dark, but even when the lights are on, the voice plays a big role. The study, the researchers said, might help explain earlier research finding that lap dancers make the best tips when they are ovulating.

Published: May 6, 2008.

Selection 1.3

Anyone who grew up on Aesop's fables can appreciate this brief about a bird that goes after what it wants and gets it. Henry Fountain, who produces the items for the weekly science column "Observatory," manages to convey much in 360 words: the study's findings and the research context, along with the methods used in the study and several quotes from the senior author. He even slips in an anecdote to show how the researcher got the idea. In an unusual move for a brief, the online version links to a YouTube video of one of the crafty birds.

Observatory
An Aesop's Fable Might Just Be True
By HENRY FOUNTAIN

Aesop was quite the fable-teller, but was he a student of bird behavior as well? A study in Current Biology suggests he might have been.

Christopher Bird of the University of Cambridge and Nathan J. Emery of Queen Mary University of London report that rooks, a relative of the crow, are able to use stones to raise the level of water in a container so they can reach a floating worm. If that sounds familiar, it's because it's similar to Aesop's fable about the crow and the pitcher, in which a thirsty bird adds stones to raise the water level in a pitcher to drink from it.

Crows, rooks and other corvids are known for their tool use— using sticks as probes, for example, or fashioning hooks out of wire. Mr. Bird knew of a 1980s study in which a rook plugged a hole in its aviary to allow a pool of water to form. That led him to wonder if a corvid could do what is described in the fable.

They experimented with four captive rooks, presenting them with clear tubes partly filled with water with a bug floating on top, and piles of stones. Within a couple of trials the birds had figured out how many stones they needed to bring the bug within reach. "It was a remarkable combination of some understanding of the task with really rapid learning," Mr. Bird said. The findings were published in Current Biology.

Rooks don't use tools in the wild, because they don't need to—they have easy access to food like carrion. But in captivity, they can be presented with a situation like this, where it pays to figure out how to perform a task. "This fits nicely with Aesop's moral," Mr. Bird said, "that necessity is the mother of invention."

He suggested that Aesop (or whoever came up with the fable, since the tales are thought to have many origins) may have seen similar behavior in a crow—or perhaps a rook. "In folklore all members of the corvid family are just called crow," he said. "So it might just as easily have been Aesop's rook."

Published: August 11, 2009.

MAKING**CONNECTIONS**

Try This. You've read some discovery stories that could work in campus publications. Now picture yourself writing for another target audience—say the parents of young children who read Parenting Magazine, or people over 50 who read The AARP Magazine. Find a newly released study on EurekAlert, the online news alert site of the American Association for the Advancement of Science, that would interest your chosen audience. (Go to EurekAlert: www.eurekalert.org.) As you scan the possibilities, also consider indicators of scientific credibility: the prominence of the scientists, their institutions and those who funded the research, and the prestige of the journal in which the research was presented. (Peer-reviewed journals are best, and top-tier journals like Science and Nature even better.) Describe the study in a way that will engage your particular audience, and justify your choice.

A Reader's Checklist: Discovery Stories

The best discovery stories explain the results in ways that enhance the public's understanding of science. Use this checklist to evaluate the information in these stories. Longer stories should mention:

☐ **Results and their significance.** The "news" is what scientists claim to have found and the apparent significance of these findings to science and/ or society. These should appear high in the story. Elaborations can come later.

☐ **Forum: Where and when findings were announced.** The date of the announcement informs audiences that the results are timely. The forum in which the study appeared provides the information needed to track down more details: the current issue (or this week's issue or the July 30 issue) of Nature. Online stories can go a step further and link to the actual article.

☐ **Research context.** Context shows how the discovery fits with, or contradicts, previous research and/or theory: The new study solves a long-standing puzzle, supports prior research, reaches a startling new conclusion, etc.

☐ **Research methods.** Readers with vested interests in the results will want to know how the study was done. Provide enough of the methods so they can figure out the quality of the evidence for themselves. But don't go overboard. In most cases, limit descriptions to a few paragraphs.

☐ **Caveats.** Emerging science is not accepted science. All studies have limitations, and their conclusions are tentative. For longer stories, especially, caveats are a must. Most caveats can go late in a piece, but with new treatments and technologies that raise hopes and alarms, caveats should come early. For example, *It is too early to know if this treatment will work in humans,* or *Scientists don't yet know the reason for the association.* Words like *may* or *suggests* also signal uncertainty.

☐ **Views of principal investigator.** Longer stories often quote authors of the study, especially senior authors. On first reference, a story is likely to say *scientists* or *researchers at the University of North Carolina.* Names will come later: *Jane Doe and a team of scientists at the University of North Carolina.*

☐ **Views of independent scientists.** The views of independent experts can support claims about the significance of the findings: *This is going to change how we treat a whole host of diseases, including x, y and z.* Or they can put research in context: *If this result is supported, it will change the way we do molecular biology.* And/or they can inject caveats: *We need more studies before we'll know for sure.* Some newsrooms require journalists to mention that these scientists had nothing to do with the research: *Experts not involved with the study said. . . .*

☐ **Ethical issues.** Few discovery stories note sources of funding, but if potential conflicts of interest exist, it's wise to include them. It's also good to note if the research raises other ethical concerns, like privacy issues related to data-gathering.

 STORY**SCAN**

Selection 1.4

This discovery story by Benedict Carey, who writes about neuroscience and mental health for The Times, reports an advance at the intersection of neuroscience and technology. A straightforward news story, the piece covers most of the bases listed on the checklist for longer discovery stories above. The annotations that accompany the story amplify what's on that this list.

Monkeys Think, Moving Artificial Arm as Own

By BENEDICT CAREY

Notice how it's not until the end of the sentence that the claim is credited to anyone, and then it is not to a named scientist, only to "scientists." Keeping identifiers general at this point is intentional; it cuts down clutter.

After summarizing what scientists have found, it's a good idea to explain, in a general way, why the finding is important. Here the writer summarizes the scientific and practical significance of the discovery.

As there are likely to be people who imagine they could benefit from this discovery, the writer makes sure we know it's not practical—yet. This is important, to avoid raising expectations beyond what the science can deliver.

Showing how a study does—or does not—conform to prior research can prevent cognitive whiplash (butter is worse than margarine; no, butter is better!). In this case, the study simply takes earlier findings one step further.

Make sure outside sources are without ties to the researchers or funders of the study in question. If there are ties, name them. If there are none, it can be a good idea to say that directly, as the writer does here.

Two monkeys with tiny sensors in their brains have learned to control a mechanical arm with just their thoughts, using it to reach for and grab food and even to adjust for the size and stickiness of morsels when necessary, scientists reported on Wednesday.

The report, released online by the journal Nature, is the most striking demonstration to date of brain-machine interface technology. Scientists expect that technology will eventually allow people with spinal cord injuries and other paralyzing conditions to gain more control over their lives.

The findings suggest that brain-controlled prosthetics, while not practical, are at least technically within reach.

In previous studies, researchers showed that humans who had been paralyzed for years could learn to control a cursor on a computer screen with their brain waves and that nonhuman primates could use their thoughts to move a mechanical arm, a robotic hand or a robot on a treadmill.

The new experiment goes a step further. In it, the monkeys' brains seem to have adopted the mechanical appendage as their own, refining its movement as it interacted with real objects in real time. The monkeys had their own arms gently restrained while they learned to use the added one.

Experts not involved with the study said the findings were likely to accelerate interest in human testing, especially given the need to treat head and spinal injuries in veterans returning from Iraq and Afghanistan.

Published: May 29, 2008.

"This study really pulls together all the pieces from earlier work and provides a clear demonstration of what's possible," said Dr. William Heetderks, director of the extramural science program at the National Institute of Biomedical Imaging and Bioengineering. Dr. John P. Donoghue, director of the Institute of Brain Science at Brown University, said the new report was "important because it's the most comprehensive study showing how an animal interacts with complex objects, using only brain activity."

The researchers, from the University of Pittsburgh and Carnegie Mellon University, used monkeys partly because of their anatomical similarities to humans and partly because they are quick learners.

Here we learn more about who the researchers are. We still don't know the individual scientists' names. Those often come later, usually with a direct quote from the senior author.

In the experiment, two macaques first used a joystick to gain a feel for the arm, which had shoulder joints, an elbow and a grasping claw with two mechanical fingers.

Notice how the description of research is in the science writer's own words, with details that help us picture what was done. This is longer than many descriptions of methods, but it works.

Then, just beneath the monkeys' skulls, the scientists implanted a grid about the size of a large freckle. It sat on the motor cortex, over a patch of cells known to signal arm and hand movements. The grid held 100 tiny electrodes, each connecting to a single neuron, its wires running out of the brain and to a computer.

The computer was programmed to analyze the collective firing of these 100 motor neurons, translate that sum into an electronic command and send it instantaneously to the arm, which was mounted flush with the left shoulder.

The scientists used the computer to help the monkeys move the arm at first, essentially teaching them with biofeedback.

After several days, the monkeys needed no help. They sat stationary in a chair, repeatedly manipulating the arm with their brain to reach out and grab grapes, marshmallows and other nuggets dangled in front of them. The snacks reached the mouths about two-thirds of the time—an impressive rate, compared with earlier work.

The writer elaborates on the findings using the anecdotal tools of a storyteller. It's not always possible to do it this way, but when it is, go for it.

The monkeys learned to hold the grip open on approaching the food, close it just enough to hold the food and gradually loosen the grip when feeding.

On several occasions, a monkey kept its claw open on the way back, with the food stuck to one finger. At other times, a monkey moved the arm to lick the fingers clean or to push a bit of food into its mouth while ignoring a newly presented morsel.

Notice the supporting quote from the journal article. This is unusual. It's more common to use quotes obtained in interviews, like the ones that follow.

The animals were apparently free-lancing, discovering new uses for the arm, showing "displays of embodiment that would never be seen in a virtual environment," the researchers wrote.

The writer finally identifies the senior author by name, title and institution.

"In the real world, things don't work as expected," said the senior author of the paper, Dr. Andrew Schwartz, a professor of neurobiology at the University of Pittsburgh. "The marshmallow sticks to your hand or the food slips, and you can't program a computer to anticipate all of that.

"But the monkeys' brains adjusted. They were licking the marshmallow off the prosthetic gripper, pushing food into their mouth, as if it were their own hand."

Scientists often want all co-authors named, as they are here, but journalists rarely have—or take—precious space to do that. You may have to explain this to scientists who aren't media-savvy.

The co-authors were Meel Velliste, Sagi Perel, M. Chance Spalding and Andrew Whitford.

The science writer returns to the caveat that was mentioned high in the story, clarifying the gap that exists between a study's findings and the practical applications.

Scientists have to clear several hurdles before this technology becomes practical, experts said. Implantable electrode grids do not generally last more than a period of months, for reasons that remain unclear.

The equipment to read and transmit the signal can be cumbersome and in need of continual monitoring and recalibrating. And no one has yet demonstrated a workable wireless system that would eliminate the need for connections through the scalp.

Yet Dr. Schwartz's team, Dr. Donoghue's group and others are working on
all of the problems, and the two macaques'
rapid learning curve in taking ownership
of a foreign limb gives scientists confidence
that the main obstacles are technical and,
thus, negotiable.

In an editorial accompanying the
Nature study, Dr. John F. Kalaska, a neuroscientist at the University of Montreal,
argued that after such bugs had been
worked out, scientists might even discover
areas of the cortex that allow more intimate, subtle control of prosthetic devices.

Studies deemed significant by journal editors are often accompanied by editorials. The scientists who write these editorials can add an additional independent voice to your account.

Such systems, Dr. Kalaska wrote,
"would allow patients with severe motor
deficits to interact and communicate with
the world not only by the moment-to-
moment control of the motion of robotic
devices, but also in a more natural and
intuitive manner that reflects their overall
goals, needs and preferences."

MAKING**CONNECTIONS**

1

Try This. Return to EurekAlert, the online news alert site of the American Association for the Advancement of Science: www.eurekalert.org/. This time, find a study that is interesting or impor-tant enough to warrant full-length treatment for your campus newspaper or other campus media. Describe the study and justify your choice.

And This. Once you've selected the press release that fits your needs, check the press release against the discovery story checklist. What's miss-ing? What would you need to check out further, and with whom? Make a list.

Selection 1.5

In this account of a neuroscience study on meditation, Sandra Blakeslee covers many of the same bases handled in the last story. But with a clear, light touch appropriate to the subject, she mimics the thoughts and sounds of breathing meditation before she quickly and deftly presents the forum in which the research was presented and the study's findings. Notice the example she uses to explain a concept central to the story, the attentional blink.

Study Suggests Meditation Can Help Train Attention

By SANDRA BLAKESLEE

In meditation, people sit quietly and concentrate on their breath. As air swooshes in and out of their nostrils, they attend to each sensation. As unbidden thoughts flutter to mind, they let them go. Breathe. Let go. Breathe. Let go.

According to a study published today in the online edition of the journal PloS Biology, three months of rigorous training in this kind of meditation leads to a profound shift in how the brain allocates attention.

It appears that the ability to release thoughts that pop into mind frees the brain to attend to more rapidly changing things and events in the world at large, said the study's lead author, Richard Davidson, a professor of psychology and psychiatry at the University of Wisconsin in Madison. Expert meditators, he said, are better than other people at detecting such fast-changing stimuli, like emotional facial expressions.

Dr. Ron Mangun, director of the Center for Mind and Brain at the University of California, Davis, who was not involved in the study, called the finding exciting. "It provides neuroscience evidence for changes in the workings of the brain with mental training, in this case meditation," he said. "We know we can learn and improve abilities of all sorts with practice, everything from driving to playing the piano. But demonstrating this in the context of meditation is interesting and novel."

Recent research has shown that meditation is good for the brain. It appears to increase gray matter, improve the immune system, reduce stress and promote a sense of well-being. But Dr. Davidson said this was the first study to examine how meditation affects attention.

The study exploited a brain phenomenon called the attentional blink. Say pictures of a St. Bernard and a Scottish terrier are flashed before one's eyes half a second apart, embedded in a series of 20 pictures of cats. In that sequence, most people fail to see the second dog. Their brains have "blinked."

Published: May 8, 2007.

Scientists explain this blindness as a misallocation of attention. Things are happening too fast for the brain to detect the second stimulus. Consciousness is somehow suppressed.

But the blink is not an inevitable bottleneck, Dr. Davidson said. Most people can identify the second target some of the time. Thus it may be possible to exert some control, which need not be voluntary, over the allocation of attention.

In the study, 17 volunteers with meditation experience spent three months at the Insight Meditation Society in Barre, Mass., meditating 10 to 12 hours a day. A novice control group meditated for 20 minutes a day over the same period.

Both groups were then given attentional blink tests with two numbers embedded in a series of letters. As both groups looked for the numbers, their brain activity was recorded with electrodes placed on the scalp.

Everyone could detect the first number, Dr. Davidson said. But the brain recordings showed that the less experienced meditators tended to grasp the first number and hang onto it, so they missed the second number. Those with more experience invested less attention to the first number, as if letting it go. This led to an increased ability to grasp the second number.

The attentional blink was thought to be a fixed property of the nervous system, Dr. Davidson said. But this study shows that it can change with practice. Attention is a flexible, trainable skill.

Just ask Daniel Levison, a staff researcher in the psychology department at the University of Wisconsin who meditated for three months as part of the study. "I'm a much better listener," he said. "I don't get lost in my own personal reaction to what people are saying."

MAKING**CONNECTIONS**

1

Consider This. Compare the types of information that the writer covers in this story with the information covered in the story about monkeys moving artificial arms. Also compare the order of the various elements. What does this comparison tell you about the information essential to full-length discovery stories and the routine construction of such stories?

And This. Compare the online presentations of the two stories as they appear on The Times Web site. What links and other features do you see that offer added value to the stories? Does anything seem unnecessary? What other ideas for online features can you imagine that would complement the writers' words?

2

Selection 1.6

The mere mention of physics could be a turn-off to many, but Kenneth Chang entices readers into this story by conjuring up "Star Trek," with its imaginary transporters, and Alexander Graham Bell's invention of the telephone. Like the writer in the story on meditation, he early on explains a concept central to the study—in this case entanglement, an aspect of quantum mechanics. He goes on to describe, in more detail, how the scientists demonstrated teleportation in their research, before pointing out, somewhat tongue in cheek, that the method almost always fails. An online animated graphic, which is alluded to in the story, shows the power of involving visuals for explaining complex physical processes.

A Leap for Teleporting, Between Ions Feet Apart
By KENNETH CHANG

Without quite the drama of Alexander Graham Bell calling out, "Mr. Watson, come here!" or the charm of the original "Star Trek" television show, scientists have nonetheless achieved a milestone in communication: teleporting the quantum identity of one atom to another a few feet away.

The contraption is a Rube Goldberg-esque mix of vacuum chambers, fiber optics, lasers and semitransparent beam splitters in a laboratory at the Joint Quantum Institute in Maryland.

Even in the far future, "Star Trek" transporters will probably remain a fantasy, but the mechanism could form an important component in new types of communication and computing.

Quantum teleportation depends on entanglement, one of the strangest of the many strange aspects of quantum mechanics. Two particles can become "entangled" into a single entity, and a change in one instantaneously changes the other even if it is far away.

Previously, physicists have shown that they could use teleportation to transfer information from one photon to another or between nearby atoms. In the new research, the scientists used light to transfer quantum information between two well-separated atoms.

"It's that hybrid approach that we've demonstrated that looks to be an interesting way to proceed," said Christopher Monroe, a University of Maryland physicist and the senior author of a paper describing the research in the Jan. 23 issue of the journal Science.

Present-day digital computers store information as zeroes and ones. In a future quantum computer, a single bit of information could be both zero and one at the same time. (In essence, a quantum coin toss would be both heads and tails until someone actually looked at the coin, at which time the coin instantly becomes one or the other.) In theory, a quantum computer could calculate certain types of problems much more quickly than digital computers.

Published: February 2, 2009. Article and graphic available at: http://www.nytimes.com/2009/02/03/ science/03teleportation.html

In the experiment, two ytterbium ions, cooled to a fraction of a degree above absolute zero, served as the two quantum coins. A microwave pulse wrote quantum information onto one; a second microwave pulse placed the ion into a state of equal probabilities of heads and tails.

A laser then induced each ion to emit exactly one photon, collected by a lens and guided through fiber optics to a beam splitter that could reflect the photons or let them pass through. Two detectors then captured and recorded the photons. Because it was not known which photon came from which atom, the photons became "entangled," meaning that the behavior of the two particles became wrapped up in a single equation even though they were not in the same place. And, oddly, because the photons were emitted by the ions, the two ions also became entangled.

"That's the magic of entanglement," Dr. Monroe said. "Now, the atoms are entangled. The photons are gone and out of the picture."

The information in the first ion was then measured in a way that did not reveal the information and that teleported the information to the second ion. (For another explanation, take a look at this animated graphic.)

By repeating the experiment many times and taking many measurements of the second ion, the researchers, from Maryland and the University of Michigan, confirmed that the second ion contained the information that had been originally written to the first ion.

The method is not particularly practical at the moment, because it fails almost all of the time. Only 1 of every 100 million teleportation attempts succeed, requiring 10 minutes to transfer one bit of quantum information.

"We need to work on that," Dr. Monroe said.

But he said that a success rate of just 1 in 10,000 would be high enough for some uses. Such systems could be used as "quantum repeaters"—reading the information from one photon and then imprinting it on a new photon for the next leg of its communications journey.

MAKING**CONNECTIONS**

Consider This. Not every full-length science story in The Times contains multiple sources. This one, for example, does not. Do you see any problems with only one source for this particular story? And if you were to consult with independent sources, what would you want to find out? Share your opinions and questions with your classmates.

Selection 1.7

The lighthearted lede to this story—about a study that tracked people's move-ments by following the signals on their cell phones—mocks the findings. But quickly we learn the significance of the research, and soon, the controversial nature of the data-gathering. The story, by writer John Schwartz, concludes with a much-needed discussion of the ethics of the research methods. The article on The Times Web site links to the original article in Nature and to a fascinating project that tracks the flow of currency as an indicator of the flow of people and provides additional context.

Cellphone Tracking Study Shows We're Creatures of Habit

By JOHN SCHWARTZ

News flash: we're boring.

New research that makes creative use of sensitive location-track-ing data from 100,000 cellphones in Europe suggests that most people can be found in one of just a few locations at any time, and that they do not generally go far from home.

"Individuals display significant regularity, because they return to a few highly frequented locations, such as home or work," the researchers found.

That might seem like science and mountains of data being mar-shaled to prove the obvious. But the researchers say their work, which also shows that people exhibit similar patterns whether they travel long distances or short ones, could open new frontiers in fields like disease tracking and urban planning.

"Slices of our behavior are preserved in these electronic data sets," said Albert-László Barabási, an author of the project and the director of the Center for Complex Network Research at Northeastern University in Boston. "This is creating huge opportunities for science."

The researchers said they used the potentially controversial data only after any information that could identify individuals had been scrambled. Even so, they wrote, people's wanderings are so subject to routine that by using the patterns of movement that emerged from the research, "we can obtain the likelihood of finding a user in any location."

The researchers were able to obtain the data from a European provider of cellphone service that was obligated to collect the infor-mation. By agreement with the company, the researchers did not disclose the country where the provider operates.

Published: June 5, 2008.

The researchers, including Dr. Barabási's Northeastern colleagues Marta C. González and César A. Hidalgo, tracked 100,000 cellphone users selected at random from a population of six million for six months. The location of the user was revealed whenever he made or received a call or text message; the telephone company would record the nearest cell tower and time. Because calls and messages tended to be sporadic, the researchers used a smaller data set that captured the location of 206 users every two hours. The results of the two data sets were similar, according to the report.

Scientists have long wondered how to measure something as ephemeral as movement. If general rules and algorithms of people's wanderings could be discerned, they could be used to create computer models for understanding emergency response, urban planning and the spread of disease, say the authors, whose work appears in the new edition of the journal Nature.

Previous efforts to find data that can shed light on the movement of large groups of people have used complex formulas to predict behavior. But more recent efforts have involved the search for data in a seemingly unrelated area.

One such paper, by Dirk Brockmann, a professor of physics at Northwestern University, tracks paper currency as a surrogate for the movement of people. Using data from the wheresgeorge.com Web site, where volunteers track the location and flow of more than 129 million bills of various denominations, Dr. Brockmann found similar routines of movement that also resemble those of animal foraging.

The cellphone researchers pointed out that the new paper moved the field forward significantly because people hold on to their phones, and so the movement of individuals is more closely tracked than it can be with paper currency that is passed from person to person. As the researchers put it in the paper, "Dollar bills diffuse, but humans do not."

Both lines of research, however, suggested that people did not really move around much.

Dr. Brockmann, who was a reviewer on the new paper, said he first approached it with some trepidation—"I said, 'Oooh, I hope this does not completely falsify what we found.' " Instead, he said, "I was very happy to see that it was consistent with what we found, even though the patterns of travel were obtained by very different sets of data."

The use of cellphones to track people, even anonymously, has implications for privacy that make this "a troubling study," said Marc Rotenberg, a founder of the Electronic Privacy Information Center in Washington. The study, Mr. Rotenberg said, "raises questions about the protection of privacy in physical spaces, when devices make possible the capture of locational data."

There are serious ethical issues as well, said Arthur Caplan, director of the Center for Bioethics at the University of Pennsylvania. While researchers are generally free to observe people in public places without getting permission from them or review from institutional ethics boards, Mr. Caplan said, "your cellphone is not something I would consider a public entity."

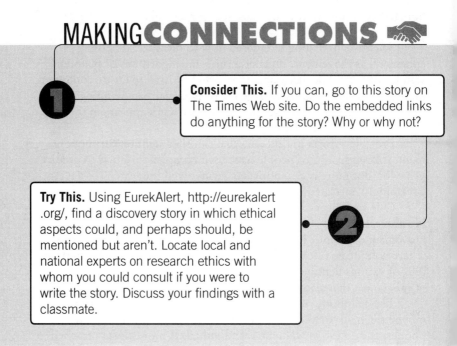

MAKING**CONNECTIONS**

1

Consider This. If you can, go to this story on The Times Web site. Do the embedded links do anything for the story? Why or why not?

Try This. Using EurekAlert, http://eurekalert .org/, find a discovery story in which ethical aspects could, and perhaps should, be mentioned but aren't. Locate local and national experts on research ethics with whom you could consult if you were to write the story. Discuss your findings with a classmate.

2

Selection 1.8

In this piece, writer Denise Grady frames the findings of a newly published survey on in vitro fertilization around the people who had participated in the research. Working with the scientists who conducted the study, Grady, who often puts people into her health and medical stories (see conversation at the end of this chapter), interviewed three subjects and made them a prominent feature in the story. The result turns a routine news story about new findings into a news feature that is both unusual and compelling. When you use real people in a story, the segue from the specific person to the broader subject is key. Notice one way Grady builds that bridge in her sixth paragraph.

Parents Torn Over Fate of Frozen Embryos

By DENISE GRADY

For nearly 15 years, Kim and Walt Best have been paying about $200 a year to keep nine embryos stored in a freezer at a fertility clinic at Duke University—embryos that they no longer need, because they are finished having children but that Ms. Best cannot bear to destroy, donate for research or give away to another couple.

The embryos were created by in vitro fertilization, which gave the Bests a set of twins, now 14 years old.

Although the couple, who live in Brentwood, Tenn., have known for years that they wanted no more children, deciding what to do with the extra embryos has been a dilemma. He would have them discarded; she cannot.

"There is no easy answer," said Ms. Best, a nurse. "I can't look at my twins and not wonder sometimes what the other nine would be like. I will keep them frozen for now. I will search in my heart."

At least 400,000 embryos are frozen at clinics around the country, with more being added every day, and many people who are done having children are finding it harder than they had ever expected to decide the fate of those embryos.

A new survey of 1,020 fertility patients at nine clinics reveals more than a little discontent with the most common options offered by the clinics. The survey, in which Ms. Best took part, is being published on Thursday in the journal Fertility and Sterility.

Among patients who wanted no more children, 53 percent did not want to donate their embryos to other couples, mostly because they did not want someone else bringing up their children, or did not want their own children to worry about encountering an unknown sibling someday.

Forty-three percent did not want the embryos discarded. About 66 percent said they would be likely to donate the embryos for research, but that option was available at only four of the nine clinics in the survey. Twenty percent said they were likely to keep the embryos frozen forever.

Embryos can remain viable for a decade or more if they are frozen properly but not all of them survive when they are thawed.

Smaller numbers of patients wished for solutions that typically are not offered. Among them were holding a small ceremony during the thawing and disposal of the embryos, or having them placed in the woman's body at a time in her cycle when she would probably not become pregnant, so that they would die naturally.

The message from the survey is that patients need more information, earlier in the in vitro process, to let them know that frozen embryos may result and that deciding what to do with them in the

Published: December 4, 2008.

future "may be difficult in ways you don't anticipate," said Dr. Anne Drapkin Lyerly, the first author of the study and a bioethicist and associate professor of obstetrics and gynecology at Duke University.

Dr. Lyerly also said discussions about the embryos should be "revisited, and not happen just at the time of embryo freezing, because people's goals and their way of thinking about embryos change as time passes and they go through infertility treatment."

Many couples are so desperate to have a child that when eggs are fertilized in the clinic, they want to create as many embryos as possible, to maximize their chances, Dr. Lyerly said. At that time, the notion that there could be too many embryos may seem unimaginable. (In Italy, fertility clinics are not allowed to create more embryos than can be implanted in the uterus at one time, specifically to avoid the ethical quandary posed by frozen embryos.)

In a previous study by Dr. Lyerly, women expressed wide-ranging views about embryos: one called them "just another laboratory specimen," but another said a freezer full of embryos was "like an orphanage."

Dr. Mark V. Sauer, the director of the Center for Women's Reproductive Care at Columbia University Medical Center in Manhattan, said: "It's a huge issue. And the wife and husband may not be on the same page."

Some people pay storage fees for years and years, Dr. Sauer said. Others stop paying and disappear, leaving the clinic to decide whether to maintain the embryos free or to get rid of them.

"They would rather have you pull the trigger on the embryos," Dr. Sauer said. "It's like, 'I don't want another baby, but I don't have it in me; I have too much guilt to tell you what to do, to have them discarded.' "

A few patients have asked that extra embryos be given to them, and he cooperates, Dr. Sauer said, adding, "I don't know if they take them home and bury them."

Federal and state regulations have made it increasingly difficult for those who want to donate to other couples, requiring that donors come back to the clinic to be screened for infectious diseases, sometimes at their own expense, Dr. Sauer said.

"It's partly reflected in the attitude of the clinics," he said, explaining that he does not even suggest that people give embryos to other couples anymore, whereas 10 years ago many patients did donate.

Ms. Best said her nine embryos "have the potential to become beautiful people."

The thought of giving them up for research "conjures all sorts of horrors, from Frankenstein to the Holocaust," she said, adding that destroying them would be preferable.

Her teenage daughter favors letting another couple adopt the embryos, but, Ms. Best said, she would worry too much about "what kind of parents they were with, what kind of life they had."

Another survey participant, Lynnelle Fowler McDonald, a case manager for a nonprofit social service agency in Durham, N.C., has one embryo frozen at Duke, all that is left of three failed efforts at the fertility clinic.

Given the physical and emotional stress, and the expense of in vitro fertilization, Ms. McDonald said she did not know whether she and her husband could go through it again. But to get rid of that last embryo would be final; it would mean they were giving up.

"There is still, in the back of my mind, this hope," she said.

At the Genetics and IVF Institute in Fairfax, Va., Andrew Dorfmann, the chief embryologist, said many patients were genuinely torn about what to do with extra embryos, and that a few had asked to be present to say a prayer when their embryos were thawed and destroyed.

Jacqueline Betancourt, a marketing analyst with a software company who took part in the survey, said she and her husband donated their embryos at Duke "to science, whatever that means." It was important to them that the embryos were not just going to be discarded without any use being made of them.

Ms. Betancourt, who has two sons, said: "We didn't ask many questions. We were just comfortable with the idea that they weren't going to be destroyed. We didn't see the point in destroying something that could be useful to science, to other people, to helping other people."

Ms. Betancourt said she wished there had been more discussion about the extra embryos early in the process. If she had known more, she said, she might have considered creating fewer embryos in the first place.

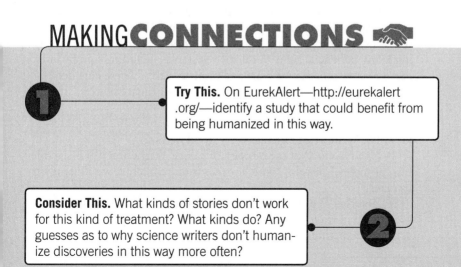

MAKING**CONNECTIONS**

1

Try This. On EurekAlert—http://eurekalert .org/—identify a study that could benefit from being humanized in this way.

Consider This. What kinds of stories don't work for this kind of treatment? What kinds do? Any guesses as to why science writers don't humanize discoveries in this way more often?

2

Selection 1.9

When scientists claimed to have extended the lives of monkeys by restricting their caloric intake, news media around the world jumped on the story. But something about the data puzzled Times science writer Nicholas Wade. Consulting with outside experts he trusted, he learned that the results were significant only if certain monkeys were excluded from the analysis. The resulting story dutifully informs Times readers of research they are likely to have learned about elsewhere, but at the same time, it lets them know that all may not be as it first appears.

Dieting Monkeys Offer Hope for Living Longer
By NICHOLAS WADE

A long-awaited study of aging in rhesus monkeys suggests, with some reservations, that people could in principle fend off the usual diseases of old age and considerably extend their life span by following a special diet.

Known as caloric restriction, the diet has all the normal healthy ingredients but contains 30 percent fewer calories than usual. Mice kept on such a diet from birth have long been known to live up to 40 percent longer than comparison mice fed normally.

Would the same be true in people? More than 20 years ago, two studies of rhesus monkeys were begun to see if primates responded to caloric restriction the same way that rodents did. Since rhesus monkeys live an average of 27 years and a maximum of 40, these are experiments that require patience.

The results from one of the two studies, conducted by a team led by Ricki J. Colman and Richard Weindruch at the University of Wisconsin, were reported Thursday in Science. The researchers say that now, 20 years after the experiment began, the monkeys are showing many beneficial signs of caloric resistance, including significantly less diabetes, cancer, and heart and brain disease. "These data demonstrate that caloric restriction slows aging in a primate species," they conclude.

Some critics say this conclusion is premature. But in an interview, Dr. Weindruch called it "very good news."

"It says much of the biology of caloric restriction is translatable into primates," he said, "which makes it more likely it would apply to humans."

In terms of deaths, 37 percent of the comparison monkeys have so far died in ways judged to be due to old age, compared with 13 percent of the dieting group.

Published: July 9, 2009.

Dr. Weindruch and his statistician, David Allison of the University of Alabama, Birmingham, said the dieting monkeys were expected to enjoy a life span extension of 10 percent to 20 percent, based on equivalent studies started in mice at the same age.

Few people can keep to a diet with 30 percent fewer calories than usual. So biologists have been looking for drugs that might mimic the effects of caloric restriction, conferring the gain without the pain. One of these drugs is resveratrol, a substance found in red wine, though in quantities too small to have any effect.

Dr. Weindruch said the study data offered "very encouraging" signs that resveratrol could duplicate in people some of the effects of caloric restriction.

Critics, however, are not yet ready to accept that the rhesus study proves caloric restriction works in primates.

If caloric restriction can delay aging, then there should have been significantly fewer deaths in the dieting group of monkeys than in the normally fed comparison group. But this is not the case. Though a smaller number of dieting monkeys have died, the difference is not statistically significant, the Wisconsin team reports.

The Wisconsin researchers say that some of the monkey deaths were not related to age and can properly be excluded. Some monkeys died under the anesthesia given while taking blood samples. Some died from gastric bloat, a disease that can strike at any age, others from endometriosis. When the deaths judged not due to aging are excluded, the dieting monkeys lived significantly longer.

Some biologists think it is reasonable to exclude these deaths, but others do not. Steven Austad, an expert on aging at the University of Texas Health Science Center, said some deaths could have been due to caloric restriction, even if they did not seem to be related to aging. "Ultimately the results seem pretty inconclusive at this point," Dr. Austad said. "I don't know why they didn't wait longer to publish."

Leonard Guarente, a biologist who studies aging at the Massachusetts Institute of Technology, also had reservations about the findings. "The survival data needs to be fleshed out a little bit more before we can say that caloric restriction extends life in primates," Dr. Guarente said. In mouse studies, people just count the number of dead animals without asking which deaths might be unrelated to aging, he said.

The second rhesus monkey study, being conducted by the National Institute on Aging, is not as advanced as the Wisconsin study. The researchers have not yet reported on the number of deaths in the dieting and normal monkey groups. But there are signs that the immune system is holding up better in the dieting group, said Julie Mattison, the leader of the institute's study.

The outcome of the rhesus monkey studies bears strongly on the prospects of finding drugs that might postpone the aging process in people. Although people are similar to mice in many ways, they differ in other ways, notably in how many cancer treatments are effective in mice but do not work in people.

Even if caloric restriction extends longevity in people as well as in mice, the extent of the effect remains unclear, though Dr. Weindruch believes the effects will be in the same general range. His monkeys were not started on the diet until 6 to 14 years of age, and seemed to be doing as well as mice that were started at equivalent ages. The most striking extensions of life span occur when the mice are put on the diet from birth.

Dietary restriction seems to set off an ancient strategy written into all animal genomes, that when food is scarce resources should be switched to tissue maintenance from breeding. In recent years biologists have had considerable success in identifying the mechanisms by which cells detect the level of nutrients available to the body. The goal is to find drugs that trick these mechanisms into thinking that famine is at hand. People could then literally have their cake and eat it, too, enjoying the health benefits of caloric restriction without the pain of forgoing rich foods.

Sirtris, a company based in Cambridge, Mass., is conducting clinical trials of resveratrol. It has developed several chemicals that mimic resveratrol and can be given in much smaller doses. On Wednesday, another such compound, the drug rapamycin, was reported to extend life span significantly in elderly mice, though it is not yet clear whether rapamycin sets off the same circuits as those that increase longevity in caloric restriction.

Dr. Weindruch joined the rhesus monkey experiment in 1990. He said he was used to being introduced as a man of incredible patience by biologists who study aging in laboratory roundworms, which live about three weeks. Dr. Weindruch will need the patience: he says he has another 15 years to go before the last monkey is expected to die.

MAKING**CONNECTIONS**

Consider This. Find a well-developed discovery story in The Times, and compare and contrast it with up to three stories that journalists have produced on the same discovery for other news media. What differences, if any, do you notice, especially with respect to the journalists' attention to research methods? Share your discoveries with others in the class, and discuss the implications of your observations for your own work as a science writer.

A Conversation with . . . **Denise Grady**

SENIOR WRITER, SCIENCE

© The New York Times

Denise Grady's journey to The New York Times science desk took many twists and turns. It began in the mid-1970s. With an undergraduate degree in biology, she secured positions as assistant editor of Physics Today, and then as assistant editor of the prestigious medical journal The New England Journal of Medicine. Along the way, she earned an M.A. in English.

In the 1980s she combined her interests in science and writing as a staff writer for the magazines Discover, The Sciences and Time. She left her staff job at Time in 1988 to spend time with her children. For the next decade, while living in New York, New Mexico and Minnesota, she worked as a freelance writer for publications that included Time, Discover, Science, Scientific American, Vogue, Reader's Digest, Parenting, Self and American Health.

Her association with The Times science desk began as a freelancer in 1996, while she was living in New Mexico. A year later, she went on contract. In 1998, when she was 46, she and her family left Minnesota for New York so she could join the science desk as a full-time writer. It was her first full-time newspaper job.

At The Times, Grady has concentrated on health, medicine, medical technologies and biology. In addition to writing news and feature stories, she produces an occasional column, "Second Opinion," about the effects of medical decisions, sometimes from a personal point of view. She has written one book, on emerging viruses,[6] and edited two Times reference books, on women's health and on alternative health.[7]

Married and the mother of two grown sons, she lives with her husband, a science teacher, in Westchester County, N.Y.

The following interview was conducted by e-mail. It has been edited for length.

You worked on staff for four magazines and then freelanced for a decade. These days many students think they can make a career freelancing from the get–go. Do you think this is a good idea, or do you advise students to work on staff for a magazine, as you did, before they launch a freelance career?
Particularly in this economy, I would advise writing students to take whatever work they can get. If you need a regular income and benefits, of course a staff

job is ideal. Until you can get one, freelancing can be a good way to accumu-late clips that will help you get more assignments and perhaps a better job. I found freelancing a tough way to make a living, but I know people who seem to do well at it, by doing a mixture of things: commercial projects like annual reports, journalism and books.

What was the best part of freelancing for you, and the most challenging part? And what led you to quit that life after so many years?
The most important thing about freelancing was that it let me be home with my kids when I wanted to be. The best part was being able to connect with certain editors I could work with—people who had a sense of what kinds of stories I was good at, who came up with assignments I liked and who were receptive to ideas that I proposed. For me, the hardest part was to man-age time and assignments in a way that would bring in a decent amount of money. Also difficult was feeling that I had to take assignments even from editors I didn't feel I worked well with. After 20 years I can still hear a grating voice on the other end of the phone saying, "Send me your outline. You don't make outlines? I always worry with a writer who doesn't make an outline."

Until I began writing for The Times, nearly all my work had been for magazines. I like magazines, but I consider them sort of a luxury. I think of newspapers as a necessity, an essential part of a democratic society. Once I started writing for The Times, I felt I had found a place where I belonged, where I was doing important work. It was a major newsgathering organization with high standards, striving for excellence, and I wanted to be part it.

On a more practical and down-to-earth level, I also found that daily deadlines suited me and made me more productive, and so did the cleaner, quicker, less pretentious approach to editing, as opposed to the layers and layers of people who seem to chew over magazine pieces, sometimes I think beyond the point of diminishing returns.

The offer of a full-time job came in 1998. At that point, my kids were just about old enough for me to consider returning to full-time work. We were living in Minnesota, and nobody wanted to move again. But I didn't think I'd ever again have such a terrific opportunity, especially since I was 46, not young in this business. And my husband had just been laid off, after 17 years with an environmental consulting company. A newspaper in Minneapolis also made me a generous job offer, but who can turn down The Times? The job was one of the best things that ever happened to me.

What is the best part of your job at The Times? The toughest part? And why?
The best part is the almost infinite variety of things to cover and the ever-changing nature of this beat. It is also wonderful to work for a well-known and respected newspaper. People call you back. A friend of mine calls working here "putting on the magic suit." People who couldn't be bothered with you

when you were freelancing are suddenly falling all over themselves to call you back. I hear there have been writers here who thought it was their own mystique and were in for a rude shock when they left and were back to being Joe Blow Freelancer minus the magic suit.

The toughest part for me is the almost infinite variety of things to cover and the ever-changing nature of this beat. It is so hard to decide what to cover and when, and there are constant distractions—news events interfering with projects, projects tempting you to ignore the news. I think some of us who like daily reporting have a little bit of attention deficit, and the onslaught of news makes it even harder to focus. Now that we have the infamous 24-hour news cycle, there is even more to sort out.

You have covered your share of scientific discoveries over the years. And as an editor at a scientific journal, you've watched other journalists write about new discoveries in science. What lessons have you taken away from these experiences that would be of benefit to aspiring science writers?
The most important thing is to put a "new" discovery into context. Where does it fit in with what was known before? Is it really new? Does it move the ball? Do reputable people in the field buy it? In medicine, the important questions are, will it affect the practice of medicine, will it affect patients, will it change the standard of care? If you had this condition, is this something you would want to know about, or want your doctor to know about?

I think medicine reporters have learned some hard lessons in recent years. Mice aren't people, and we've got to be awfully careful to avoid making too much of things that cure cancer or other diseases in mice or other animals, or in cells in test tubes. We've also got to be careful to look for conflicts of interest. Who paid for the study? Do the authors take money from drug or device makers, do they have patents on the tests or treatments concerned, or do they stand to benefit in any other way from the findings that they are presenting?

Observational studies can be a mine field. By observational, I mean the kind of study where subjects fill out surveys or questionnaires about their habits and then researchers look for associations with diseases or conditions. Do people who take vitamins or eat a lot of chocolate or fish have fewer heart attacks (or more)? This is in contrast to a randomized controlled trial, in which people are picked at random to be in groups that have one treatment or another, and are then followed and compared. Randomized controlled studies are considered the gold standard. They are certainly not perfect, but the findings are usually more reliable than the ones from observational studies.

One of the problems with observational studies is that the people are not picked at random: They take certain pills or eat certain foods for reasons that may reflect other differences that affect their health. People who take vitamins may also take better care of themselves in other ways, for instance. So it's hard to tell what the findings mean. The famous saying is, association doesn't prove cause and effect. In an ideal scientific world, findings from observational studies are supposed to be used to generate ideas that can be tested in controlled trials. They aren't supposed to be regarded as conclusive. But there are media reports all the time saying that a new observational study has just "proved" something. A notorious example was an observational study suggesting that beta carotene could prevent lung cancer. A later controlled study found the opposite: It increased the risk in smokers.[8] Doctors take an oath to do no harm. Maybe science writers should, too.

What about covering new technologies? How does writing about technological innovations compare with covering new scientific discoveries? Any tips for beginning science writers?
I am going to restrict myself once again to medicine, because that's what I'm most familiar with. My advice is, research, research, research, particularly when it comes to medical devices. There are huge sums of money involved, vested interests all over the place, and you have to work hard not to be taken in. It's amazing how many medical devices turn out to have problems or to not be what they first appeared.

One thing that you seem to do often (more often than many) is incorporate ordinary people into your stories. This seems to be true whether you are writing a routine feature story, or a story about a new scientific discovery or technological innovation. Is this something you consciously do, and if so, how did you come to do this, and why?
Because I write about medicine, I've got to include people. A treatment or other advance that sounds great on paper (or terrible) may seem very different once you hear what it's like to be on the receiving end. You think you know what it's all about, but talking to patients will often surprise you, and your readers. A study of a brain stimulator implanted to stop seizures may sound mildly interesting, but the real meaning of it was not clear to me until I interviewed a middle-aged man who had suddenly become epileptic, so severely that he lost his career and his marriage, and was desperate enough to try just about anything.[9] People like stories, and they like reading about people. Why not try to bring science to life when you can? The best accounts of the Manhattan Project, in my opinion, are the ones that show the scientists' personalities and interactions. The bomb is fascinating, but the people behind it make the story even more so.

If you could give but one piece of advice to aspiring science writers, what would it be?
Strive to be clear. Hold in your mind an ideal reader—mine is someone who is smart but not a specialist in what I'm writing about. And look at your writing with an eye as to whether or not that person will understand it and find it interesting enough to finish. I think clarity and a simple, straightforward style

that most people can understand are my strong points, and I think it comes from growing up in a working-class family with parents and sisters who were smart but not college-educated, who read tabloids and mystery novels and had a great wealth of common sense. They detested stuffiness and pretense. They expected to be able to understand things, and you couldn't put anything over on them. If you couldn't explain yourself, you didn't know what you were talking about. I think of them when I write. My mother had only an eighth-grade education, and I believe she could understand everything I write.

The New York Times

meetings

AS TRAVEL BUDGETS AT MANY NEWS MEDIA have shrunk, so has the number of science writers attending major scientific meetings in the hotels and convention centers of big cities. But on the campuses of research universities and many colleges, scientists continue to gather for small symposia and other specialized conferences. Socially minded scientists also occasionally mingle with nonscientists in public places large and small.

All such gatherings, as these stories show, make great fishing grounds for science writers trawling for stories. Specialized scientific meetings in particular make it easy to net a lot of experts on a topic. They also offer a way to become quickly familiar with a subject, and familiarity leads to more story ideas—features about individual scientists, or trend or issue stories, to name just a few.

In this chapter, you will find two stories based on university conferences, one on the melting of Arctic ice and the other related to art and neuroscience. There are also stories about meetings in which scientists mixed with nonscientists, one a conference on happiness, and the other a gathering of global climate skeptics.

With all the complexities and information overload that conferences present, deciding what to focus on, whom to interview and what to write can be a challenge. Writers at The Times typically take a couple days to make these decisions, ones that would be made in the heat of a deadline at other media outlets. The resulting stories are part breaking news, part feature. As you read them, notice the different approaches, from stories that are written as grand overviews of an area of research to the story that is an on-the-ground look at one specific topic. Whether you are writing on deadline or with a few days' grace, these models can guide you.

Selection 2.1

Surrounded by scientists at a symposium on sea ice at the University of Alaska, Andrew Revkin talked to more than a dozen of them. The resulting story focuses on experts' views on the unexpectedly rapid retreat of Arctic sea ice, a subject Revkin writes about often and well, both in the print edition of The Times and in his blog on the environment, Dot Earth. It may look like it was easy to bring all these different voices together, but Revkin had to sort through and synthesize the Everest of information he heard and read at the meeting and then summarize it in everyday language. He then had to figure out where to punctuate the story with quotes from the participating scientists. Accompanying the online story are researcher-supplied visuals: a photograph of melting sea ice that would be soothing were it not for what it depicts, and a stunning interactive graphic that vividly demonstrates the loss of sea ice and other changes in the Arctic.

Arctic Melt Unnerves the Experts

By ANDREW C. REVKIN

The Arctic ice cap shrank so much this summer that waves briefly lapped along two long-imagined Arctic shipping routes, the Northwest Passage over Canada and the Northern Sea Route over Russia.

Over all, the floating ice dwindled to an extent unparalleled in a century or more, by several estimates.

Now the six-month dark season has returned to the North Pole. In the deepening chill, new ice is already spreading over vast stretches of the Arctic Ocean. Astonished by the summer's changes, scientists are studying the forces that exposed one million square miles of open water—six Californias—beyond the average since satellites started measurements in 1979.

At a recent gathering of sea-ice experts at the University of Alaska in Fairbanks, Hajo Eicken, a geophysicist, summarized it this way: "Our stock in trade seems to be going away."

Scientists are also unnerved by the summer's implications for the future, and their ability to predict it.

Complicating the picture, the striking Arctic change was as much a result of ice moving as melting, many say. A new study, led by Son Nghiem at NASA's Jet Propulsion Laboratory and appearing this week in Geophysical Research Letters, used satellites and buoys to show that winds since 2000 had pushed huge amounts of thick old ice out of the Arctic basin past Greenland. The thin floes that formed on the resulting open water melted quicker or could be shuffled together by winds and similarly expelled, the authors said.

The pace of change has far exceeded what had been estimated by almost all the simulations used to envision how the Arctic will respond to rising concentrations of greenhouse gases linked to global warming. But that disconnect can cut two ways. Are the models overly conservative? Or are they missing natural influences that can cause wide swings in ice and temperature, thereby dwarfing the slow background warming?

The world is paying more attention than ever.

Russia, Canada and Denmark, prompted in part by years of warming and the ice retreat this year, ratcheted up rhetoric and actions aimed at securing sea routes and seabed resources.

Published: October 2, 2007. Graphic available at: www.nytimes.com/interactive/2007/10/01/science/ 20071002_ARCTIC_GRAPHIC.html.

Proponents of cuts in greenhouse gases cited the meltdown as proof that human activities are propelling a slide toward climate calamity.

Arctic experts say things are not that simple. More than a dozen experts said in interviews that the extreme summer ice retreat had revealed at least as much about what remains unknown in the Arctic as what is clear. Still, many of those scientists said they were becoming convinced that the system is heading toward a new, more watery state, and that human-caused global warming is playing a significant role.

For one thing, experts are having trouble finding any records from Russia, Alaska or elsewhere pointing to such a widespread Arctic ice retreat in recent times, adding credence to the idea that humans may have tipped the balance. Many scientists say the last substantial warming in the region, peaking in the 1930s, mainly affected areas near Greenland and Scandinavia.

Some scientists who have long doubted that a human influence could be clearly discerned in the Arctic's changing climate now agree that the trend is hard to ascribe to anything else.

"We used to argue that a lot of the variability up to the late 1990s was induced by changes in the winds, natural changes not obviously related to global warming," said John Michael Wallace, a scientist at the University of Washington. "But changes in the last few years make you have to question that. I'm much more open to the idea that we might have passed a point where it's becoming essentially irreversible."

Experts say the ice retreat is likely to be even bigger next summer because this winter's freeze is starting from such a huge ice deficit. At least one researcher, Wieslaw Maslowski of the Naval Postgraduate School in Monterey, Calif., projects a blue Arctic Ocean in summers by 2013.

In essence, Arctic waters may be behaving more like those around Antarctica, where a broad fringe of sea ice builds each austral winter and nearly disappears in the summer. (Reflecting the different geography and dynamics at the two poles, there has been a slight increase in sea-ice area around Antarctica in recent decades.)

While open Arctic waters could be a boon for shipping, fishing and oil exploration, an annual seesawing between ice and no ice could be a particularly harsh jolt to polar bears.

Many Arctic researchers warned that it was still far too soon to start sending container ships over the top of the world. "Natural variations could turn around and counteract the greenhouse-gas-forced change, perhaps stabilizing the ice for a bit," said Marika Holland, of the National Center for Atmospheric Research in Boulder, Colo.

But, she added, that will not last. "Eventually the natural variations would again reinforce the human-driven change, perhaps leading to even more rapid retreat," Dr. Holland said. "So I wouldn't sign any shipping contracts for the next 5 to 10 years, but maybe the next 20 to 30."

While experts debate details, many agree that the vanishing act of the sea ice this year was probably caused by superimposed forces including heat-trapping clouds and water vapor in the air, as well as the ocean-heating influence of unusually sunny skies in June and July. Other important factors were warm winds flowing from Siberia around a high-pressure system parked over the ocean. The winds not only would have melted thin ice but also pushed floes off-shore where currents and winds could push them out of the Arctic Ocean.

But another factor was probably involved, one with roots going back to about 1989. At that time, a periodic flip in winds and pressure patterns over the Arctic Ocean, called the Arctic Oscillation, settled into a phase that tended to stop ice from drifting in a gyre for years, so it could thicken, and instead carried it out to the North Atlantic.

The new NASA study of expelled old ice builds on previous measurements showing that the proportion of thick, durable floes that were at least 10 years old dropped to 2 percent this spring from 80 percent in the spring of 1987, said Ignatius G. Rigor, an ice expert at the University of Washington and an author of the new NASA-led study.

Without the thick ice, which can endure months of nonstop summer sunshine, more dark open water and thin ice absorbed solar energy, adding to melting and delaying the winter freeze.

The thinner fresh-formed ice was also more vulnerable to melting from heat held near the ocean surface by clouds and water vapor. This may be where the rising influence of humans on the global climate system could be exerting the biggest regional influence, said Jennifer A. Francis of Rutgers University.

Other Arctic experts, including Dr. Maslowski in Monterey and Igor V. Polyakov at the University of Alaska, Fairbanks, also see a role in rising flows of warm water entering the Arctic Ocean through the Bering Strait between Alaska and Russia, and in deep currents running north from the Atlantic Ocean near Scandinavia.

A host of Arctic scientists say it is too soon to know if the global greenhouse effect has already tipped the system to a condition in which sea ice in summers will be routinely limited to a few clotted passageways in northern Canada.

But at the university in Fairbanks—where signs of northern warming include sinkholes from thawing permafrost around its Arctic research center—Dr. Eicken and other experts are having a hard time conceiving a situation that could reverse the trends.

"The Arctic may have another ace up her sleeve to help the ice grow back," Dr. Eicken said. "But from all we can tell right now, the means for that are quite limited."

Selection 2.2

At a Columbia University symposium on art and neuroscience, writer Natalie Angier zeros in on one topic: change blindness. With characteristic good humor, she pulls readers into her disorienting experience of not seeing something that was, in fact, there. (Notice as she does this the whoops, the um and her No, wait, and . . . could it? Few other writers risk such chattiness.) Much as Angier makes this story fun, she is also careful to point out that this research matters. A natural for visuals, the online story is accompanied by a mind-bending pop-art quiz devised by neuroscientists quoted in the story.

Blind to Change, Even as it Stares Us in the Face
By NATALIE ANGIER

Leave it to a vision researcher to make you feel like Mr. Magoo.

When Jeremy Wolfe of Harvard Medical School, speaking last week at a symposium devoted to the crossover theme of Art and Neuroscience, wanted to illustrate how the brain sees the world and how often it fumbles the job, he naturally turned to a great work of art. He flashed a slide of Ellsworth Kelly's "Study for Colors for a Large Wall" on the screen, and the audience couldn't help but perk to attention. The checkerboard painting of 64 black, white and colored squares was so whimsically subtle, so poised and propulsive. We drank it in greedily, we scanned every part of it, we loved it, we owned it, and, whoops, time for a test.

Dr. Wolfe flashed another slide of the image, this time with one of the squares highlighted. Was the highlighted square the same color as the original, he asked the audience, or had he altered it? Um, different. No, wait, the same, definitely the same. That square could not now be nor ever have been anything but swimming-pool blue . . . could it? The slides flashed by. How about this mustard square here, or that denim one there, or this pink, or that black? We in the audience were at sea and flailed for a strategy. By the end of the series only one thing was clear: We had gazed on Ellsworth Kelly's masterpiece, but we hadn't really seen it at all.

The phenomenon that Dr. Wolfe's Pop Art quiz exemplified is known as change blindness: the frequent inability of our visual system to detect alterations to something staring us straight in the face. The changes needn't be as modest as a switching of paint chips. At the same meeting, held at the Italian Academy for Advanced Studies in America at Columbia University, the audience failed to notice entire stories disappearing from buildings, or the fact that one poor chicken

Published: April 1, 2008. Pop quiz available at: www.nytimes.com/interactive/2008/03/31/science/20080331_ANGIER_GRAPHIC.html#step1.

in a field of dancing cartoon hens had suddenly exploded. In an interview, Dr. Wolfe also recalled a series of experiments in which pedestrians giving directions to a Cornell researcher posing as a lost tourist didn't notice when, midway through the exchange, the sham tourist was replaced by another person altogether.

Beyond its entertainment value, symposium participants made clear, change blindness is a salient piece in the larger puzzle of visual attentiveness. What is the difference between seeing a scene casually and automatically, as in, you're at the window and you glance outside at the same old streetscape and nothing registers, versus the focused seeing you'd do if you glanced outside and noticed a sign in the window of your favorite restaurant, and oh no, it's going out of business because, let's face it, you always have that Typhoid Mary effect on things. In both cases the same sensory information, the same photonic stream from the external world, is falling on the retinal tissue of your eyes, but the information is processed very differently from one eyeful to the next. What is that difference? At what stage in the complex circuitry of sight do attentiveness and awareness arise, and what happens to other objects in the visual field once a particular object has been designated worthy of a further despairing stare?

Visual attentiveness is born of limited resources. "The basic problem is that far more information lands on your eyes than you can possibly analyze and still end up with a reasonable sized brain," Dr. Wolfe said. Hence, the brain has evolved mechanisms for combating data overload, allowing large rivers of data to pass along optical and cortical corridors almost entirely unassimilated, and peeling off selected data for a close, careful view. In deciding what to focus on, the brain essentially shines a spotlight from place to place, a rapid, sweeping search that takes in maybe 30 or 40 objects per second, the survey accompanied by a multitude of body movements of which we are barely aware: the darting of the eyes, the constant tiny twists of the torso and neck. We scan and sweep and perfunctorily police, until something sticks out and brings our bouncing cones to a halt.

The mechanisms that succeed in seizing our sightline fall into two basic classes: bottom up and top down. Bottom-up attentiveness originates with the stimulus, with something in our visual field that is the optical equivalent of a shout: a wildly waving hand, a bright red object against a green field. Bottom-up stimuli seem to head straight for the brainstem and are almost impossible to ignore, said Nancy Kanwisher, a vision researcher at M.I.T., and thus they are popular in Internet ads.

Top-down attentiveness, by comparison, is a volitional act, the decision by the viewer that an item, even in the absence of flapping parts or strobe lights, is nonetheless a sight to behold. When you are looking for a specific object—say, your black suitcase on a moving baggage carousel occupied largely by black suitcases—you apply a top-down approach, the bouncing searchlights configured to specific parameters, like a smallish, scuffed black suitcase with one broken wheel. Volitional attentiveness is much trickier to study than is a simple response to a stimulus, yet scientists have made progress through improved brain-scanning technology and the ability to measure the firing patterns of specific neurons or the synchronized firing of clusters of brain cells.

Recent studies with both macaques and humans indicate that attentiveness crackles through the brain along vast, multifocal, transcortical loops, leaping to life in regions at the back of the brain, in the primary visual cortex that engages with the world, proceeding forward into frontal lobes where higher cognitive analysis occurs, and then doubling back to the primary visual centers. En route, the initial signal is amplified, italicized and annotated, and so persuasively that the boosted signal seems to emanate from the object itself. The enhancer effect explains why, if you've ever looked at a crowd photo and had somebody point out the face of, say, a young Franklin Roosevelt or George Clooney in the throng, the celebrity's image will leap out at you thereafter as though lighted from behind.

Whether lured into attentiveness by a bottom-up or top-down mechanism, scientists said, the results of change blindness studies and other experiments strongly suggest that the visual system can focus on only one or very few objects at a time, and that anything lying outside a given moment's cone of interest gets short shrift. The brain, it seems, is a master at filling gaps and making do, of compiling a cohesive portrait of reality based on a flickering view.

"Our spotlight of attention is grabbing objects at such a fast rate that introspectively it feels like you're recognizing many things at once," Dr. Wolfe said. "But the reality is that you are only accurately representing the state of one or a few objects at any given moment." As for the rest of our visual experience, he said, it has been aptly called "a grand illusion." Sit back, relax and enjoy the movie called You.

Selection 2.3

In the dopamine-laden city of San Francisco, Patricia Leigh Brown couldn't resist attending a public conference on happiness. With a keen eye for contrasts, she describes the many earnest efforts to find and explain happiness that she found there. Brown is not a science writer, which may explain why her story conveys as much interest in the multifaceted and sometimes goofy happiness industry as it does in the serious science of happiness. But she does summarize science presented at the meeting, and that—along with cameos of participants like Aymee Coget, who offers "happiness makeovers"—makes for a great, galloping read. In the online version of the story, embedded links take readers to other Times stories on everything from dopamine and Oprah to stress and hypertension.

Even if You Can't Buy it, Happiness Is Big Business

By PATRICIA LEIGH BROWN

SAN FRANCISCO—The stock market has been on a roller coaster, banks are going under, unemployment is skyrocketing, and foreclosed homes pepper the landscape. What better time for a happiness conference?

In this dopamine-laden city, where the pursuit of well-being is something of a high art, a motley array of scientists, philosophers, doctors, psychologists, navel-gazing Googlers and Tibetan Buddhists addressed the latest findings on the science of human happiness—or eudaemonia, the classical Greek term for human flourishing.

Planned before the current crises, the first American "Happiness and Its Causes" conference was equal parts Aristotle and Oprah. It brought together heavy hitters like Paul Ekman, the psychologist known for deciphering facial "microexpressions" that reveal feelings, and Robert Sapolsky, the Stanford biologist. They considered topics like "Compassion and the Pursuit of Happiness" and "Why Zebras Don't Get Ulcers."

The conference is the latest manifestation of the booming happiness industry, subject of a growing number of books, scholarly research papers and academic courses. The concept began in Sydney in 2006 and has since expanded, its profile raised by the participation of the Dalai Lama in Sydney in 2007.

The two-day gathering in San Francisco this week, which cost $545, benefited a nonprofit group offering Buddhist teachings to prisoners. It knitted together many currents in the cultural ether: positive psychology, neuroplasticity, mindfulness-based stress reduction, the role of emotional support in cancer and the yogic ideal of "being in the present moment."

"We know more about gloominess than cheerfulness," Dr. Ekman said before exploring cross-cultural definitions of happiness, including nachas, the Yiddish expression of pride in the achievements of one's offspring.

Fortunately, given recent events, a growing number of studies over the past decade have suggested that money does not equal happiness, among them one concluding that the Inuit of northern Greenland and the Masai in Kenya were just as happy as members of the Forbes 400 list of richest Americans.

The latest word on happiness from the frontlines of medicine and science was condensed, à la SparkNotes, into user-friendly 15-minute nuggets.

Published: November 27, 2008.

Dr. David Spiegel, a professor at the Stanford School of Medicine and the director of its Center on Stress and Health, discussed the positive effects of group therapy on metastatic breast cancer patients, and his belief that people can live longer if they face their illnesses directly with proper emotional support. "I've never lost a patient to terminal crying," Dr. Spiegel said. "Suppressing sadness is the devil's bargain."

Professor Sapolsky of Stanford made a similar point about humans and baboons. Modern stress disorders contributing to hypertension, heart disease and other illnesses are the result of a disjuncture between primitive conditions and our own—or, as he put it, "running for your life in the savannah versus 30-year mortgages."

The relatively new field of behavioral neurogenetics is exploring a handful of genes that seem to be related to depression, anxiety, addictive personality, sensation seeking and other traits. But, Professor Sapolsky said in a follow-up e-mail message, a person's risk seems not predetermined but rather the result of interactions of genes and the environment, especially stressors in childhood.

Social support is vital, no matter how healthy you are, he told the crowd. "How much you groom somebody else is more important than who grooms you."

The audience, composed largely of the helping professions, also included a senior vice president of a large mortgage company, who would not give her name. She said she had laid off more than 500 people in the last six months, and was there to learn how to boost the morale of employees working weekends and holidays and making do with bonuses cut in half. "What truly makes people happy is a higher calling," she said, adding that companies like hers were not totally at fault for the mortgage crisis. "Western society is too focused on blame," she said. "In order for our customers to be happy, they have to understand that they're accountable."

"Happiness entrepreneurs" promoted themselves in the tea break that ended with the ting of a Tibetan prayer bell. Aymee Coget, who wants to be the Suze Orman of happiness, handed out fliers for her "Happiness Makeover," a three-month route to "sustainable eudaemonia." Ms. Coget, dressed to the nines in pink silk, said, "I guarantee happiness in three months."

In the Bay Area, the happiness business has been in full flower. James Baraz, a revered meditation teacher, has a 10-month course in Berkeley on "Awakening Joy." Among the exercises and meditations are suggestions for improving your life, including singing every day, making lists of things that made you happy and getting a "joy buddy."

The course is a bona fide phenomenon since an article appeared in O, Oprah Winfrey's magazine, with 300 people taking it in Berkeley and 2,500 taking it online.

"Neuroscience and spirituality are coming together," Mr. Baraz said by telephone. "It's not airy-fairy stuff."

Nevertheless, a few renegades at the conference suggested that happiness was overrated. "Unhappiness about not being happy is a modern condition," said Darrin M. McMahon, a professor of history at Florida State University. "We cannot feel good all the time, nor should we."

Yet the national embrace of "Yes We Can" hung in the air. "We've had a period of borrowing money, personal gratification, consumption and self-interest," said Dacher Keltner, a professor of psychology at the University of California, Berkeley, and a director of the Greater Good Science Center. "Now we will have a president who is talking about sacrifice."

"Human beings are wired to care and give," Dr. Keltner added, "and it's probably our best route to happiness."

Selection 2.4

To cover a conference of global warming skeptics, reporter Andrew Revkin understood he would need to put skeptics' contentious views into a larger scientific perspective. As he has written about repeatedly in book chapters and on his blog Dot Earth, context is critical in the reporting of science that is as highly politicized as global warming: You don't just pit opposing scientists against one another in an artificial show of balance; you let your audience know if the accumulated evidence supports one side more than another,[1] even if it risks inciting charges of politically inspired bias. The challenges of covering a conference of skeptics who berate the majority view were formidable. Revkin needed to find a way to air the skeptics' views, while at the same time conveying the reality and urgent risks of human-induced global warming, which the vast majority of studies now support. His resulting story picks a careful path between participating skeptics, who appeared united in their opposition to regulation if not in their views of the science, and those who have decided to no longer attend as evidence of global warming has mounted. The online story links to Revkin's blog post on climate skeptics of the prior day and to a list of other Times stories on global warming.

Skeptics Dispute Climate Worries and Each Other
By ANDREW C. REVKIN

More than 600 self-professed climate skeptics are meeting in a Times Square hotel this week to challenge what has become a broad scientific and political consensus: that without big changes in energy choices, humans will dangerously heat up the planet.

The three-day International Conference on Climate Change— organized by the Heartland Institute, a nonprofit group seeking

Published: March 8, 2009.

deregulation and unfettered markets—brings together political figures, conservative campaigners, scientists, an Apollo astronaut and the president of the Czech Republic, Vaclav Klaus.

Organizers say the discussions, which began Sunday, are intended to counter the Obama administration and Democratic law-makers, who have vowed to tackle global warming with legislation requiring cuts in the greenhouse gases that scientists have linked to rising temperatures.

But two years after the United Nations Intergovernmental Panel on Climate Change concluded with near certainty that most of the recent warming was a result of human influences, global warming's skeptics are showing signs of internal rifts and weakening support.

The meeting participants hold a wide range of views of climate science. Some concede that humans probably contribute to global warming but they argue that the shift in temperatures poses no urgent risk. Others attribute the warming, along with cooler temperatures in recent years, to solar changes or ocean cycles.

But large corporations like Exxon Mobil, which in the past financed the Heartland Institute and other groups that challenged the climate consensus, have reduced support. Many such companies no longer dispute that the greenhouse gases produced by burning fossil fuels pose risks.

From 1998 to 2006, Exxon Mobil, for example, contributed more than $600,000 to Heartland, according to annual reports of char-itable contributions from the company and company foundations.

Alan T. Jeffers, a spokesman for Exxon Mobil, said by e-mail that the company had ended support "to several public policy research groups whose position on climate change could divert attention from the important discussion about how the world will secure the energy required for economic growth in an environmentally responsible manner."

Joseph L. Bast, the president of the Heartland Institute, said Exxon and other companies were just shifting their stance to improve their image. The Heartland meeting, he said, was the last bastion of intellectual honesty on the climate issue.

"Major corporations are painting themselves green around global warming," Mr. Bast said, adding that the companies have shifted their lobbying and public relations efforts toward trying to shape climate legislation in their favor. He said that contributions, over all, had continued to rise.

But Kert Davies, a climate campaigner for Greenpeace, who is attending the Heartland event, said that the experts giving talks were "a shrinking collection of extremists" and that they were "left talking to themselves."

Organizers expected to top the attendance of about 500 at the first Heartland conference, held last year. They also point to the speaker's roster, which included Mr. Klaus and Harrison Schmitt, a geologist, Apollo astronaut and former senator.

A centerpiece of the 2008 meeting was the release of a report, "Nature, Not Human Activity, Rules the Planet." The document was expressly designed as a challenge to the reports from the Intergovernmental Panel on Climate Change.

This year, the meeting will focus on a more nuanced question: "Global warming: Was it ever a crisis?"

Most of the talks at the meeting will challenge climate orthodoxy. But some presenters, including prominent figures who have been vocal in their criticism in the past, say they will also call on their colleagues to synchronize the arguments they are using against plans to curb greenhouse gases

In a keynote talk Sunday night, Richard S. Lindzen, a professor at M.I.T. and a longtime skeptic of the mainstream consensus that global warming poses a danger, first delivered a biting attack on what he called the "climate alarm movement."

There is no solid scientific evidence to back up the models used by climate scientists who warn of dire consequences if warming continues, he said. But Dr. Lindzen also criticized widely publicized assertions by other skeptics that variations in the sun were driving temperature changes in recent decades. To attribute short-term variation in temperatures to a single cause, whether human-generated gases or something else, is erroneous, he said.

Speaking of the sun's slight variability, he said, "Acting as though this is the alternative" to blaming greenhouse gases "is asking for trouble."

S. Fred Singer, a physicist often referred to by critics and supporters alike as the dean of climate contrarians, said that he would be running public and private sessions on Monday aimed at focusing participants on which skeptical arguments were supported by science and which were not.

"As a physicist, I am concerned that some skeptics (a very few) are ignoring the physical basis," Dr. Singer said in an e-mail message.

"There is one who denies that CO_2 is a greenhouse gas, which goes against actual data," Dr. Singer said, adding that other skeptics wrongly contend that "humans are not responsible for the measured increase in atmospheric CO_2."

There are notable absences from the conference this year. Russell Seitz, a physicist from Cambridge, Mass., gave a talk at last year's meeting. But Dr. Seitz, who has lambasted environmental campaigners as distorting climate science, now warns that the skeptics are in danger of doing the same thing.

The most strident advocates on either side of the global warming debate, he said, are "equally oblivious to the data they seek to discount or dramatize."

John R. Christy, an atmospheric scientist at the University of Alabama who has long publicly questioned projections of dangerous global warming, most recently at a House committee hearing last month, said he had skipped both Heartland conferences to avoid the potential for "guilt by association."

Many participants said that any division or dissent was minor and that the global recession and a series of years with cooler temperatures would help them in combating changes in energy policy in Washington.

"The only place where this alleged climate catastrophe is happening is in the virtual world of computer models, not in the real world," said Marc Morano, a speaker at the meeting and a spokesman on environmental issues for Senator James M. Inhofe, Republican of Oklahoma.

But several climate scientists who are seeking to curb greenhouse gases strongly criticized the meeting. Stephen H. Schneider, a climatologist at Stanford University and an author of many reports by the intergovernmental climate panel, said, after reviewing the text of presentations for the Heartland meeting, that they were efforts to "bamboozle the innocent."

Yvo de Boer, head of the United Nations office managing international treaty talks on climate change, said, "I don't believe that what the skeptics say should provide any excuse to delay further" action against global warming.

But he added: "Skeptics are good. It's important to give people the confidence that the issue is being called into question."

MAKING**CONNECTIONS** 🤝

Try This. Talk to your campus conference bureau and see if you can find an upcoming scientific conference or symposium whose subject matter would appeal to a general interest audience of students and faculty. Ask the organizers for a program description and list of participants. Search the participants online to get a better feel for what they are likely to discuss. Now write a short query to the editor of your campus newspaper. The query should include what is important, interesting and/or timely about the meeting, and should suggest ways you might cover the gathering. If you need inspiration, look at the meeting stories in this chapter and notice how the writers conveyed the importance and significance of the meetings they covered, and how they also worked to engage reader interest.

Part II

features

It's a truism of journalism: One story leads to another. As science writers monitor journals and meetings for breaking news in science, they often get ideas for other kinds of stories. Some of these stories explain the basic science behind the discoveries. Some introduce the scientists who have done the research. Still others convey entire trends in scientific thinking.

Events happening outside of science also spark ideas. Modifications to a state's educational standards may prompt a behind-the-scenes look at the teaching of evolutionary biology in public schools. A calamity in which people risk their lives to save total strangers may give rise to a piece on altruism. A parent's diagnosis of Alzheimer's may inspire a story about treatments for this dreaded disease.

While events both public and personal can prompt such stories, the pieces themselves may or may not be dominated by them. Even if timely, many such stories are not so tightly bound to a deadline that they must be written with little or no delay. Journalists call these less event-driven, less time-sensitive stories "features."

The features that science writers produce give the public a view of science and technology that would otherwise be closed to them, a view that is alive with people and ideas, with illumination and conflict. Because the success of these stories depends as much on presentation as the facts, they both invite and demand the kind of deep reporting and creative play that nourishes many of us as writers. They also cultivate skills of explanation useful to any journalistic effort.

In this chapter you will find four kinds of science features: explanatory features, features about scientists, trend and issue stories and extended narratives. Each offers its own opportunities and challenges.

- **Explanatory features** offer the chance to explain everything from the workings of chromosomes to the unsung virtues of viruses, basic principles and processes that scientists don't need to spell out when talking to other scientists and only rarely take the time to explain to the public. To work, they require the skills of the best science teachers you have ever known—the ability to define things clearly, to use vivid comparisons to explain unfamiliar concepts and processes, even to use humor if it will put people at ease. With experience and a little help from scientists, it is possible to cultivate most of them.

- **Features about scientists** explain science, too, but their primary purpose is to show the men and women who bend over the slides and collect the insects, people who are anything but the "mad" and "goofy genius" stereotypes of scientists that pervade popular culture. These stories range from

Q&As, which require strong questions posed in an order that makes sense; to narrative interviews, which demand both good questions and close attention to the people in their environments; to traditional profiles, which make use of anecdotes and often the full-blown scenes of storytellers. The mantra for those who produce features about scientists is *details, details, details:* Notice them, collect them, then choose those most telling.

• **Trend and issue stories** are Big Picture stories that make sense of the buzzing, blooming confusion of developing science and of the many ways that science and society intersect. Because they do, they demand yet additional skills—the capacity to spot problems and patterns of change that might otherwise go unnoticed, and the ability to zero in on those aspects most important to the story and to audiences. But Big Picture stories don't have to tarry in Abstraction Land. The best bring patterns and problems down to earth, using many of the same skills required of stories about scientists. Again: *details, details, details.*

• **Extended narratives** can reveal the dramas in the lives of scientists and nonscientists alike. These features often read like fiction, with carefully crafted characters, scenes, dialogue, even suspense. They aren't fiction, of course; they are solidly rooted in reality. As such, they are hard to report and even harder to write. Extended narratives (which some call "creative nonfiction") may be the most challenging of all feature stories, for they are a long time in the making as the writers document with meticulous care what people say, do, think and feel (even more *details*), and as they labor to craft a deeply involving, even gripping, tale. But if writers succeed, they know they can move readers and forever change how they view their world. They may also win a Pulitzer Prize.

All of these stories do their best work when they shuttle between abstractions and specifics and when they rely on vivid language that captures the juicy reality of scientific knowledge in the making—strong nouns like whiff, splash, volley, sphere, gash, and verbs that conjure up sounds or images, like flattens, stretches, stoops, snatches, whips, squats, billows, plops.

The features in this chapter do not exhaust the possibilities for feature writing, for features are protean forms, limited only by writers' imaginations and their willingness to experiment. But all reveal writers who are applying their skills to show us aspects of science that more event- and deadline-driven stories only rarely convey. Because they do, we see with new eyes.

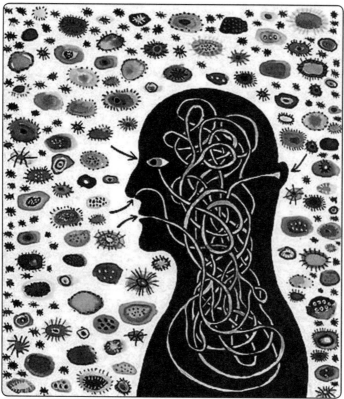

explanatory features

SCIENTISTS OFTEN STUDY THINGS WE CANNOT SEE. What they learn is not always intuitively obvious, and their conversations with other scientists can sound like hums from outer space. So how do science writers take the often strange and difficult ideas of science and explain them so that they both engage the public and enhance our understanding?

While few science journalists think of themselves as educators, the most skilled among them use explanatory techniques that the most effective biology, chemistry and physics teachers have always used to draw students in and keep them learning:

- **Familiar Comparisons.** They take concepts and processes that are strange or difficult and connect them to what is familiar and easy to understand: comparing the X chromosome to a harried mother, for example, or a virus to a freeloading schemer.

- **Clear Definitions.** They define things clearly. So they may define a primary cilia both by what it is ("solitary slivers that poke out of almost every cell in the body") and by what it is not ("the wisps that wave Rockette-like in our airways").

- **Vivid, Conversational Language.** They explain things conversationally, often using strong, sensory language to help us to visualize in our mind's eye unseen physical and biological processes: Chromosomes "prod" genes, for example, and viruses "jimmy" cellular locks.

- **Humor.** And if they've got the talent and it fits, they may even embellish their words with humor, the better to calm the nerves of the edgy.

But these aren't the only techniques good science writers use.

- **Visuals.** Increasingly, many supplement their words with visuals. Indeed, writers at The Times and elsewhere often collaborate with graphic artists to create visual models that reinforce, and sometimes even amplify, their descriptions of how science, technology and nature work. Some of the resulting graphics are interactive and involve readers in learning about processes that would be much more difficult to absorb if left to words. (See, for example, the graphic on teleportation in Chapter 1 and the graphic on melting sea ice in Chapter 2.)

• **Transformative Explanations.** Finally, when trying to explain science that violates people's ordinary understandings of the world, science writers often pull out yet another trick of effective science teachers—the "transformative explanation." Few working science journalists are likely to know this technical term, but most have experienced at one time or other the necessity of righting people's mistaken views when the findings of science defy conventional wisdom, as they often do. Indeed, the best science writers instinctively take steps that have been found effective for transforming wrong ideas: They identify an incorrect or incomplete idea that people may have, acknowledging (if it exists) its apparent plausibility. They reveal how the idea is wrong or insufficient. They then present the counterintuitive but more scientifically accurate idea, showing why this second notion is better or more complete. We all tend to think earthquakes are bad, for example, and it's true—they can be. But in the long run they are also a good thing, essential for the evolution of complex life, and so essential for humanity. Likewise, many of us think manatees are as stupid as sweet potatoes—everything about them seems to say so. However, when you look at the emerging scientific evidence, it's clear that they are good at what they need to be good at; they are perfectly adapted to their environment.

The stories in this chapter are explanatory features, ones that explicitly focus on explaining nature or natural processes. They are offered here to prompt discussion of these and other explanatory strategies that science writers bring to the stories they write. One of the features has been annotated to highlight some of these techniques. If you pay close attention to this story and to the others, they will sensitize you to explanatory tools that top-flight science writers use, not only in this collection, but in fine science writing everywhere.

 STORY**SCAN**

Selection 3.1

This Times piece, one of the first in a series of occasional explanatory features on the secrets of the cell, focuses on primary cilia. These tiny slivers extend from almost every cell in our bodies and play an important role in the formation of neurons, the organization of the brain and the healing of wounds. As writer Wallace Ravven explains these cellular extensions, he reveals himself to be a master of both definition and metaphor. His story is annotated to show these and other explanatory techniques. A Times graphic showing the work of primary cilia, and other cilia too, amplifies the written explanations.

SECRETS OF THE CELL
Antenna on Cell Surface Is Key to Development and Disease

By WALLACE RAVVEN

At first they cannot see at night. Then daytime vision fails, and by age 5 or 10, these children are blind. Some become extremely obese and develop diabetes and kidney disease.

The crushing condition is known as Bardet-Biedl syndrome, and it is caused by inherited defects in the child's primary cilia— solitary slivers that poke out of almost every cell in the body. These are not the wisps that wave Rockette-like in our airways. They are stiff, tiny, nearly transparent structures, sometimes as little as one-thousandth the size of the cell. Only one sticks out of each cell, and it acts as both an antenna and a machine to process signals essential for development and survival.

Largely ignored for a century as vestigial, primary cilia are now emerging as pivotal players in the subtle shifts of signaling that shape the fetus and assure normal adult cell growth. Powerful genetic and imaging tools have opened a window into these machines, fueling a flurry of research intended to clarify their role in health and disease.

"Primary cilia are turning out to be a kind of signaling machine that no one had appreciated," said Matthew Scott, a geneticist at Stanford Medical School. "It's as if there was a shed out back with all sorts of weird machinery, and hardly anyone had ever looked in. But the farm can't work without it."

In the last few years, scientists have discovered that the single cilium on each cell receives and reconfigures the signals that form neurons, sculpt the body plan and organize the brain. In adults, cilia are required to heal wounds and grow cells, and when they malfunction, they can help cause cancer. Damage to primary cilia is now also linked to kidney disease, obesity and even the failure of adult neuron development.

When audiences might confuse one concept with another, it can help to define the concept both by what it is and by what it is not. Ravven does that here, and in addition uses a vivid comparison to enliven our understanding.

Scientists don't always speak in jargon. In fact, they can often offer great comparisons. Still, you may have to ask lots of questions and try out your own metaphors before you get something this clear and engaging.

Published: May 19, 2009. Graphic available at: www.nytimes.com/imagepages/2009/05/18/ science/19cilia.ready.html.

If you can extend a metaphor multiple ways without distorting the science, it can facilitate understanding.

A quick succession of discoveries in the past 10 years has revealed an intricate architecture within each cilium that supports two-way trafficking of proteins up and down tubes that run the cilium's length. Molecular motors push particles along the tubes. These motor proteins are linked to the cilium's outer envelope, so they can move material up and down the membrane itself.

More startling than the finding of this elaborate system was the discovery a few years later that traffic on the cilia highway includes the signals that switch on genes to drive development of the embryo. These signals are themselves proteins, like the highly important Sonic hedgehog.

The writer introduces the technical term intraflagellar transport *only after he defines it. This reflects a basic principle of explanation: Start with the familiar; it will make the unfamiliar information that follows easier to understand.*

The cilia trafficking system, now known as intraflagellar transport, was discovered in the green algae Chlamydomonas, which has long, thin flagella, accessible to study. Flagella and cilia have the same structure, part of life's toolkit for more than a billion years.

In the mid-1990s, Keith Kozminski, a graduate student in the Yale laboratory of Joel Rosenbaum, placed small beads on the membrane of Chlamydomonas, and under a powerful microscope he saw that some of them moved along the surface of the membrane.

He and Dr. Rosenbaum knew that meant motors must have been at work inside the cilium. Motor proteins had been discovered elsewhere in cells. Among other tasks, they are responsible for pushing paired chromosomes apart during cell division.

When a source explains something more vividly than you can, consider putting it in quotes. This quote visualizes both the traffic up and down the cilium and the moment of discovery. It is the stuff of storytelling.

"We were using the very best optics available," Dr. Rosenbaum said. "Keith told me he could see particles under the membrane, moving up from the bottom to the tip of the cilium and back down again. My first response was, 'Almost certainly that is an optical artifact.' "

All transport systems are engineered, and have "architecture," so this noun works.

But it was for real. Douglas Cole in Dr. Rosenbaum's lab and Gregory Pazour at the University of Massachusetts Medical School soon identified a number of flagellum genes needed for the architecture that made the transport system possible.

In 2000, with George Witman of the University of Massachusetts, they found the first link between primary cilia and disease. They showed that a gene connected to transport within the Chlamydomonas flagellum was a close relative of a mouse gene that causes a severe kidney disease when it is defective. A mutated flagellum or cilium gene, then, could cause a serious, recognized illness.

Polycystic kidney disease affects about 600,000 people in the United States. It is the most common life-threatening disease caused by a single gene mutation, and the reason for most of the need for dialysis. The disease develops when cysts grow in the kidney and block its filtering capacity. Cilia normally protrude into the kidney tubules and bend in the urine flow. If a mutation prevents cilia from bending, kidney cells needlessly divide, and cysts form.

The connection of cilia to kidney disease extended the prevailing view that cilia were antennas capable of sensing the environment. But a few years later, the discovery of a far more pervasive cilia role startled developmental biologists and geneticists. In 2003, Kathryn Anderson of the Sloan-Kettering Institute and a graduate student, Danwei Huangfu, went on a kind of genetic fishing expedition.

They were looking for genes that affect early development of mouse embryos, so they exposed the embryos to a chemical mutagen and found mutated genes that caused early neural defects. Some of the mutated genes were somehow connected to the pathways followed by Sonic hedgehog, an extremely important growth-promoting protein involved in embryonic development. And among these genes were two that affected the construction of cilia.

The conclusion was that cilia were involved in an important way in the Sonic hedgehog system, which reaches into so many aspects of cell biology. "Kathryn Anderson's discovery was astounding," said Dr. Frédéric de Sauvage, the vice president for molecular biology at the biotech company Genentech. "Virtually all basal cell carcinomas—the most common form of skin

If you can create a picture in words, it can help readers to understand unfamiliar processes in nature. In this passage, we actually see how malfunctioning cilia contribute to a disease of the kidney. Nothing fancy, but clear.

"Sonic hedgehog" in a story that talks of "heavy traffic" mixes metaphors in an unfortunate way for those who don't know the scientific term. (Picture a poor hedgehog in the headlights. Some readers may also conjure up "Sonic the Hedgehog," the video game.) But when scientists name things this way, what can you do?

cancer—have mutated genes involved in processing hedgehog signals. Mutations in components of the hedgehog pathway keep it turned on all the time."

Genentech is now running clinical trials of a compound that inhibits unrestrained signaling in the hedgehog pathway for potential treatment of basal cell carcinoma, colorectal cancer and ovarian cancer.

Arturo Alvarez-Buylla, a neuroscientist at the University of California, San Francisco, recently began studying how primary cilia affect the brain's neural stem and progenitor cells. He suspects damaged primary cilia may cause some types of brain tumors. In related research, working with Young-Goo Han, a postdoctoral fellow, he discovered that neural stem cells that lack primary cilia failed to give rise to adult neurons in the hippocampus, a region of the brain required for memory formation.

He sees strong evidence that cilia also help orient neuronal stem cells in tissues in the direction in which they will grow.

Comparisons to Rube Goldberg contraptions are overused in science writing, and it's not clear how this one helps understanding here, but at least it offers something vivid and concrete to break up the abstractions.

Since Dr. Anderson's discovery, reported in Nature, scientists have begun to decipher how the cilium's Rube Goldberg-like mechanism, on the fringes of the cell, controls genes that are cradled in the cell's nucleus.

Bradley Yoder of the University of Alabama at Birmingham discovered that the protein units that ultimately deliver hedgehog's commands to the genes actually reside in the cilium's tip. Jeremy Reiter at the University of California, San Francisco, and Dr. Scott at Stanford have shown that hedgehog's arrival—at a different site on the cilium—turns on this gene-switching protein.

Again, we are led to see a process. The verbs are plain, but active.

The protein messengers move down the cilium tube to the nucleus, where they light up or turn off dozens of genes.

Scientists zeroing in on different diseases are encountering more cilia defects. For example, the hormone leptin circulates throughout the body, gauging fat deposition and docking onto neurons to convey that the body has adequate food. One of leptin's targets is a class of neurons in the hypothalamus. Dr. Yoder and Val Sheffield at the University of Iowa have found in mice that when the lone cilium on each such neuron is disrupted, the animals seem unable to sense leptin as they normally would. They overeat and become obese.

At a meeting in February in Italy focusing on the latest primary cilia research, Soren Christensen of the University of Copenhagen discussed cell culture studies showing that primary cilia are essential for wound healing. He studies a signaling molecule that, like Sonic hedgehog, diffuses to tissue to spur growth and division. In Italy, he reported that cells lacking cilia failed to migrate normally toward a wound, a process that usually is the first step in healing. He and Dr. Yoder have now confirmed this in live mice.

"If you look at mutated cells that cannot make the primary cilium, they are blindfolded," Dr. Christensen said. They cannot sense the signals from the wound. "They don't migrate. They just run in place."

Once more, scientists are often your best sources for metaphors.

Other research reported in Italy focused on primary cilia's effect on another signaling molecule, called Wnt, which orients cells in developing tissue and enables them to sense their three-dimensional location. Kimberly McDermott of the University of California, San Francisco, described research showing that primary cilia are essential for Wnt to control normal mouse mammary gland branching in puberty and pregnancy. Although the cilium appears to be far removed from the heart of the cell, it is tightly tied to cell division. As the cell prepares to divide, the cilium disassembles, and rebuilds only after division.

Another visualization of a process, this time in the words of a scientist.

"This little antenna is poking out of the cell surface and may well communicate when and in what orientation the cell should divide," said Wallace Marshall at the University of California, San Francisco.

Dr. Marshall recently helped clarify a classic discovery 10 years ago of how the embryo "knows" left from right. This sense enables normal placement and structure of the heart. Unlike most primary cilia, the subset of cilia involved in this process move. The original discovery had revealed that thousands of individual cilia in the week-old mouse embryo rotate from their base, similar to the way a stiff arm rotates around the shoulder.

When the rotation of cilia in mouse embryos is likened to "the way a stiff arm rotates around the shoulder," we gain an immediate sense of how left-right asymmetry is established.

The net effect is a leftward flow of embryonic fluid that establishes left-right asymmetry. Dr. Marshall and his colleagues confirmed that each cilium projected out at a left-leaning angle to the cell surface, and they used fluid dynamics models to demonstrate that the angle and motion accounted for the flow observed in the embryos.

Some scientists are exploring the possibility that cilia may do more than regulate master signaling molecules. They may actually coordinate protein signals for proper fetal development.

Dr. Yoder said he was confident that cilia coordinated different signals. But what interests him most is homing in on the mutations affecting the cilia.

"We need that to identify those genes so we can develop drugs to counter defective signals," he said. "That could help us attack severe obesity, polycystic kidney disease, Bardet-Biedl syndrome and even cancer."

Selection 3.2

In this explanatory feature, Pulitzer Prize–winning science writer Natalie Angier takes advantage of an unpleasant personal experience to explain the norovirus, a nasty bug that felled her husband and herself following a New Year's Eve party. Angier's explanatory style has been likened to a "romp." She is usually playful and, more often than most science writers, funny. But if you read enough of her work, you quickly see that there's a serious science educator at work. As with the previous story on cilia, she defines her subject both by what it is and by what it is not, and she makes much use of metaphor. But in addition, she describes viruses as "tiny enough to fit millions on board a single fleck of spit," a move that intentionally evokes a visceral response. (In a Q&A at the end of this chapter, Angier discusses why sensory language so often works to explain science.) Then, in magnanimous deference to emerging findings in virology, she suggests that viruses are more than the easy-to-hate freeloaders that we imagine them to be when they bring us down. In truth, they are "delicate" and "needy," even useful. With these additional explanatory strokes, Angier illuminates a biological phenomenon that might otherwise remain no more than a puke-inducing misery.

Tiny Specks of Misery, Both Vile and Useful

By NATALIE ANGIER

I spent New Year's Eve with friends and family. A couple of days later, my pathologically healthy mother called to say she'd gotten very sick after the party, like nothing she'd experienced before. She thought it had been a stomach bug. Hey, it's just like in "The Devil Wears Prada," I said lightly, the perfect way to jump-start your new diet!

Hardy har. By that afternoon, my husband and I had been drafted into the same violent weight-loss program, and for the next 18 hours would treat the mucosal lining of our stomachs like so much pulp in a pumpkin, while our poor daughter ran around scrubbing her hands and every surface in sight as she sought to stay healthy. I am relieved to report that she succeeded, and that her parents lost 10 pounds between them.

The agent of our misery was a virus, very likely a type of norovirus. Named for Norwalk, Ohio, the site of a severe outbreak of vomiting, nausea and diarrhea among schoolchildren in the late 1960s, the norovirus is a small, spherical, highly contagious virus that targets the digestive system. Its sour suite of symptoms is often referred to as "stomach flu," but norovirus infection is distinct from the flu, which is caused by the influenza virus and targets not the gut but the lungs.

Well, not that distinct. Noroviruses, flu viruses, the rhino and corona viruses that cause the common cold, the herpes virus that causes the cold sore, all are active players in the wheezing ambient pleurisy of January.

As viruses, all of them are, by definition, infectious parasitic agents tiny enough to pass through a microfilter that would trap bacteria and other microbes, tiny enough to fit millions on board a single fleck of spit. All viruses have at their core compact genetic instructions for making more viruses, some of the booklets written in DNA, others in the related nucleic language of RNA. Our cells have the means to read either code, whether they ought to or not. Encasing the terse viral genomes are capsids, protective coats constructed of interlocking protein modules and decorated with some sort of docking device, a pleat of just the right shape to infiltrate a particular cell. Rhinoviruses dock onto receptors projecting from the cells of our nasal passages, while hepatitis viruses are shaped to exploit portholes on liver cells.

Their ergonomic specificity stems from the competition for a niche in a virus-packed world. Viruses very likely arose along with or possibly just before the appearance of the first living cells, nearly four billion years ago, and they have been jimmying cellular locks ever since. "Viruses are found everywhere, in every tree of life," said Phillip

Published: January 8, 2008.

A. Sharp of the Center for Cancer Research at M.I.T., "and every virus has to have a scheme."

It's easy to hate viruses for those freeloading schemes: nice trick, forcing me to throw up just so you can get out and mingle. How about if I name an entire class of computer problems after you? Yet viruses can seem almost tragic. Many strains, it turns out, are surprisingly delicate.

"Microbes like the anthrax bacterium can remain dormant in the soil for years" and still retain their power to kill, said Marlene Zuk, author of "Riddled With Life" and a professor of biology at the University of California, Riverside. "But viruses are really fragile, and they can't survive outside their host for very long." A few hours, maybe a couple of days left unclaimed on a cup or keyboard, and the average viral spore falls apart.

And they are so nakedly needy. They depend on our cells to manufacture every detail of their offspring, to print up new copies of the core instruction booklets, to fabricate the capsid jackets and to deliver those geometrically tidy newborn virions to fresh host shores. Through us, viruses can transcend mere chemistry and lay claim to biology. Many scientists view viruses, with their lack of autonomous means of metabolism or reproduction, as straddling the border between life and nonlife. But if there is ever a case to be made for the liveliness of viruses, it is when they are replicating and mutating and evolving inside us.

Yet viruses have not only taken; they have also repaid us in ways we are just beginning to tally. "Viral elements are a large part of the genetic material of almost all organisms," said Dr. Sharp, who won a Nobel Prize for elucidating details of our genetic code. Base for nucleic base, he said, "we humans are well over 50 percent viral."

Scientists initially dismissed the viral elements in our chromosomes as so much tagalong "junk DNA." But more recently some researchers have proposed that higher organisms have in fact co-opted viral genes and reworked them into the source code for major biological innovations, according to Luis P. Villarreal, director of the Center for Virus Research at the University of California, Irvine.

Some genes involved in the growth of the mammalian placenta, for example, have a distinctly viral character, as do genes underlying the recombinant powers of our adaptive immune system—precisely the part that helps us fight off viruses.

In fact, it may well have been through taking genomic tips from our viral tormentors that we became so adept at keeping them at bay.

"Our bodies spontaneously recover from viruses more so than overwhelming bacterial infections," said Anthony S. Fauci, director of the National Institute of Allergy and Infectious Diseases. "Viral infections have shaped the nature of the human immune system, and we have adapted to mount a very effective response against most of the viruses that we confront." Vaccines accentuate this facility, he added, which is why vaccination programs have been most successful in preventing viral diseases.

Should prevention elude you, well, you may at least lose some weight.

Selection 3.3

In addition to her other talents, Natalie Angier has mastered the art of the extended comparison, one that can structure an entire piece. A case in point is her explanation of the X chromosome, written near Mother's Day as part of her biweekly column, "Basics." In the piece, Angier compares the chromosome to an overworked and underappreciated mother. It's an amusing comparison, illustrating Angier's frequent and deliberate use of humor to make readers feel comfortable with science. While purists might object to this playful personification, as an organizing metaphor that enhances our understanding of the X, it works. Adding to the mood is an accompanying drawing of toy-inspired acrobats who fly through the air, then link their bodies to make the letter X.

BASICS
For Motherly X Chromosome, Gender Is Only the Beginning
By NATALIE ANGIER

As May dawns and the mothers among us excitedly anticipate the clever e-cards that we soon will be linking to and the overpriced brunches that we will somehow end up paying for, the following job description may ring a familiar note:

Must be exceptionally stable yet ridiculously responsive to the needs of those around you; must be willing to trail after your loved ones, cleaning up their messes and compensating for their deficiencies and selfishness; must work twice as hard as everybody else; must accept blame for a long list of the world's illnesses; must have a knack for shaping young minds while in no way neglecting the less glamorous tissues below; must have a high tolerance for babble and repetition; and must agree, when asked, to shut up, fade into the background and pretend you don't exist.

As it happens, the above precis refers not only to the noble profession of motherhood to which we all owe our lives and guilt complexes. It is also a decent character sketch of the chromosome that allows a human or any other mammal to become a mother in the first place: the X chromosome.

Published: May 1, 2007. Drawing is featured at the beginning of this chapter.

The X chromosome, like its shorter, stubbier but no less conspicuous counterpart, the Y chromosome, is a so-called sex chromosome, a segment of DNA entrusted with the pivotal task of sex determination. A mammalian embryo outfitted with an X and Y chromosomal set buds into a male, while a mammal bearing a pair of X chromosomes emerges from the maternal berth with birthing options of her own.

Yet the X chromosome does much more than help specify an animal's reproductive plumbing. As scientists who study the chromosome lately have learned, the X is a rich repository of genes vital to brain development and could hold the key to the evolution of our particularly corrugated cortex. Moreover, the X chromosome behaves unlike any of the other chromosomes of the body—unlike little bigman Y, certainly, but also unlike our 22 other pairs of chromosomes, the self-satisfied autosomes that constitute the rest of our genome, of the complete DNA kit packed into every cell that we carry. It is a supple, switchbacking, multitasking gumby doll patch of the genome; and the closer you look, the more Cirque du Soleil it appears.

Although the precise details of its chemical structure and performance are only just emerging, the X chromosome has long been renowned among geneticists, who named it X not because of its shape, as is commonly presumed—the non-sex chromosomes also vaguely resemble an "X" at times during cell division—but because they were baffled by the way it held itself apart from the other chromosomal pairs. "They called it X for unknown," said Mark T. Ross of the X Chromosome Group at the Wellcome Trust Sanger Institute in Cambridge. (When its much tinier male counterpart was finally detected, researchers simply continued down the alphabet for a name.) Many of the diseases first understood to be hereditary were linked to X's span, for the paradoxical reason that such conditions showed their face most often in those with just a single X to claim: men.

Scientists eventually determined that we inherit two copies of our 23,000 or so genes, one from each parent; and that these genes, these chemical guidelines for how to build and maintain a human, are scattered among the 23 pairs of chromosomes, along with unseemly amounts of apparent chemical babble.

Having two copies of every gene proves especially handy when one of those paired genes is defective, at which point the working version of the gene can step in and specify enough of the essential bodybuilding protein that the baby blooms just fine and may never know its DNA is hemi-flawed. And here is where the Y's petite stature looms large. Because it holds a mere 50ish different genes against its counterpart's 1,100, the vast majority of X-based genes have no potential pinch-hitter on the Y. A boy who inherits from his mother an X chromosome that enfolds a faulty gene for a bloodclotting factor, say, or for a muscle protein or for a color receptor won't find succor in the chromosomal analogue bestowed by Dad. He will be born with hemophilia, or muscular dystrophy, or color-blindness. But, hey, he will be a boy, for male-making is the task to which the Y chromosome is almost exclusively devoted.

In fact, it is to compensate for the monomania of the Y that the X chromosome has become such a mother of a multitasker. Over the 300 million years of evolution, as the Y chromosome has shrugged off more of its generic genetic responsibilities in pursuit of sexual specialization, the X has had to pick up the slack. It, too, has pawned off genes to other chromosomes. But for those genes still in its charge, the X must double their output, to prod each gene to spool out twice the protein of an ordinary gene and thus be the solo equivalent of any twinned genes located on other, nonsexy chromosomes.

Ah, but women, who have two X chromosomes, two copies of those 1,100 genes: What of them? With its usual Seussian sense of playfulness, evolution has opted to zeedo the hoofenanny. In a girl's cells, you don't see two pleasantly active X chromosomes behaving like two ordinary nonsex chromosomes. You see one hyperactive X chromosome, its genes busily pumping out twice the standard issue of protein, just as in a boy's cells; and you see one X chromosome that has been largely though not wholly shut down, said Laura Carrel, a geneticist at Penn State College of Medicine.

Through an elaborate process called X inactivation, the chromosome is blanketed with a duct tape of nucleic acid. In some cells of a woman's body it may be the chromosome from Dad that's muffled, while in other cells the maternal one stays mum.

Every daughter, then, is a walking mosaic of clamorous and quiet chromosomes, of fatherly sermons and maternal advice, while every son has but his mother's voice to guide him. Remember this, fellows: you are all mama's boys.

Selection 3.4

Erica Goode's feature on manatees is an example of an entire story built around the challenge of changing people's ideas about a subject. With a wealth of detail, her story completely transforms conventional wisdom about manatees—that they are big, lumbering dunces. Like all good, transformative explanations, this one begins with the incorrect but plausible view people have of the subject. There is nothing abstract or dull about how Goode does this. Using vivid details, like oohs and ahs, she shows, rather than tells, how sleeker, faster sea mammals get all the praise. The rest of the story uses emerging scientific evidence to right, one by one, the many wrong views of this giant sea creature. By the end of the story, it is hard to deny that manatees are a lot more complex than any of us knew. By circling back to the lede, the final quote, terrific by any standard, nails the story's focus. This feature was one of the most read science/technology stories on The Times Web site in 2006. A Times graphic and an audio slideshow narrated by one of Goode's scientist-sources nicely reinforce this message on the Web.

Sleek? Well, No. Complex? Yes, Indeed.

By ERICA GOODE

It is a good thing the manatee has thick skin.

To the dolphins, the whales, the sea otters go the admiring oohs and ahs, the cries of, "How sleek!" "How beautiful!"

The manatee, sluggish, squinty-eyed and bewhiskered, is more likely to have its rotund bulk compared to "a sweet potato," its homely, almost fetal looks deemed "prehistoric"—terms applied by startled New Yorkers this month to a Florida manatee that made an unexpected appearance in the Hudson River.

Cleverness is unhesitatingly ascribed to the dolphin. But the manatee is not seen leaping through hoops or performing somersaults on command, and even scientists have suspected it may not be the smartest mammal in the sea. Writing in 1902, a British anatomist, Grafton Elliot Smith, groused that manatee brains—tiny in proportion to the animals' bodies and smooth as a baby's cheek—resembled "the brains of idiots."

Yet the conception of the simple sea cow is being turned on its head by the recent work of Roger L. Reep, a neuroscientist at the University of Florida at Gainesville, and a small group of other manatee researchers, including Gordon B. Bauer, a professor of psychology at New College of Florida, and David Mann, a biologist at the University of South Florida.

In studies over the last decade, they have shown that the endangered Florida manatee (Trichechus manatus latirostris) is as unusual in its physiology, sensory capabilities and brain organization as in its external appearance.

Far from being slow learners, manatees, it turns out, are as adept at experimental tasks as dolphins, though they are slower-moving and, having no taste for fish, more difficult to motivate. They have a highly developed sense of touch, mediated by thick hairs called vibrissae that adorn not just the face, as in other mammals, but the entire body, according to the researchers' recent work.

And where earlier scientists saw in the manatee's brain the evidence of deficient intelligence, Dr. Reep sees evolution's shaping of an animal perfectly adapted to its environment.

Dr. Reep—a co-author, with Robert K. Bonde, a biologist at the Sirenia Project of the United States Geological Survey, of a recently published book, "The Florida Manatee: Biology and Conservation" (University Press of Florida)—argues that the small size of the manatee brain may have little or nothing to do with its intelligence.

Published: August 29, 2006. Graphic available at www.nytimes.com/imagepages/2006/08/28/science/ 20060829_MANA_GRAPHIC.html. Audio slideshow available at www.nytimes.com/packages/khtml/ 2006/08/28/science/20060829_MANA_AUDIOSS.html.

Brain size has been linked by some biologists with the elaborateness of the survival strategies an animal must develop to find food and avoid predators. Manatees have the lowest brain-to-body ratio of any mammal. But, as Dr. Reep noted, they are aquatic herbivores, subsisting on sea grass and other vegetation, with no need to catch prey. And with the exception of powerboats piloted by speed-happy Floridians, which kill about 80 manatees a year and maim dozens more, they have no predators.

"Manatees don't eat anybody, and they're not eaten by anybody," Dr. Reep said.

But he also suspects that rather than the manatee's brain being unusually small for its body, the situation may be the other way around: that its body, for sound evolutionary reasons, has grown unusually large in proportion to its brain.

A large body makes it easier to keep warm in the water—essential for a mammal, like the manatee, with a glacially slow metabolism. It also provides room for the large digestive system necessary to process giant quantities of low-protein, low-calorie food.

The manatee must consume 10 percent of its 800-pound to 1,200-pound body weight daily. Hugh, 22, and Buffett, 19, captive manatees at the Mote Marine Laboratory in Sarasota, Fla., are fed 72 heads of lettuce and 12 bunches of kale a day, their trainers say. And in a 2000 study, Iske Larkin, a researcher in Dr. Reep's laboratory, used colored kernels of corn to determine that food took an average of seven days to pass through a captive manatee's intestinal tract—a leisurely digestive pace comparable to that of a koala or a two-toed sloth.

The smooth surface of the manatee's brain—it generally has only one main vertical fissure, or sulcus, and no surface ridges to speak of—is more puzzling, Dr. Reep concedes. The brains of virtually every other mammal bigger than a small rodent show some degree of folding. And scientists have generally taken the human cortex, a study in ridges and crevasses, as a model of higher-order mental process, assuming accordingly that brain convolution is a sign of intelligence.

"I would make a guess that if you showed a manatee brain to a modern neuroscientist, to this day, most would consider that the manatee is not very smart, that idea is so ingrained," Dr. Reep said.

But he added that scientists still know almost nothing about what drives the development of brain formation. Evolutionary lineage appears to have an influence. The brains of primates tend to have different patterns of convolution than those of carnivores, for example. And mechanical factors like brain size and the denseness of neural tissue in the cortex may play a role.

Manatees have a relatively thick cerebrum, with multiple layers that may, Dr. Reep suspects, indicate complexity despite a lack of folding.

In any case, he said, brain convolution "doesn't seem to be correlated with the capacity to do things."

More to the point, intelligence—in animals or in humans—is hard to define, much less compare between species, Dr. Reep said. Is the intelligence of a gifted concert pianist the same as that of a math whiz? Is a lion's cunning the same as the cleverness of a Norwegian rat?

The manatee is good at what it needs to be good at.

Sirenia, a biological order that includes the dugong and three extant species of manatees, appear in the fossil record in the early to middle Eocene, about 50 million years ago, around the same time as whales, horses and other mammals, said Daryl P. Domning, a professor of anatomy at Howard University who has collected and studied the fossils of manatees and other sirenians around the world.

Four-legged land mammals that returned to the sea, the sirenians shed their hind legs but retained vestigial pelvic bones and, in two manatee species, nails on their flippers. Manatees count among their close relatives the elephant and the rock hyrax. Another sirenian, Steller's sea cow, lived in the Bering Sea and exceeded 5,000 pounds. It was hunted into extinction in the 1700's.

Although dugongs appear in the folklore of Palau, sirenians in general "don't seem to have inspired the amount of awe that other animals did, like pumas and jaguars and things like that," Dr. Domning said. "You don't find them putting up monuments or statues to them."

Florida manatees, a subspecies of the West Indian manatee, thrive in warm, shallow coastal waters and migrate when the temperature drops. They spend a great deal of time eating, with frequent naps between meals. Their social world is relatively straightforward. Males mate with females in a violent affair that resembles a gang rape; manatee calves stick close to their mothers for about two years, then head off on their own.

Groups of manatees may cluster, playing, grazing and dozing at a warm-water source—a power plant, for example. But they are just as likely to be loners, striking out wherever the warm currents take them, even if that means passing the Statue of Liberty and heading up the East River to Rhode Island, as an earlier northward manatee pioneer, Chessie, did in 1995. (The manatee spotted in the Hudson in early August was seen on Aug. 17 even farther north, off Cape Cod. But two days later it had turned south again to Rhode Island. The last reported sighting was the afternoon of Aug. 25, in Bristol Harbor, R.I.)

The manatee's sensory capacities and brain organization, researchers are learning, are perfectly suited to its style of life.

In the dim, muddy shallows where manatees feed, for example, sharp eyes are less than useful. And sight is not a manatee's strong suit, though the heavy-lidded wrinkled dimples that serve as eyes are undoubtedly part of the animal's charm.

Manatees distinguish colors. The orange of carrots in a trainer's hand can inspire a captive manatee to an uncharacteristic speed. But they are bad at distinguishing brightness, and they are clumsy, frequently bumping into things.

In 2003, Dr. Bauer and four colleagues, including Debborah Colbert and Joseph Gaspard III of the Mote Marine Laboratory, reported in The International Journal of Comparative Psychology on the visual testing of the Mote manatees, Hugh and Buffett. The manatees were trained to discriminate between two underwater panels of evenly spaced vertical lines, swimming toward the correct panel for a reward of apples, beets, carrots and monkey biscuits. By varying the distance between the lines, the researchers showed that Buffett's eyesight was about 20/420, similar to a cow's and far worse than a human's.

Poor Hugh, Dr. Bauer said, was blind "even by manatee standards."

Yet far more valuable than sight in murky water is an acute sense of touch, and it is here that manatees excel. Their mastery of the tactile world, Dr. Reep and his colleagues have recently established, comes from the thick, bristly hairs called vibrissae. Unlike normal hair fibers, each vibrissa is a finely calibrated sensory device, its follicle surrounded by a blood-filled pocket or blood sinus. The movement of the hair produces changes in the fluid that are registered by receptors around the hair follicle, which transmit the information to the brain via hundreds of nerve fibers. An increase in blood pressure increases the sensitivity of the hairs.

In research over the last five years, Dr. Reep and his colleagues have shown that manatees have 2,000 facial vibrissae of varying thickness, 600 of them in the so-called oral disk, a circular region between mouth and nose that the manatee uses much like an elephant's trunk, to grasp or explore objects. Each facial vibrissa is linked with 50 to 200 nerve fibers. An additional 3,000 vibrissae are spaced less densely over the rest of the body.

Rats, dogs, sea lions and other whiskered animals also have vibrissae, but not in such large numbers and typically only on the face. In research not yet published, Diana Sarko, a graduate student in Dr. Reep's lab, confirmed that another mammal has vibrissae dispersed over its body, the rodent-faced, rabbit-size rock hyrax, the manatee's distant cousin.

Like the manatee, the hyrax, which inhabits rocky outcroppings, spends much of its time in dim light and has poor vision.

"Rock hyraxes live in little cave dwellings, so they probably use these hairs to navigate in these dark surroundings," Ms. Sarko said.

In testing, Buffett, Hugh and other captive animals have proved just how acute a manatee's tactile sense can be. Using the bristles on the oral disk and the upper lips, manatees can detect minute differences in the width of grooves and ridges on an underwater panel. A manatee tested by a team of researchers in Germany could distinguish differences as small as 0.05 millimeters, as well as an elephant performing the same task with its trunk, and almost as well as a human. Hugh and Buffett did even better, outperforming the elephant and, in Buffett's case, the human.

The findings were presented at the 16th Biennial Conference on the Biology of Marine Mammals in 2005.

A sensory modality that is so important should be prominently represented in the brain. And, confirming an observation first made by a German scientist in 1912, Dr. Reep's research team has identified large clusters of cells called Rindenkerne in sensory processing areas in the deep layers of the manatee's cerebral cortex. These clusters, the researchers suspect, are the manatee equivalents of the cell groupings called barrels found in other whiskered species like mice and rats, regions that process sensory information from the vibrissae.

Even more tantalizing is that, in the manatee, these clusters extend into a region of the brain believed to be centrally involved with sound perception.

"Either these things have nothing to do with the hair at all, or the more exciting possibility is that perhaps somatic sensation is so important that the specialized structure is overlapping with processing going on in auditory areas," Dr. Reep said.

The normal hearing of manatees is known to be quite good in certain ranges, better than that of humans. In studies published in 1999 and 2000, Edmund and Laura Gerstein of Florida Atlantic University found that the underwater hearing of two captive manatees in a pool was sharpest at high frequencies—in the 16-to-18-kilohertz range—findings that have complicated the debate about powerboats. Though Florida has spent years trying to persuade boaters to slow down in areas that manatees frequent, the high frequencies emitted by a boat moving at high speed may be easier for the animals to hear (although having the time to get out of the way is a different matter).

But in a study also presented at the marine mammal meetings, Dr. Bauer, Dr. Reep and colleagues have found hints that manatees can also "hear" low-frequency sounds, perhaps by using the vibrissae on their bodies to detect subtle changes in water movement. Hugh and Buffett were able to determine the location of three-second low-frequency vibrations in the 23-to-1,000-hertz range with up to 100 percent accuracy. The researchers plan to repeat these experiments with the vibrissae covered, to see whether the manatees still score highly.

If they do, it will suggest that they have a capacity unique among mammals and may help biologists explain, among other things, how they navigate back to their favorite patches of sea grass each year and how they monitor the movements of other manatees in cloudy water. Fish and some amphibians have similar sensory systems, mediated by cells running down the sides of their bodies. Called the lateral line, this system is "the reason why we can sneak up behind a fish but cannot grab it," Dr. Reep writes.

For now, the question of how intertwined the sensory abilities of manatees might be remains unanswered. Yet even what is known reveals a degree of complexity that argues against labeling them as sweet but dumb—peaceable simpletons.

Dr. Domning of Howard could not agree more.

"They're too smart to jump through hoops the way those dumb dolphins do," he said.

Selection 3.5

Just weeks after an underwater earthquake triggered a deadly tsunami, William Broad wrote this feature on the value of earthquakes. The timing of the story posed an especially daunting challenge. The scientists Broad interviewed were keenly aware of the difficulties of explaining killer quakes as useful, but they also were willing to supply evidence to support what they knew to be true: Earthquakes can be catastrophic in the short run, yes, but in the long run they are of great benefit. Notice how Broad introduces this touchy topic before he works to transform the way we think about it.

Deadly and Yet Necessary, Quakes Renew the Planet
By WILLIAM J. BROAD

They approach the topic gingerly, wary of sounding callous, aware that the geology they admire has just caused a staggering loss of life. Even so, scientists argue that in the very long view, the global process behind great earthquakes is quite advantageous for life on earth— especially human life.

Powerful jolts like the one that sent killer waves racing across the Indian Ocean on Dec. 26 are inevitable side effects of the constant recycling of planetary crust, which produces a lush, habitable planet. Some experts refer to the regular blows—hundreds a day—as the planet's heartbeat.

The advantages began billions of years ago, when this crustal recycling made the oceans and atmosphere and formed the continents. Today, it builds mountains, enriches soils, regulates the planet's temperature, concentrates gold and other rare metals and maintains the sea's chemical balance.

Published: January 11, 2005.

Plate tectonics (after the Greek word "tekton," or builder) describes the geology. The tragic downside is that waves of quakes and volcanic eruptions along plate boundaries can devastate human populations.

"It's hard to find something uplifting about 150,000 lives being lost," said Dr. Donald J. DePaolo, a geochemist at the University of California, Berkeley. "But the type of geological process that caused the earthquake and the tsunami is an essential characteristic of the earth. As far as we know, it doesn't occur on any other planetary body and has something very directly to do with the fact that the earth is a habitable planet."

Many biologists believe that the process may have even given birth to life itself.

The main benefits of plate tectonics accumulate slowly and globally over the ages. In contrast, its local upheavals can produce regional catastrophes, as the recent Indian Ocean quake made clear.

Even so, scientists say, the Dec. 26 tsunamis may prove to be an ecological boon over the decades for coastal areas hardest hit by the giant waves.

Dr. Jelle Zeilinga de Boer, a geologist at Wesleyan University who grew up in Indonesia and has studied the archipelago, says historical evidence from earlier tsunamis suggests that the huge waves can distribute rich sediments from river systems across coastal plains, making the soil richer.

"It brings fertile soils into the lowlands," he said. "In time, a more fertile jungle will develop."

Dr. de Boer, author of recent books on earthquakes and volcanoes in human history, added that great suffering from tectonic violence was usually followed by great benefits as well. "Nature is reborn with these kinds of terrible events," he said. "There are a lot of positive aspects even when we don't see them."

Plate tectonics holds that the earth's surface is made up of a dozen or so big crustal slabs that float on a sea of melted rock. Over ages, this churning sea moves the plates as well as their superimposed continents and ocean basins, tearing them apart and rearranging them like pieces of a puzzle.

The process starts as volcanic gashes spew hot rock that spreads out across the seabed. Eventually, hundreds or thousands of miles away, the cooling slab collides with other plates and sinks beneath them, plunging back into the hot earth.

The colliding plates grind past one another about as fast as fingernails grow and over time produce mountains and swarms of earthquakes as frictional stresses build and release. Meanwhile, parts of the descending plate melt and rise to form volcanoes on land.

The recent cataclysm began in a similar manner as volcanic gashes in the western depths of the Indian Ocean belched molten rock to form the India plate. Its collision with the Burma plate created the volcanoes of Sumatra as well thousands of earthquakes, including the magnitude 9.0 killer.

But despite such staggering losses of life, said Robert S. Detrick Jr., a geophysicist at the Woods Hole Oceanographic Institution, "there's no question that plate tectonics rejuvenates the planet."

Moreover, geologists say, it demonstrates the earth's uniqueness. In the decades after the discovery of plate tectonics, space probes among the 70 or so planets and moons that make up the solar system found that the process existed only on earth—as revealed by its unique mountain ranges.

In the book "Rare Earth" (Copernicus, 2000), which explored the likelihood that advanced civilizations dot the cosmos, Dr. Peter D. Ward and Dr. Donald Brownlee of the University of Washington argued in a long chapter on plate tectonics that the slow recycling of planetary crust was uncommon in the universe yet essential for the evolution of complex life.

"It maintains not just habitability but high habitability," said Dr. Ward, a paleontologist. (Dr. Brownlee is an astronomer.) Most geologists believe that the process yielded the earth's primordial ocean and atmosphere, as volcanoes spewed vast amounts of water vapor, nitrogen, carbon dioxide and other gases. Plants eventually added oxygen. Meanwhile, many biologists say, the earth's first organisms probably arose in the deep sea, along the volcanic gashes.

"On balance, it's possible that life on earth would not have originated without plate tectonics, or the atmosphere, or the oceans," said Dr. Frank Press, the lead author of "Understanding Earth" (Freeman, 2004) and a past president of the National Academy of Sciences.

The volcanoes of the recycling process make rich soil ideal for producing coffee, sugar, rubber, coconuts, palm oil, tobacco, pepper, tea and cocoa. Water streaming through gashes in the seabed concentrates copper, silver, gold and other metals into rich deposits that are often mined after plate tectonics nudges them onto dry land.

Experts say the world ocean passes through the rocky pores of the tectonic system once every million years or so, increasing nutrients in the biosphere and regulating a host of elements and compounds, including boron and calcium.

Dr. William H. Schlesinger, dean of the Nicholas School of the Environment and Earth Sciences at Duke, says one vital cycle keeps adequate amounts of carbon dioxide in the atmosphere. Though carbon dioxide is thought to cause excessive greenhouse-gas warming of the planet, an appreciable level is needed to keep the planet warm enough to support life.

"Having plate tectonics complete the cycle is absolutely essential to maintaining stable climate conditions on earth," Dr. Schlesinger said. "Otherwise, all the carbon dioxide would disappear and the planet would turn into a frozen ball."

Dr. Press, who was President Jimmy Carter's science adviser, said the challenge in the coming decades would be to keep enjoying the benefits of plate tectonics while improving our ability to curb its deadly byproducts.

"We're making progress," Dr. Press said. "We can predict volcanic explosions and erect warning systems for tsunamis. We're beginning to limit the downside effects."

MAKING**CONNECTIONS**

1

Consider This. Compare and contrast these stories with respect to their use of definitions, comparisons, transformative explanations and other explanatory techniques. And don't be afraid to improve on some of them. Do the same for the multimedia extras that accompany these stories on the Web.

Try This. Come up with a topic that gets a bum rap in the natural world and would, if the science supports it, make a good explanatory feature for your campus newspaper. Do background research and develop a story proposal, with a list of expert sources. Be sure to include what most people think, with the evidence to support an alternative view. If visuals could reinforce your explanation, come up with a rough sketch for an explanatory graphic as well.

2

A Conversation with . . . **Natalie Angier**

SCIENCE WRITER

© Katherine Angier

As a college student, Natalie Angier felt herself to be something of an anomaly. An English major who also studied physics and astronomy, she had an obvious affinity for both the humanities and the sciences. Seeking a career that might allow her to indulge her twin passions, she began to dream of starting a popular magazine about science for smart lay readers. Instead of starting such a magazine, though, she soon went to work for one—a new science magazine called Discover, founded by Time Inc. in 1980.

At Discover, by her own account, she overcame a natural shyness and learned to avoid the "sin of clichés."[1] Her editor also encouraged her as she experimented with wordplay and metaphor. Within five years, she was working as a senior science writer at Time Magazine, and embarking on the first of several award-winning books and collections of science writing.[2]

The New York Times came calling in 1990, hiring her to cover evolutionary biology, genetics, medicine and other fields. Just ten months later, she won a Pulitzer Prize for her explanatory features on scorpions, parasites, philandering and other topics. In her years at The Times, Angier has covered a dazzling range of subjects, including (according to her personal Web site): "polar bears, jaguars, tigers, cheetahs, lions, hyenas, crocodiles, turtles, pit vipers, why we curse, why we laugh, why we play, why I'm a crybaby, why I hate the beach, why women's shoes don't fit their feet, cuteness vs. beauty, empathy, altruism, anthropomorphism, laziness" and more.

In everything she does, Angier displays a blend of keen intelligence, childlike passion for science and a love of language. Much of her writing possesses an almost rollicking quality, filled with exuberant metaphors, puns and on occasion, even laugh-out-loud humor.[3]

Angier works out of her home in Tacoma Park, Md., where she lives with her husband, Rick Weiss, a science policy analyst, and their daughter, Katherine Ida Weiss Angier.

The following interview was conducted by telephone. It has been edited for length and flow. Other interviews with this writer can be found on Angier's personal Web site: www.natalieangier.com.

The Boston Globe once quoted you as saying writing about science gives meaning to your life. I wonder if you could say a little bit more about that?
One of the things that I like about writing about science, as I have said, is it's good news with a forebrain. People often complain that the news is full of bad news; it's the human race getting things wrong. But science is the human race getting things right. So I like the fact that writing about science gives me hope for the future.

The fact that we have got the tools for understanding not just our world but our universe—that we can look at the lights in the night sky as sources of information about not only stars that are very distant but that are not even there anymore—it's an incredible accomplishment, and it does make me hope that we will eventually get past this kind of logjam in cultural evolution and start to appreciate the facts of our existence.

I just feel that science is a way of knowing, a way of understanding life that doesn't have any other parallel because it is thoroughly based in reality. And yet it is not just the everyday, because science deals in a lot of things that you can't see, that are either too small or too big or too ancient or too new. It deals with scales that are way beyond our experience. So it's not just that. It's not just this kind of mechanical view. It's understanding the very fabric of life. And it's very exciting because when you do get beyond the everyday, it is as transporting as anything that has ever been written in any religious text, if not much more so.

People have to realize when they dismiss science as just a bunch of molecules and atoms, it's *not* just anything. The fact that we can even talk about molecules and atoms is extraordinary, and what does it mean that we are made up of these particles and these particles have these interactions? You can start to understand the world from a conceptual level as well as just a mechanical or anatomical level. As a science writer I am always trying to get the background and the larger context, what it all means, the big picture, and so this is a constant source of excitement, of stimulation, intellectual and emotional.

I'm a glum person by nature, but when I hear something has been discovered that is unexpected, it gives me this feeling of transporting to a different dimension because science does think in other dimensions. In a sense it is a kind of an out-of-body experience.

So what is it then that you're actually trying to do for your readers when you do your science writing? What are you trying to convey either intellectually or emotionally?
One of the things I try to do, particularly with the column [the biweekly column, "Basics"], is to get people to think about their own lives and their own experiences and how science may fit into the story. So if we're going to understand the nature of taxation, just what does taxation mean? We have this kneejerk response against it, but let's look at it in a larger context—O.K., this is part of the price we pay for being a social animal and what other social animals pay similar prices.[4] So I try to bring readers to think about science themselves and

to feel most importantly that they have a right to think about it—that science is not just for scientists, that science is a way of thinking about the world, of putting ideas together, of seeing what evidence is there, of coming to some kind of tentative hypothesis about reality that will enrich your own life.

I really feel that in that sense science is like art. You may not be an artist, but you can use art to enrich your own life because it can give you a different perspective. It can take you out of the kind of prison of the self and put you into some other perspective. So I do try to do that, and to the extent that I can, I use humor because if you can laugh about something, you feel comfortable with it and you will start to feel in possession of it.

A lot of creative people have talked about the need to play. I wonder if you could talk a little bit more about play and its importance to you and to your audience?

Playing with language, with ideas, with comparisons, trying to put the essence of your being into your work and to make it just lift off the page is the important thing. So that means taking risks, and it also means this constant *do-si-do* of back and forth between, on the one hand, letting yourself go, opening yourself up, and on the other hand, reining yourself back in and being disciplined. I feel that process going on throughout any particular writing project. I have to force myself to open up, and then I have to also be very, very rigorous and ask what exactly am I trying to say, because one of the problems with writing is that you have this amorphous idea and then you have to put it into this serial narrative format and you have to really put one foot in front of the other to get across the point.

So there is a very strong need for discipline, but also for freedom and for play. Those two pitted against one another is the thing that makes it difficult but also the thing that makes it ultimately very rich and rewarding. You owe it to your reader to do that, which is why when I used to teach I would say look, writing takes time and there is no way around that. You have to build that into your schedule.

What tips have you given aspiring science writers over the years for explaining things clearly, starting with how you work with scientists to understand what they are saying?

One of the expressions that I once heard another reporter using that I think is very good is, "Can you hold my hand and walk me through this?" It is helpful to say, "O.K., let's start from the beginning. Can you hold my hand and walk me through this so that I get it to the extent possible?"

Another thing that every science reporter is going to run up against is the scientist asking you how much science background you have. They're going to tailor what they say to that. This is dangerous if you have a general audience. You don't want the scientist speaking to you in technical language because, for one thing, you'll never be able to quote the scientist directly in your article. So to the extent possible, you could say to the scientist, "Well you know I'm pretty good with science, but let's just sort of talk about it from the general public's point of view. What should they know about your work? What do you see is the central concept here that you're trying to get across with your research?" Really, keep it at that level, not only to avoid jargon in the interview but also to avoid getting into all of the dotted i's and crossed t's that readers aren't going to care about. Sometimes you may think that you already know it, but have them walk you through it anyway because they may come up with a connection or with a way of putting it that you haven't heard before that will be useful.

In one of the interviews on your Web site, you were quoted as advising writers to make the invisible visible, by using your senses. . . .
To the extent that you can use all five senses to understand anything, do it. We are embodied minds. One of the interesting things to come out of research recently is that you learn better when you gesture. They have shown through studies that even students explaining to other students about something with math, if they use gestures to show, for example, that this part of the equation is equal to that (I'm gesturing as I'm speaking) those students actually do better. The kids who are learning learn more when gestures are used. So obviously using our bodies to understand even something that seems very cerebral is important. So to the extent that you can use your body, any of the senses, what would it look like? What would it sound like, smell like? Any of the senses that you can use. Anything you can do to bring it back to really kind of physically absorbing and metabolizing the material is really helpful.

Like the "snot" comparison? [Angier once asked a biologist, "What would a cell look like if it were blown up big enough to place on your desk?" and the scientist replied "snot."][5]
Yes, and when you're explaining things, never assume that people know anything. Explain it vividly but explain it in a way that doesn't sound patronizing or condescending or tutorial or kindergarten-ese. You have to do it almost like you're talking among friends about something that you're all part of rather than I'm explaining this and here's what you need to know. So I think that's important. That's why I think humor comes into it.

Any other tips for beginning writers?
To the extent that you can use pre-existing interest to get points across in the same way that you can use the five senses, it's probably not a bad idea. I'm also in my own life constantly thinking about how to make a story out of something. I used to tell this to students: If you're looking for story ideas, think about your own life. Think about what interests you. For example, in the early '90s, when I was working at The Times in New York, I always used to keep a pair of sneakers in the office and change into them when I was leaving to be able to walk around. I was taking off these uncomfortable shoes and putting on my sneakers and complaining to my editor who was sitting there. Then it suddenly occurred to me. I said to him, "Oh you know what? I should write something about why women's shoes don't fit women's feet!" He said, "That's

a great idea." That was one of the most popular stories I ever wrote because it was not just obvious things like high heels are bad, but all sorts of other elements of the female shoe.[6]

So think about your own life. Many times in the middle of summer, I was feeling very lazy, didn't want to work, the usual thing: I don't want to do it. I thought laziness! How about laziness in nature, the evolution of laziness? That was a hugely popular story. It also turned out to be an enormous amount of work to do that story, but it was really worth it to look at the amount of time that different animals work and the conditions under which they do or don't. It was just using my own experience to try to explore the world.[7] So to the extent that you can do that, you're probably going to come up with a better story.

What parting advice do you have for someone who aspires to do what you do?
I believe that no matter what happens with the format, whether it's Web-based or anything else, good writing is good writing. It takes time and you need to work at it, and to keep working at it, and you need to read, read, read, read and to always be looking as you read for how other people do things and how they accomplished something that you admire. I used to tell my students you have to read a lot, but they would say, "We don't have time." What do you mean you don't have time? It's your job! Do you have time for your job? You do! You just have to make time for it and read promiscuously.

Also keep experimenting in your own work. The editor that I mentioned earlier, Jesse Birnbaum, used to say that it was easier for an editor to take a little air out of an overinflated tire than to pump up a flat one. So I think that there is some truth in that. You really just try to fill it up with as much as you can give it and you might have to let some of the air out, but it's better to err on the side of excess. So those are eternal verities of good writing that will, I hope, be useful.

stories about scientists
Q&As, Narrative Interviews and Profiles

FOR PEOPLE WITHOUT ACCESS TO SCIENTISTS, there are only a few ways to get a sense of the men and women behind the telescopes, species counts and human rat labs: There are science and nature documentaries. There are the entertainment programs of television and film, where scientists come off as either "mad, bad and dangerous"[1] (think "Jurassic Park") or as brilliant, fumbling nerds (think "Honey, I Shrunk the Kids"). And then there is the news.

For news consumers, the stories about scientists that science writers produce offer a nice antidote to the distorting images of the profession that pervade popular culture. And they're an easy way to convey the science, too, because people tend to enjoy listening to others talk about their passions, and few scientists work as hard as they do without being excited about their work.

Over the decades, science writers have found a range of ways to turn our attention to the people who bring us science and technology. This chapter contains examples of three such approaches, loosely arranged from simplest to most demanding in terms of the amount and complexity of the reporting they require.

- **Q&As** are increasingly popular as a way to convey the stories of scientists. That's because they are relatively short and easy to read. They also tend to be easier than other kinds of stories to produce, simply because you don't have to spend a lot of time observing the person or noodling over story structure. But a few caveats: Q&As require an excellent subject to interview, someone who is newsworthy, a good translator and a good storyteller. Selection is everything. Well, almost everything. Your questions, and the order you put them in, also matter mightily. So does the introduction you write, which must engage readers and convey the person's significance.

- **Narrative interviews** are a step up from Q&As in terms of the complexity of the reporting. These snapshot portraits take readers along as you spend time with a scientist in the lab or in the field. Narrative interviews require you to simultaneously ask questions and observe keenly, a tricky juggling act if you've never done it before. But they unroll fairly easily once you have laid out the general direction of your questions and have picked a good spot for the interview, one where your subject is comfortable and will be able to talk about what he or she is seeing and doing. They are fairly easy to write too. This is because—unlike most features—you organize them chronologically, as you conducted the interview itself. The only tricky part is usually slipping the significance of your interview subject into your story and figuring out a good place to end. This is slightly more complex than a Q&A, but still easier than a full-blown profile.

• **Profiles** are much more than snapshots. Unlike narrative interviews, they strive to draw a full-bodied portrait of your interview subject, complete with back story of how and why the person came to do their work, and details and insights usually gathered from observing the person in multiple settings and talking to others. Profiles demand an ability to ask the kinds of probing questions that elicit anecdotes, the little stories within the big story that reveal a person's past and their enthusiasms. If a story in the person's personal history is important enough, a writer might even reconstruct scenes, an even greater challenge requiring consummate interviewing skills.

There are two Q&As are in this chapter. One, with a neurologist who was a woman when he began his life as a scientist, offers a unique perspective on the issue of sexism in science. The other, with a psychologist famous for inducing sadistic behavior in college students, probes the situational causes of wrongdoing.

A classic narrative interview with the world-famous ant man, E. O. Wilson, follows. In this interview, the writer accompanies the aging Wilson as he stoops to hunt for insects on the forest floor near Walden Pond. With riveting detail, the story captures the man's youthful curiosity. This story is followed by a feature on a scientist who studies the blinks of amorous fireflies. This is a hybrid piece, part narrative like the two stories that precede it, and part profile because it aims to reveal more of the scientist's life.

The chapter's final selection—the story of the chief repairman on the Hubble Space Telescope—is a full-blown profile. The writer, who at the end of the chapter talks about his work as a science writer, wasn't on the scene with the physicist-astronaut. But he worked tenaciously to gather the arresting details needed to bring to life key moments in the life of the scientist and the history of the National Aeronautics and Space Administration (NASA). The resulting story illuminates an unsung hero of the U.S. space program.[2]

Selection 4.1

One of the most read science/technology stories of 2006, this Q&A by Cornelia Dean lingers, if only for the selection of its subject—a man who grew up as a woman and so knows firsthand the different ways people treat men and women in science. Notice how Dean establishes Ben Barres' news value in the introduction and lays the ground for subsequent questions. Notice, too, the matter-of-fact nature of her questions about highly personal issues, and her willingness to tackle basics like: Why are you a scientist? (Sometimes what readers most want to know are the basics.) Photos of the scientist as a woman and as a man accompanied the story. The online version of the story also linked to the scientist's commentary, on sexism in science, in the journal Nature.

A Conversation With Ben A. Barres
Dismissing "Sexist Opinions" About
Women's Place in Science

By CORNELIA DEAN

Perhaps it is inevitable that Ben A. Barres would have strong opinions on the debate over the place of women in science. Dr. Barres has a degree in biology from M.I.T., a medical degree from Dartmouth and a doctorate in neurobiology from Harvard. He is a professor of neurobiology at Stanford. And until his surgery a decade ago, his name was Barbara, and he was a woman.

Now he has taken his unusual perspective to the current issue of the journal Nature, in a commentary titled "Does Gender Matter?"

Dr. Barres (pronounced BARE-ess), 51, who grew up in West Orange, N.J., said he had been thinking about the gender issue for over a year, since Lawrence H. Summers, then the president of Harvard, gave a talk in which he suggested that one explanation for women's relative absence at the upper ranks of science might be innate intellectual deficiencies. Assertions of innate differences by other researchers—"sexist opinions," Dr. Barres calls them—fueled his anger, especially because they came from scientists.

Dr. Barres discussed his commentary, his career and sexism in science in a telephone interview from his home in Stanford, Calif.

Q. What's your response to people who say you rely too much on your own experience and should take scientific hypotheses less personally?

A. They should learn that scientific hypotheses require evidence. The bulk of my commentary discusses the actual peer-reviewed data.

Published: July 18, 2006.

Q. Why do some people attribute differences in professional achievement to innate ability?

A. One of the reasons is the belief by highly successful people that they are successful because of their own innate abilities. I think as a professor at Stanford I am lucky to be here. But I think Larry Summers thinks he is successful because of his innate inner stuff.

Q. What about the idea that men and women differ in ways that give men an advantage in science?

A. People are still arguing over whether there are cognitive differences between men and women. If they exist, it's not clear they are innate, and if they are innate, it's not clear they are relevant. They are subtle, and they may even benefit women.

But when you tell people about the studies documenting bias, if they are prejudiced, they just discount the evidence.

Q. How does this bias manifest itself?

A. It is very much harder for women to be successful, to get jobs, to get grants, especially big grants. And then, and this is a huge part of the problem, they don't get the resources they need to be successful. Right now, what's fundamentally missing and absolutely vital is that women get better child care support. This is such an obvious no-brainer. If you just do this with a small amount of resources, you could explode the number of women scientists.

Q. Why isn't there more support for scientists who have children?

A. The male leadership is not doing it, but women are not demanding it. I think if women would just start demanding fairness, they might get it. But they might buy in a little bit to all this brainwashing. They are less self-confident. And when women speak out, men just see them as asking for undeserved benefits.

Q. Why are you a scientist?

A. I knew from a very young age—5 or 6—that I wanted to be a scientist, that there was something fun about it and I would enjoy doing it. I decided I would go to M.I.T. when I was 12 or 13.

Q. As a girl, were you pressured not to try for M.I.T.?

A. Of course. I was a very good math and science student, maybe the best in my high school. And despite all that, when it came time to talk to my guidance counselor, he did not encourage me. But I said, I want to go to M.I.T.; I don't want to go anywhere else. So I just ignored him. Fortunately, my parents did not try to dissuade me.

Q. Were there girls at M.I.T. then?

A. Very few, but M.I.T. from its very start took women. I loved it. I am not saying it is perfect, but it was a great place to go to school.

Q. Why did you decide to specialize in neuroscience? Did the fact that you were a transgendered person spark your interest in the brain?

A. I think all transgendered people and gay people are aware from childhood that something is going on. But I thought I would be a chemist or an engineer. It was when I took a course from a fabulous neuroscientist that I just got interested in understanding the brain and how disease affected the brain.

Q. When you were a woman did you experience bias?

A. An M.I.T. professor accused me of cheating on this test. I was the only one in the class who solved a particular problem, and he said my boyfriend must have solved it for me. One, I did not have a boyfriend. And two, I solved it myself, goddamn it! But it did not occur to me to think of sexism. I was just indignant that I would be accused of cheating.

Then later I was in a prestigious competition. I was doing my Ph.D. at Harvard, which would nominate one person. It came down to me and one other graduate student, and a dean pulled me aside and said, "I have read both applications, and it's going to be you; your application is so much better." Not only did I not win, the guy got it, but he dropped out of science a year later.

But even then I did not think of sexism.

Q. Why didn't you see these episodes as sexism?

A. Women who are really highly successful, they are just as bad as the men. They think if they can do it, anyone can do it. They don't see that for every woman who makes it to the top there are 10 more who are passed over. And I am not making this up, that's what the data show.

And it may be that some women—and African-Americans, too—identify less strongly with their particular group. From the time I was a child, from the littlest, littlest age, I did not identify as a girl. It never occurred to me that I could not be a scientist because I was a woman. It just rolled off my back.

Now I wonder, maybe I just didn't take these stereotypes so seriously because I did not identify myself as a woman.

Q. As a transgendered person, are you viewed as having an unusually valuable perspective?

A. I think because I am transgendered some people view anything I say with suspicion. I am very different from the average person. But I have experienced life both as a woman and as a man. I have some experience of how both sexes are treated.

Q. What about the idea that male scientists are more competitive?

A. I think that's just utter nonsense. Men just make this stuff up. But when women are made to feel less confident, they are less likely to enter the competition. I think a lot of this is just the way men and women are treated from the time they are very young.

Take my experience with M.I.T. If I had been a guy who had been the only one in the class to solve that problem, I am sure I would have been pointed out and given a pat on the back. I was not only not given positive feedback, I was given negative feedback. This is the kind of thing that undermines women's self-confidence.

Q. What about the idea that women are too emotional to be hard-headed scientists?

A. It is just patently absurd to say women are more emotional than men. Men commit 25 times the murders; it's shocking what the numbers are. And if anyone ever sees a woman with road rage, they should write it up and send it to a medical journal.

Q. Are men more careerist?

A. I think people do what they are rewarded for doing, and I think women realize, whether it's conscious or unconscious, they are not going to get the rewards. So they put the hours into their families or whatever. That's just a guess.

Science is like art, it's just something you have to do. It's a passion. When I go into a lab, I'll go without sleep, I'll go hours and hours, day after day. And I think women would do that if they weren't given so much negative feedback.

Q. You write that as a man, you can complete a sentence without being interrupted. Are you treated differently in other ways?

A. It's when people don't know that I was a woman that I can really see the difference. Even in just stupid things. You go into a department store and people are more likely to wait on you.

Q. As a woman and then as a man, you have been a scientist for about three decades. Do you see things improving for women in science?

A. Slowly, but not nearly at the rate one would expect. In biology, something like 50 percent of the best postdocs are women. It's still very bad in physics and engineering and chemistry, but even in biology you don't see women making the leap to tenure. And this disturbs me greatly. These women have worked very hard. They have fulfilled their side of the social contract. I think what we've got is just a lot more highly trained, frustrated women.

Selection 4.2

In this Q&A, Claudia Dreifus, who writes most of the Q&As for Science Times,[3] interviews psychologist Philip G. Zimbardo. In the early 1970s, in an experiment that would never pass muster today with tightened regulations on the treatment of human subjects, Zimbardo induced college students to engage in sadistic behavior. What does Zimbardo think of his research decades later? Does he have any guilt? Are the findings still relevant? With one question building nicely to the next, Dreifus gets to all these matters, and more. When this story appeared, the Web site posted black and white photos from the 1971 experiment, photos that today eerily resemble soldiers' snapshots from the infamous prison, Abu Ghraib.

A Conversation With Philip G. Zimbardo
Finding Hope in Knowing the Universal Capacity for Evil

By CLAUDIA DREIFUS

SAN FRANCISCO—At Philip G. Zimbardo's town house here, the walls are covered with masks from Indonesia, Africa and the Pacific Northwest.

Dr. Zimbardo, a social psychologist and the past president of the American Psychological Association, has made his reputation studying how people disguise the good and bad in themselves and under what conditions either is expressed.

His Stanford Prison Experiment in 1971, known as the S.P.E. in social science textbooks, showed how anonymity, conformity and boredom can be used to induce sadistic behavior in otherwise wholesome students. More recently, Dr. Zimbardo, 74, has been studying how policy decisions and individual choices led to abuse at the Abu Ghraib prison in Iraq. The road that took him from Stanford to Abu Ghraib is described in his new book, "The Lucifer Effect: Understanding How Good People Turn Evil" (Random House).

"I've always been curious about the psychology of the person behind the mask," Dr. Zimbardo said as he displayed his collection. "When someone is anonymous, it opens the door to all kinds of antisocial behavior, as seen by the Ku Klux Klan."

Q. For those who never studied it in their freshman psychology class, can you describe the Stanford Prison Experiment?

A. In the summer of 1971, we set up a mock prison on the Stanford University campus. We took 23 volunteers and randomly divided them into two groups. These were normal young men, students. We asked them to act as "prisoners" and "guards" might in a prison environment. The experiment was to run for two weeks.

By the end of the first day, nothing much was happening. But on the second day, there was a prisoner rebellion. The guards came to me: "What do we do?"

"It's your prison," I said, warning them against physical violence. The guards then quickly moved to psychological punishment, though there was physical abuse, too.

In the ensuing days, the guards became ever more sadistic, denying the prisoners food, water and sleep, shooting them with fire-extinguisher spray, throwing their blankets into dirt, stripping them naked and dragging rebels across the yard.

Published: April 3, 2007.

How bad did it get? The guards ordered the prisoners to simulate sodomy. Why? Because the guards were bored. Boredom is a powerful motive for evil. I have no idea how much worse things might have gotten.

Q. Why did you pull the plug on the experiment?

A. On the fifth night, my former graduate student Christina Maslach came by. She witnessed the guards putting bags over the prisoners' heads, chain their legs and march them around. Chris ran out in tears. "I'm not sure I want to have anything more to do with you, if this is the sort of person you are," she said. "It's terrible what you're doing to those boys." I thought, "Oh my God, she's right."

Q. What's the difference between your study and the ones performed at Yale in 1961? There, social psychologist Stanley Milgram ordered his subjects to give what they thought were painful and possibly lethal shocks to complete strangers. Most complied.

A. In a lot of ways, the studies are bookends in our understanding of evil. Milgram quantified the small steps that people take when they do evil. He showed that an authority can command people to do things they believe they'd never do. I wanted to take that further. Milgram's study only looked at one aspect of behavior, obedience to authority, in short 50-minute takes. The S.P.E., because it was slated to go for two weeks, was almost like a forerunner of reality television. You could see behavior unfolding hour by hour, day by day.

Here's something that's sort of funny. The first time I spoke publicly about the S.P.E., Stanley Milgram told me: "Your study is going to take all the ethical heat off of my back. People are now going to say yours is the most unethical study ever, and not mine."

Q. From your book, I sense you feel some lingering guilt about organizing "the most unethical study" ever. Do you?

A. When I look back on it, I think, "Why didn't you stop the cruelty earlier?" To stand back was contrary to my upbringing and nature.

When I stood back as a noninterfering experimental scientist, I was, in a sense, as drawn into the power of the situation as any prisoners and guards.

Q. What was your reaction when you first saw those photographs from Abu Ghraib?

A. I was shocked. But not surprised. I immediately flashed on similar pictures from the S.P.E. What particularly bothered me was

that the Pentagon blamed the whole thing on a "few bad apples."
I knew from our experiment, if you put good apples into a bad
situation, you'll get bad apples.

That was why I was willing to be an expert witness for Sgt. Chip
Frederick, who was ultimately sentenced to eight years for his role at
Abu Ghraib. Frederick was the Army reservist who was put in charge
of the night shift at Tier 1A, where detainees were abused. Frederick
said, up front, "What I did was wrong, and I don't understand why
I did it."

Q. Do you understand?

A. Yeah. The situation totally corrupted him. When his reserve
unit was first assigned to guard Abu Ghraib, Frederick was exactly
like one of our nice young men in the S.P.E. Three months later, he
was exactly like one of our worst guards.

Q. Aren't you absolving Sergeant Frederick of personal responsibility for his actions?

A. You had the C.I.A., civilian interrogators, military intelligence saying to the Army reservists, "Soften these detainees up for
interrogation."

Those kinds of vague orders were the equivalent of my saying to
the S.P.E. guards, "It's your prison." At Abu Ghraib, you didn't have
higher-ups saying, "You must do these terrible things." The authorities, I believe, created an environment that gave guards permission to
become abusive—plus one that gave them plausible deniability.

Chip worked 40 days without a single break, 12-hour shifts. The
place was overcrowded, filthy, dangerous, under constant bombardment. All of that will distort judgment, moral reasoning. The bottom
line: If you're going to have a secret interrogation center in the middle
of a war zone, this is going to happen.

Q. You keep using this phrase "the situation" to describe the
underlying cause of wrongdoing. What do you mean?

A. That human behavior is more influenced by things outside of
us than inside. The "situation" is the external environment. The inner
environment is genes, moral history, religious training. There are times
when external circumstances can overwhelm us, and we do things we
never thought. If you're not aware that this can happen, you can be
seduced by evil. We need inoculations against our own potential for
evil. We have to acknowledge it. Then we can change it.

Q. So you disagree with Anne Frank, who wrote in her diary,
"I still believe, in spite of everything, that people are truly good at
heart?"

A. That's not true. Some people can be made into monsters. And
the people who abused, and killed her, were.

MAKING**CONNECTIONS**

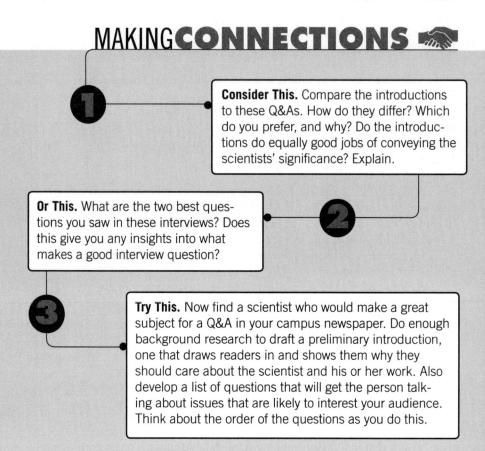

1

Consider This. Compare the introductions to these Q&As. How do they differ? Which do you prefer, and why? Do the introductions do equally good jobs of conveying the scientists' significance? Explain.

Or This. What are the two best questions you saw in these interviews? Does this give you any insights into what makes a good interview question?

2

3

Try This. Now find a scientist who would make a great subject for a Q&A in your campus newspaper. Do enough background research to draft a preliminary introduction, one that draws readers in and shows them why they should care about the scientist and his or her work. Also develop a list of questions that will get the person talking about issues that are likely to interest your audience. Think about the order of the questions as you do this.

Selection 4.3

When this story was written, the eminent evolutionary biologist E. O. Wilson had just published a book that began with a letter to Henry David Thoreau. In the letter, Thoreau described how he was a lover of little things and the world of the forest floor. That—and Wilson's description of microwildernesses and microreserves—caught the eye of deputy science editor James Gorman. When Gorman called Wilson, he asked him if there was a favorite place where they could explore and talk about microwildernesses. Wilson, a writer himself, suggested Waldon Pond. The resulting narrative interview shows the then 73-year-old scientist—whose accomplishments are intentionally piled on in the lede—"on his hands and knees, pawing in leaf litter." As you read the story, notice other contrasts, between the man as aging scientist and the man as youthful explorer, between the civilized world above the forest floor and the wilderness underfoot. Notice, too, the use of specific names for creatures the two encounter on their walk, and the writer's own musings and associations that are woven into the narrative. Like the scientist in his enthusiasm, this story draws us into a microworld that, when one takes the time to notice, is nothing less than astonishing.

INTO THE WOODS WITH: EDWARD O. WILSON
A Wild, Fearsome World Under Each Fallen Leaf
By JAMES GORMAN

Dr. Edward O. Wilson, Pellegrino University research professor and honorary curator in entomology of the Museum of Comparative Zoology at Harvard University, winner of two Pulitzer prizes and scientific honors too numerous to recount, is on his hands and knees, pawing in the leaf litter near Walden Pond.

He eases into a half-sitting, half-reclining position and holds out a handful of humus and dirt. "This," he says, "is wilderness."

Just a dozen yards from the site of Thoreau's cabin Dr. Wilson is delving into the ground with a sense of purpose and pleasure that would instantly make any 10-year-old join him. His smile suggests that at age 73, with a troublesome right knee, he still finds the forest floor as much to his liking as a professor's desk.

These woods are not wild; indeed they were not wild in Thoreau's day. Today, the beach and trails of Walden Pond State Reservation draw about 500,000 visitors a year. Few of them hunt ants, however. Underfoot and under the leaf litter there is a world as wild as it was before human beings came to this part of North America.

Dr. Wilson is playing guide to this micro-wilderness—full of ants, mites, millipedes and springtails in a miniature forest of fungal threads and plant detritus in order to make a point about the value of little creatures and small spaces. If he wrote bumper stickers, rather than books, his next might be "Save the Microfauna" or "Sweat the Small Stuff."

He begins his most recent book, "The Future of Life," with a "Dear Henry" letter, talking to Thoreau about the state of the world and the Walden Pond woods.

"Untrammeled nature exists in the dirt and rotting vegetation beneath our shoes," he writes. "The wilderness of ordinary vision may have vanished—wolf, puma and wolverine no longer exist in the tamed forests of Massachusetts. But another, even more ancient wilderness lives on."

In their world, centipedes are predators as fearsome as saber-toothed tigers, ants more numerous than the ungulates of African plains. And, in contrast to the vast preserves required by the world's most revered megafauna—grizzlies and elephants, jaguars and condors—maintaining biodiversity among the little creatures, shockingly rich in unexplored behavior and biochemistry, can be done on the cheap, in relatively tiny patches, as small as a few acres, around the world.

Published: September 24, 2002.

Dr. Wilson is by no means turning from the grand plans for conservation. Indeed, he has suggested that 50 percent of the globe ought to be reserved for nonhuman nature. But he is a realist, and, as he describes himself, "a lover of little things."

He has been turning over logs and rocks looking into the world of insects and other tiny creatures since he was a boy in Alabama and Florida. And he has not stopped. During the walk, he talks enthusiastically about a coming field trip to the Dominican Republic to investigate ants there, and about the publication this fall of a book-length monograph on the genus Pheidole describing all 625 species of ants, including 341 new to science.

Researchers tend to share a kind of acquisitive passion to see, touch, grasp the world. Nothing passes without comment. As he strolled along the shore of Walden Pond, on the way to the woods, Dr. Wilson spotted a butterfly and interrupted his discussion of the sizes of reserves needed for mammals, reptiles and amphibians, complete with references and citations to scientific studies.

When the butterfly landed on the beach, Dr. Wilson stopped, leaning forward like a heron on the hunt, and peered at it. "It's hard to identify," he said. "It's a very beat-up little butterfly," probably the variety called a question mark, because of the design on its wings.

Having reached the woods and having begun to talk about what lay under the surface of the forest floor, he held the crumbled leaf litter and humus in his hand as if he were savoring what lovers of certain wines call the "goût de terroir," or taste of the soil, a certain earthy specificity that the wine owes to the ground, not the grape.

"When I go on a field trip," he said, "providing you can get me up to the edge of a natural environment, I usually don't go more than a hundred yards or so in, because when I settle down immediately I start finding interesting stuff."

"This ground," he said, "we see it as two-dimensional because we're gigantic, like Godzilla. When you just go a few centimeters down, then you're in a three-dimensional world where the conditions change dramatically almost millimeter by millimeter. In one square foot of this litter you're looking at into the tens of thousands of small creatures that you can still spot with your naked eye."

The ground was drier than usual, and Dr. Wilson speculated that the drought might have affected insects. Some he had hoped to see were not there. "If we looked long enough," he said, breaking open several rotting acorns, "we would find entire colonies of very small ants living in an acorn."

As he moved on, from log to log, he uncovered relatives of cave crickets, predatory rove beetles, termites, several varieties of ants, spiderlings, beetle larvae—not quite in the abundance he had hoped for. Still, the small wilderness was teeming.

"The exact perception of wilderness is a matter of scale," he writes in "The Future of Life," going on to say that "microaesthetics" is "an unexplored wilderness to the creative mind." But he also notes that while microreserves are "infinitely better than nothing at all, they are no substitute for macro- and megareserves." He continues, "People can acquire an appreciation for savage carnivorous nematodes and shape-shifting rotifers in a drop of pond water, but they need life on the larger scale to which the human intellect and emotion most naturally respond."

Dr. Wilson is no sentimentalist, about nematodes or people. His proposals for microreserves are practical and hard-headed. The idea is fairly simple. While areas of nearly 25,000 acres are needed to have a good chance at preserving most large forms of life, plants and insects can sometimes be preserved in plots of 25 or even 2.5 acres.

In the Amazon, for instance, Dr. Wilson said, where the land is being savaged, "You'll see hanging on the side of a ravine somewhere a patch a farmer hasn't farmed, one hectare, to maybe 10." Such a small area may not catch the eye of most conservationists, he said, but, he added, "The entomologist and the botanist is likely to say, hold on a minute."

A researcher, he said, may find species not found anywhere else, and such plots can grow, with care and reseeding of the surrounding area. "You can do this in most parts of the world, in most developing countries, where a farmer or village elders would happily take a thousand bucks for you to set aside 10 or 100 hectares and even hire them to help with the reseeding," he said.

But it is not just the developing world where biodiversity can be preserved, bit by bit. City parks may hold small wonders. Even at Walden Pond, in the midst of the Massachusetts suburbs, he said: "Many of the species you find here are new to science. The basic biology of most of these things is poorly known or not known at all."

In the Walden woods live two relatively unknown ant species in the genus Myrmica. "They've been noticed, but not named or described," he said. As to the nematodes and mites, he said, lifetimes can be spent and careers can be made studying them.

It is not, of course, entomologists, or even weekend naturalists, who need convincing about the richness of the forest floor. And there are many reasons to try to preserve biological diversity at the near-microscopic level and below. There is always potential economic value in new biochemical discoveries. There is real and present economic value in clean air and water, to which the plants and insects and microbes contribute. In fact, Dr. Wilson points out, the life of the planet is built on a foundation of tiny creatures. In ecological systems it is the giants that stand on the shoulders of mites.

Finally, there is the simplest argument of all, that life itself, in all its variations, is astonishing and mysterious, and that humans have a responsibility to preserve it.

Under one log turned over on our walk, the environment was moist enough to provide a widely varied selections of insects. Dr. Wilson picked up a gooey white worm without a trace of discomfort. "That is a fly larva, a maggot actually," he said. "I don't know the kind of fly. It's very slimy."

Asked if he might be demonstrating the very reason many people do not like to turn over logs and dig under leaves, he laughed. "I'll admit it's an acquired taste," he said. "Don't mistake me, I don't expect legions of people, particularly Americans, going out and seeing how many different kinds of oribatid mites or fly larvae they can find."

"But," he continued, "they can get a feel, one way or the other, that what's at their feet is not dead leaves and dirt, but a living world with a diversity of creatures, some of which are so strange to the average experience that they beat most of the things you see in Star Wars."

It is not so hard to imagine. Butterfly fanciers are legion. Dragonflies are now attracting watchers with binoculars. "But mainly," he said, "there's got to be some sense of the beauty and integrity and the extreme age of these areas."

At the next and last log, he pointed out a predatory rove beetle, a millipede (a detritovore), a spiderling, a nematode he caught only a glimpse of ("like a very tiny silvery strand"), more ants and a wood cockroach. As he began to describe the thousands of inoffensive species of cockroach throughout the world, a siren went off on a nearby street, a reminder of where he was.

Dr. Wilson looked up from the timeless environment under the log, "That's sure a sound that Thoreau never heard."

MAKING**CONNECTIONS** 🤝

1

Consider This. Examine a more recent narrative interview with E. O. Wilson, "Taking a Cue from Ants on Evolution of Humans," July 15, 2008.[4] Now compare it to this story. Which lingers more in your mind, and why? Which do you prefer, and why? Any tips you'll take away for your own narrative interviews?

Selection 4.4

This piece neatly blends the tale of a scientist with the story of what she studies, the communication of fireflies. The lede—"Sara Lewis is fluent in firefly"—segues nicely into a scene of the scientist ambling through a farm field, reading the language of sexual selection from the flashes of these intriguing insects. Another nice segue follows, as we learn it was "on a night much like this one" years before that the scientist came "under the spell of fireflies." After exploring some of the scientific and personal reasons for the scientist's fascination, the story returns to the meadow. There the scientist snatches a net and chases a predator firefly that lures his female prey with a triple flash. In the course of this story, which contains elements of both narratives and profiles, we learn a lot about a phenomenon that anyone who has tried to capture fireflies on a warm summer evening has witnessed, but few have understood. After the story was published, National Public Radio interviewed writer Carl Zimmer on what he'd learned while working on the story. That six-minute interview is on The Times Web site, along with a longer podcast that uses Zimmer's article as background for an interview with the scientist herself. The Times site also links to a citizen science project called the Firefly Watch Project, an activity of the Boston Museum of Science.

Blink Twice if You Like Me
By CARL ZIMMER

LINCOLN, Mass.—Sara Lewis is fluent in firefly. On this night she walks through a farm field in eastern Massachusetts, watching the first fireflies of the evening rise into the air and begin to blink on and off. Dr. Lewis, an evolutionary ecologist at Tufts University, points out six species in this meadow, each with its own pattern of flashes.

Along one edge of the meadow are Photinus greeni, with double pulses separated by three seconds of darkness. Near a stream are Photinus ignitus, with a five-second delay between single pulses. And near a forest are Pyractomena angulata, which make Dr. Lewis's favorite flash pattern. "It's like a flickering orange rain," she said.

The fireflies flashing in the air are all males. Down in the grass, Dr. Lewis points out, females are sitting and observing. They look for flash patterns of males of their own species, and sometimes they respond with a single flash of their own, always at a precise interval after the male's. Dr. Lewis takes out a penlight and clicks it twice, in perfect Photinus greeni. A female Photinus greeni flashes back.

Published: June 30, 2009.

"Most people don't realize there's this call and response going on," Dr. Lewis said. "But it's very, very easy to talk to fireflies."

For Dr. Lewis, this meadow is the stage for an invertebrate melodrama, full of passion and yearning, of courtship duets and competitions for affection, of cruel deception and gruesome death. For the past 16 years, Dr. Lewis has been coming to this field to decipher the evolutionary forces at play in this production, as fireflies have struggled to survive and spread their genes to the next generation.

It was on a night much like this one in 1980 when Dr. Lewis first came under the spell of fireflies. She was in graduate school at Duke University, studying coral reef fish. Waiting for a grant to come through for a trip to Belize, she did not have much else to do but sit in her backyard in North Carolina.

"Every evening there was this incredible display of fireflies," Dr. Lewis said. She eventually started to explore the yard, inspecting the males and females. "What really struck me was that in this one-acre area there were hundreds of males and I could only find two or three females," she said. "I thought, 'Man, this is so intense.' "

When a lot of males are competing for the chance to mate with females, a species experiences a special kind of evolution. If males have certain traits that make them attractive to females, they will mate more than other males. And that preference may mean that those attractive males can pass down their traits to the next generation. Over thousands of generations, the entire species may be transformed.

Charles Darwin described this process, which he called sexual selection, in 1871, using male displays of antlers and feathers as examples. He did not mention fireflies. In fact, fireflies remained fairly mysterious for another century. It was not until the 1960s that James Lloyd, a University of Florida biologist, deciphered the call and response of several species of North American firefly.

Dr. Lewis, realizing that other firefly mysteries remained to be solved, switched to fireflies from fish in 1984, when she became a postdoctoral researcher at Harvard. She taught herself Dr. Lloyd's firefly code and then began to investigate firefly mating habits. North American fireflies spend two years underground as larvae, then spend the final two weeks of their lives as adults, flashing, mating and laying eggs. When Dr. Lewis started studying fireflies, scientists could not say whether the females mated once and then laid all their eggs, or mated with many males. "Nobody knew what happened after the lights went out," Dr. Lewis said.

She searched for mating fireflies in the evening, marked their locations with surveyor's flags and then revisited them every half-hour through the night. They were still mating at dawn.

"It was cool to watch the sun rise and see the couples breaking up and the females crawling down the grass to lay their eggs," Dr. Lewis said.

Many Americans are familiar with the kinds of fireflies Dr. Lewis studies, but they represent only a tiny fraction of the 2,000 species worldwide. And there is enormous variation in these insects. "There are some species that produce flashes when they're adults, and there are some that simply glow as adults," Dr. Lewis said. "Then there are a whole bunch of species where the adults don't produce any light at all."

In recent years scientists have analyzed the DNA of fireflies to figure out how their light has evolved. The common ancestor of today's fireflies probably produced light only when they were larvae. All firefly larvae still glow today, as a warning to would-be predators. The larvae produce bitter chemicals that make them an unpleasant meal.

As adults, the earliest fireflies probably communicated with chemical signals, the way some firefly species do today. Only much later did some firefly species gain through evolution the ability to make light as adults. Instead of a warning, the light became a mating call. (An enzyme in the firefly's tail drives a chemical reaction that makes light.)

The more Dr. Lewis watched firefly courtship, the clearer it became that the females were carefully choosing mates. They start dialogues with up to 10 males in a single evening and can keep several conversations going at once. But a female mates with only one male, typically the one she has responded to the most.

Dr. Lewis wondered if the female fireflies were picking their mates based on variations in the flashes of the males. To test that possibility, she took female fireflies to her lab, where she has computer-controlled light systems that can mimic firefly flashes. "You can play back specific signals to females and see what they respond to," Dr. Lewis said.

The female fireflies turned out to be remarkably picky. In many cases, a male flash got no response at all. In some species, females preferred faster pulse rates. In others, the females preferred males that made long-lasting pulses.

If females preferred some flashes over others, Dr. Lewis wondered why those preferences had evolved in the first place. One possible explanation was that the signals gave female fireflies a valuable clue about the males. Somehow, mating with males with certain flash patterns allowed females to produce more offspring, which would inherit their preference.

It is possible that females use flashes to figure out which males can offer the best gifts. In many invertebrate species, the males provide females with food to help nourish their eggs. Dr. Lewis and her colleagues discovered that fireflies also made these so-called nuptial gifts—packages of protein they inject with their sperm.

Dr. Lewis is not sure why she and her colleagues were the first to find them. The gifts form coils that can take up a lot of space in a male firefly's abdomen. "They're incredibly beautiful," she said.

Receiving nuptial gifts, Dr. Lewis and her colleagues have shown, can make a huge difference in the reproductive success of a female firefly. "It just about doubles the number of eggs a female can lay in her lifetime," she said. One reason the effect is so big is that fireflies do not eat during their two-week adulthood. A slowly starving female can use a nuptial gift to build more eggs.

In at least some species, females may use flashes to pick out males with the biggest gifts. Dr. Lewis has tested this hypothesis in two species; in one, males with conspicuous flashes have bigger gifts. In another species, she found no link.

"In some cases they could be honest signals, and in some cases they could be deceptive signals," Dr. Lewis said.

Deception may, in fact, evolve very easily among fireflies. It turns out that a male firefly does not need to burn many extra calories to make flashes. "It takes some energy, but it's tiny. It's less costly for a male than flying around," Dr. Lewis said.

If making light is so cheap for males, it seems odd that they have not all evolved to be more attractive to females. "What is it that keeps their flashes from getting longer and longer or faster and faster?" Dr. Lewis asked.

Scanning the meadow, she grabbed her insect net and ran after a fast-flying firefly with a triple flash. She caught an animal that may offer the answer to her question. Dr. Lewis dropped the insect into a tube and switched on a headlamp to show her catch. Called Photuris, it is a firefly that eats other fireflies.

"They are really nasty predators," Dr. Lewis said. Photuris fireflies sometimes stage aerial assaults, picking out other species by their flashes and swooping down to attack. In other cases, they sit on a blade of grass, responding to male fireflies with deceptive flashes. When the males approach, Photuris grabs them.

"They pounce, they bite, they suck blood—all the gory stuff," Dr. Lewis said. She has found that each Photuris can eat several fireflies in a night. Photuris kills other fireflies only to retrieve bad-tasting chemicals from their bodies, which it uses to protect itself from predators.

To study how Photuris predation affects its firefly prey, Dr. Lewis and her colleagues built sticky traps equipped with lights that mimicked courtship signals of Photuris's victims. The scientists found that Photuris was more likely to attack when flash rates were faster. In other words, conspicuous flashes—the ones females prefer—also make males more likely to be killed.

"At least where Photuris predators are around," Dr. Lewis said, "there's going to be a strong selection for less conspicuous flashes."

MAKING**CONNECTIONS**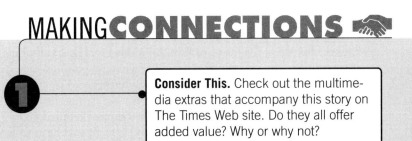

1 **Consider This.** Check out the multimedia extras that accompany this story on The Times Web site. Do they all offer added value? Why or why not?

Selection 4.5

For years, writer Dennis Overbye had in mind profiling the physicist who was the official repairman for the Hubble Space Telescope. But Overbye, who regularly covered the Hubble, had to wait for the right moment. When that moment finally arrived, he supplemented his personal knowledge of the man with interviews of others who knew him well. In long conversations with the scientist himself, he also fleshed out critical anecdotes and recreated pivotal scenes. So thorough was Overbye's interviewing that he was able to convey how on one critical day the scientist felt "as if he had been hit by a two-by-four." He was also able to report that five years later, when the scientist reported for work at a $6 million indoor pool, he was wearing "long underwear and a baseball cap bearing an image of Curious George in a spacesuit." The resulting story, of a physicist who was once asked to bury a project for which he'd risked his life, does what all good profiles do: It gives us a strong sense of the person—in this case, a man who is something of a hero. On The Times Web site, another Times reporter interviews the scientist about his upcoming space mission. The scientist also narrates an audio slideshow that takes readers into the training pools and into space as documented on prior missions.

SCIENTIST AT WORK: JOHN GRUNSFELD
Last Voyage for the Keeper of the Hubble
By DENNIS OVERBYE

HOUSTON—John Grunsfeld was sitting in an astronomical meeting in Atlanta in January of 2004 when he got a message to come back to headquarters in Washington to talk about the Hubble Space Telescope.

To say that he was excited would be an understatement. As an astronaut, Dr. Grunsfeld had twice journeyed to space to make repairs

Published: April 14, 2009. Slideshow available at: http://www.nytimes.com/2009/04/14/science/space/14prof.html

on humanity's most vaunted eye on the cosmos, experiences he had described to a high-level panel pondering Hubble's fate only a few months before as the most meaningful in his life. He was looking forward to leading the third and final servicing mission, which had been delayed by the loss of the shuttle Columbia and its crew the year before.

Thinking that the mission was now being scheduled, Dr. Grunsfeld raced to Washington, only to learn that Sean O'Keefe, NASA's administrator, had canceled it on the ground that it was too risky. Wearing his other hat as NASA's chief scientist, Dr. Grunsfeld now had the job of telling the world that the space agency was basically abandoning its greatest scientific instrument at the same time that it was laying plans for the even riskier and more expensive effort to return humans to the Moon.

He said he felt as if he had been hit by a two-by-four.

"Being an astronaut, there are not a lot of things that have really shocked me in my life," Dr. Grunsfeld said in a recent interview. But, he added, "I don't think anybody could ever prepare themselves for, you know, trying to bury something that they have said, 'Hey, this is worth risking my life for.' "

He went home that January night and wondered whether he should resign.

Five years later, Dr. Grunsfeld reported for work at a six million-gallon indoor pool near the Johnson Space Center in his long underwear and a red baseball cap bearing an image of Curious George in a spacesuit. The pool's blue depths contained sunken replicas of the Hubble and the International Space Station. Surrounded by divers and helpers, Dr. Grunsfeld squirmed into a 400-pound set of overalls known as a space suit. He was preparing to practice for his return to space.

On May 12, he and six other astronauts commanded by Scott Altman are scheduled to ride to the telescope's rescue one last time aboard the shuttle Atlantis. This will be the fifth and last time astronauts visit Hubble. When the telescope's batteries and gyros finally run out of juice sometime in the middle of the next decade, NASA plans to send a rocket and drop it into the ocean.

If all goes well in what Dr. Grunsfeld described as "brain surgery" in space, Hubble will be left at the apex of its scientific capability. As chief Hubble repairman for the past 18 years, he has been intertwined with the Hubble telescope physically, as well as intellectually and emotionally. "He might be the only person on Earth who has observed with Hubble and touched Hubble," said Bruce Margon, an astronomer at the University of California, Santa Cruz, and former deputy director of the Space Telescope Science Institute.

Last September, Dr. Grunsfeld and his crewmates were two weeks from blasting off for Hubble when a data router failed, shutting down the telescope until a backup could be booted up. The servicing mission was postponed so that NASA could prepare a replacement router, adding another degree of difficulty to an already crowded and high-stakes agenda.

To accommodate installing the new router, mission planners had to cut into the time allotted for the repair and resurrection of Hubble's main camera, the Advanced Camera for Surveys. That repair was originally scheduled to happen over two spacewalks, and now planners are hoping to be able to do it a few hours on one spacewalk.

If it cannot be done, Dr. Grunsfeld said grimly, the pictures that have inspired people around the world, pinpointed planets around other stars and helped investigate the fate of a cosmos dominated by dark energy will be lost.

If anybody is up to the challenge, it seems to be Dr. Grunsfeld, who will be making his fifth trip to space.

Michael Turner, a cosmologist and former colleague at the University of Chicago, described Dr. Grunsfeld's career as "Mr. Smith goes to space." He said: "Everything turns to magic even when things go bad. In the end it gets righted and he gets to lead the team."

Dr. Grunsfeld's whole life has led to Hubble. Born in Chicago in 1958 into a family of architects—his grandfather designed the Adler Planetarium—Dr. Grunsfeld said he yearned from age 6 to be an astronaut. Science soon beckoned as an alternative. By the time he reached college at the Massachusetts Institute of Technology his interests were centered on physics and cosmology. To make some money as an undergraduate, he took a job for $4 an hour on the graveyard shift in the control room for a small satellite, known as Sas-3, which was observing X-rays. Sometimes he took his dates there.

The job led to a year in Tokyo, where he lived in a Zen monastery, meditating in the morning and teaching and working with an X-ray astronomer, Minoru Oda, at the University of Tokyo in the afternoon. When he came home early one day and found the monks watching baseball on television, a spell was broken. He returned to Chicago to get a Ph.D. doing cosmic ray research at the University of Chicago. Along the way he married a woman he had known in high school, Carol Schiff. They now have two children, and she is an accountant at the Johnson Space Center. Dr. Grunsfeld then took a job at the California Institute of Technology, and he and his wife both learned to fly.

When NASA invited him to an interview in 1991, Dr. Grunsfeld flew his own plane to Houston. On his first space flight, a 16-day mission in 1995 tending a suite of small telescopes, Dr. Grunsfeld did not want to come down. "I had this real feeling of peace, you know, that I never had here on planet Earth."

Dr. Grunsfeld went up again on a 10-day mission to the Mir space station, in 1997.

Then, he said, "I got lucky and got assigned to Hubble."

Hubble had already been through high drama. Launched to great fanfare in 1990 as the greatest advance in astronomy since Galileo first used a telescope, it had turned out to have a misshapen mirror and was branded a "technoturkey." In 1993, in the first on-orbit telescope servicing, astronauts installed corrective optics on Hubble, restoring the telescope's vision and promise, and astronomers' faith in NASA.

"The only reason Hubble works is because we have a space shuttle," Dr. Grunsfeld said. "And of all things we do, I think Hubble is probably the best thing we use it for."

By December 1999, however, Hubble was in trouble again. Four of the six gyroscopes that keep the telescope pointed had broken down, and the telescope had gone into a so-called safe mode, suspending science operations. As a result NASA officials split a planned servicing mission into two parts and rushed the astronauts up to the telescope to replace the gyros and perform other vital tasks. Coming out of the hatch on his first spacewalk, Dr. Grunsfeld had a moment of unreality. "I mean it was just too magical. Three hundred miles below me is the Earth. There I was a meter away from the Hubble Space Telescope. I couldn't resist. I had to take a finger and reach out and touch it."

In one of the longest spacewalks to date, more than eight hours, Dr. Grunsfeld and his spacewalking partner, Steven Smith, replaced the telescope's gyros, a job that Dr. Grunsfeld described as "an icky task" because the gyros are in a delicate and awkward spot. He discovered that he had a knack for getting things done Out There.

Dr. Grunsfeld said he could get so involved in his task that he would forget he was in a space suit wearing gloves, a feeling he calls the Zen of space. "And once you're outside working, you know, all the rest of the world disappears."

"Once in a while the universe lets you be free alone and in peace," he said.

On his second mission to the telescope, in 2002, the cooling system in Dr. Grunsfeld's spacesuit sprang a leak as he was about to leave the airlock, necessitating a quick change before mission control could cancel the spacewalk.

Outside the airlock, the Zen of space took over. He thought of nothing except his task of replacing 34 tightly packed connectors in a power control unit that had not been designed to be repaired in space. "And the Zen part," he explained, "is that I had trained myself in the challenge of connecting all these connectors to only think about one connector." It would simply be too overwhelming to think about them all at once. "So I only ever had one connector to do."

An ideal job, Dr. Grunsfeld said, would be to spend six months on the International Space Station. "I would like to live in space," he said.

One of the attractions of that lifestyle is unique to physicists. When the shuttle passes through a zone in its orbit called the South Atlantic Anomaly, astronauts are exposed to large doses of cosmic rays, high-energy particles from the Sun or distant galaxies, which leave a wake of visible light as they pass through a dark-adapted human eyeball.

"In space you can get in touch with your quantum self," Dr. Grunsfeld said. "I was a human cosmic ray detector." He said he could identify the different kinds of particles zooming through his eyeball by how bright the flashes were.

The loss of the space shuttle Columbia and its crew of seven in February 2003 threw the American space program into crisis. Ultimately, as a result, the Hubble Telescope faced its greatest perils on the ground.

Busy with his chief scientist duties and helping to roll out the scientific aspects to President George W. Bush's Moon-Mars initiative in the winter of 2003–2004, Dr. Grunsfeld, who describes himself as "fat, dumb and happy," did not see the decision to cancel Hubble coming.

When it happened, he called John Bahcall, the late astrophysicist at the Institute for Advanced Study and behind-scenes-eminence for Hubble, and asked his advice. He could either stay and fight, probably losing, Dr. Grunsfeld told Dr. Bahcall, "Or I throw my badge down and, you know, walk away."

Dr. Bahcall told him not to worry. If he left, the astronomical community would regard him as a hero, he would be able to get a job anywhere he wanted.

"And then there was the pregnant pause. But—" Dr. Grunsfeld recalled.

If he left, Dr. Bahcall warned, he would lose all his ability to help the rest of the science NASA was doing, X-ray satellites and gravitation-wave observatories that were dear to his heart as a high-energy physicist. There was no guarantee that anybody else would be there to protect this work.

"And that had a very calming effect on me," Dr. Grunsfeld said, "and he was absolutely right."

A week later, Dr. Grunsfeld presided over a news conference, defending the decision that Hubble would be abandoned. "It's a sad day that we have to announce this," he said. The decision meant the telescope was doomed to die in orbit by 2007 or 2008 when its batteries and gyros gave out, and it sparked worldwide consternation and criticism of Dr. Grunsfeld as well as Mr. O'Keefe.

The criticism of Dr. Grunsfeld was resented by astronomy insiders. "There was never any doubt that he was one of us," said Dr. Margon, who was then deputy director of the Space Telescope Science Institute. "He handled it all with tremendous grace."

Dr. Grunsfeld decided that his new job was to work within the system to save Hubble. With the support of Mr. O'Keefe, who was shaken by news reports of schoolchildren offering to pool their pennies to keep Hubble alive and working, Dr. Grunsfeld pushed a proposal by Frank Cepollina of the Goddard Spaceflight Center in Greenbelt, Md., to send a robot to service the telescope. The robot mission was eventually scotched by a National Academy of Sciences panel of experts. Mr. O'Keefe resigned and was replaced by Michael Griffin, who reinstated the Hubble mission. In the meantime, the engineering team at Goddard and its expertise needed for Hubble servicing had been kept alive.

"If we hadn't gone down that road," Dr. Grunsfeld said, "NASA would have terminated all the contracts, the big contracts, and there would be no recourse."

Since Dr. Griffin's decision, more has gone wrong with Hubble than could have been fixed by a robot, anyway. Two of the telescope's most important instruments—a spectrograph named STIS, which made the first atmospheric measurements of a planet around another star, and the Advanced Camera for Surveys—have failed. Neither was designed to be repaired in space. When the advanced camera stopped working in 2007, the Hubble engineers first said that prospects for repair were poor. Now they have a plan. "For the first time," Dr. Grunsfeld said, "we're going to go in and open boxes of tiny screws, take circuit cards out and replace the circuit cards."

The spectrograph has only one card, but the camera has four. Moreover, the camera is around a corner and behind a strut where it cannot be seen.

Before the recent underwater rehearsal on a sunken replica of the Hubble, Dr. Grunsfeld was showing off a pair of ultra-sensitive gloves that will help him to feel around the corners during the mission. When he climbed back out of the water, he reported that he and Dr. Andrew Feustel, his spacewalking partner, had once again managed the camera repair, and in jig time, although a foot restraint had broken partway through. That, he said, was good practice for the frustrations of real space work.

It will be with mixed emotions, Dr. Grunsfeld said, that he hugs Hubble for the last time—the last time that any human will touch it. "I try and tell myself it's just a satellite," he said.

But his involvement with Hubble will continue. He has been given observing time on the telescope, which he said he will use to study the Moon's Tycho crater, formed by an impact 70 million or 90 million years ago, about the time that an asteroid is thought to have wiped out the dinosaurs on Earth.

Dr. Grunsfeld said that this would probably be his last flight.

"I achieved everything I ever wanted after my first spaceflight," he said, wearing his space monkey hat. "To be the Hubble repairman is really just unbelievable."

MAKING**CONNECTIONS**

1

Consider This. Identify the anecdotes and the scenes that the writer had to reconstruct for this piece. Now pick out those details that you think work especially well in these anecdotes and scenes. What questions do you imagine the reporter had to ask to get those details?

Or This. Check out the audio slideshow that accompanies this piece online. Notice the sources of the many slides and how they are perfectly timed to work with the voice-over of the scientist. Can you imagine reasons that a slideshow might have been used in this case instead of a video-taped interview of the scientist?

A Conversation with . . . **Dennis Overbye**

SCIENCE CORRESPONDENT

© The New York Times

Dennis Overbye could easily have become a career scientist. He earned a B.S. in physics from M.I.T. in 1966, took short-lived positions with Boeing and other companies and studied briefly in a graduate program in astronomy. But the would-be scientist had another side. He was an avid reader who had always had a strong urge to write. Unable to resist the muse, he dropped his astronomy studies and wrote a novel. When that didn't work out (the novel, he says, remains in a drawer), he took a position as an assistant typesetter at Sky and Telescope magazine. A few years later, he became a founding staff writer and eventually senior editor at Discover Magazine in New York City.

In 1985 he moved to Woodstock, N.Y., where he freelanced science pieces to The New York Times Magazine and other publications, and wrote two award-winning books, "Lonely Hearts of the Cosmos: The Scientific Search for the Secret of the Universe" (HarperCollins 1991, and Little, Brown, 1999), and "Einstein in Love, A Scientific Romance" (Viking, 2000).

Thirteen years later, in 1998, he joined the The New York Times as deputy science editor. Overbye held this position until 2001, when he has said he realized "that the reporters were having more fun and got to take cooler trips than editors," and he once again returned to full-time writing.

Today Overbye covers his two greatest loves in science, physics and cosmology, writing about dark matter, dark energy, the fog of microwaves, the proliferation of planets beyond our universe, the distribution of galaxies, multiple universes and a lot more. He writes about all these challenging topics in news stories, features and essays, with what one reviewer of his work has called "the precision of a scientist and the ear of a musician."

With his wife, Nancy Wartik, and daughter, Mira, he lives in New York City.

A Q&A between Overbye and Times readers, mostly about physics and astronomy, can be found on the "Talk to the Newsroom" page of The Times Web site. The following Q&A was conducted by telephone and has been edited for length and flow.

Physics and cosmology seem far removed from everyday life and concerns ordinary people have for the planet's future. Why is it important for the public to know about these things?

Well, I hate to quote myself, but I did write in one of my books once that we're all cosmologists in our hearts. We're all looking for the answer to where we came from and where we're going and what we're doing here and what this place is that we find ourselves in, and science is one response to that predicament.

Also science is certainly as relevant as great art or music or any cultural pursuit, and it has the advantage over those of being progressive and cumulative, so that each generation doesn't start over inventing the quest, which has its own power. So you should care about it because as a friend of mine said in his book, when a child asks "What is the world?" you actually want to be able to say something, that we actually do know answers to that question.

Anyway, it's important to know because it makes you a more informed citizen, and I think science also teaches values and teaches you to be humble and curious and tolerant of opposing viewpoints. It really does teach you how to live, which is especially important for a democratic society. Because I have a philosophical bent, I'm drawn to the big questions. It's kind of presumptuous to take these on, but they let me.

And what does it take to write well about physics and cosmology for ordinary folks?

I don't think background is such a big deal, because whatever you learned in school is obsolete. The most important things I think are a sense of humor about your own ignorance. You have to be willing to make a fool of yourself by asking foolish questions. But I've never heard a scientist actually say "That is a foolish question," because scientists really are expecting questions, and the more foolish the better because some really great things in science have been discovered by people who asked questions that we would have thought were foolish, but turned out to have some traction on the world.

It sounds like you're pretty comfortable with your own ignorance. Was that hard to come by?

Yeah, because I always thought I was pretty smart. I was once intending to be a physics student, and now I spend a lot of time interviewing people that might have been my co-students, and now would be my professors. I do kind of try to show off my knowledge in the field. But generally, that's not helpful to the reader.

So how do you get the kind of information your reader *is* going to need?

You really want the scientist to do the work for you. Make them make up the metaphors and explanations if at all possible; let them do the heavy lifting. After I wrote my first book, I sent the early drafts out for other people to look at. The response I often got is "Oh, let me tell you about this or here's a great story you'd like." And I thought if that's the way you write a book, to just write it first and then do the reporting by sending it around to people, they will see all the stuff that is left out and they will tell you all this good stuff.

That may work for books, but does that work for articles too?

No, no. But you could start out trying to tell them what your understanding is of something and fall on your face, and hopefully they'll try to help you up.

You've worked for both science magazines and for a general interest newspaper. I wonder if you could talk about some of the differences?

Well, of course when you're writing for science magazines you presume that the audience has more sophistication and background. At the newspaper you are speaking to a more general audience, and it has to make sense to somebody who's coming in cold.

How do you think of your audience, and how do you actually avoid writing over their heads, or do you think of your audience as like well-informed readers of the sports section?

That's a very good question, because I feel like my audience includes the world's scientific community *and* people who don't know anything. And I would like the more sophisticated readers to learn something as well as, say, the more general readers—people like my wife who don't have a scientific background. When I'm writing the story, I'm really thinking of my editors, or I'm thinking of somebody who doesn't know anything. At the same time, Thomas Pynchon and Henry Kissinger are reading these stories, but maybe they'll learn something because they don't know the details of some field or some new twist in the how we're structured in the astronomical establishment or whatever. So I get e-mails from people who are pretty sophisticated and who say they have learned stuff they didn't know. I don't feel that my job is to teach people science, *per se.*

If your job isn't to teach people science, then what *is* your job?
My job is to tell them what the scientists are doing. It's the scientists' job to watch nature. My job is to watch the scientists. So that's what I tell myself my mission is—to know what scientists are thinking or finding out, and what it may mean to people.

With so many changes in the media these days, do you think science writing remains a viable career option?
Well, I think science writing *is* a viable career for people. Somebody's got to keep track of these people and what's going on, and I don't think you can depend on volunteer bloggers to tell you. Some of them are good. But some of them are bad—they push their theories or their views of the world. You can't count on any of them to stay up all night working on an account of the latest discovery somewhere, reporting something that you might actually need to know.

You once talked about the difficulties of deciding what to write about. You said it was like you're at the end of a giant funnel with all these things coming at you. So how *do* you make those decisions?
Badly, I think. A lot of it is just wherever the most pressure is coming from. I mean today I've got the World Science Festival on, I've got Hubble. I've got the publicist for the film "Angels and Demons," who's wanting to know if I want to talk to director Ron Howard. I've got a woman who wants to have a zero-gravity wedding this summer, and something else, I forget. There's always all these things floating around that I feel I should be doing, and so about half of them wind up getting done. There's a mysterious blob that astronomers discovered that I was going to write about. Then there were all these rumors that Stephen Hawking was going to die, and that took precedence over everything for a while. I realize you can't do everything, and actually a newspaper doesn't have room for everything either, so it's kind of like when I was a student in M.I.T. and there was way too much homework. The best students did triage. They came home, and they did what they could do. I went home and didn't do any of it. So I wasn't a very good example. It

seems like there's always undone homework hanging over your head that you'll have to forget about as there's always more coming.

Doesn't sound real attractive. There has to be something . . .
It's all interesting stuff. And I suppose it's clearly what I want to do.

Well, you certainly have united two things that you really like. Judging from your bio, you really like to write, and you really appreciate science, and you found a way to do both.
I think I'm useful in the world, and that's actually quite meaningful to me, and I appreciate that.

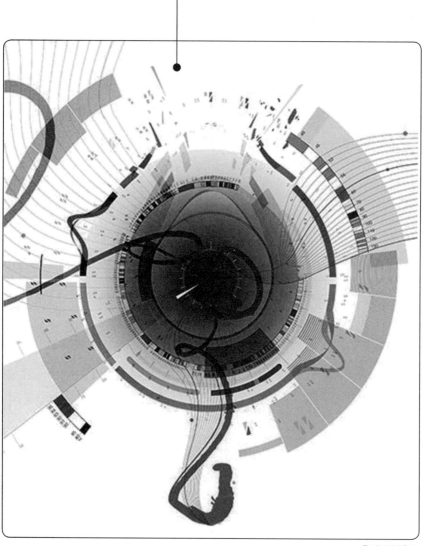

trends, issues and other stories

IN MINES AND CAVES ACROSS THE COUNTRY, bats die by the thousands, and scientists scratch their heads, then dig in to figure out why. In an ocean, a British research vessel registers one of the biggest waves ever recorded; soon oceanographers around the world are holding conferences to study monster waves that sometimes make ships look like "corks in a bathtub." And in a laboratory in Italy, a monkey watches a graduate student lick an ice cream cone and the part of his brain responsible for movement ignites; before long, scientists swarm to study "mirror neurons" in a huge range of scientific disciplines.

Writers who cover wildlife biology, oceanography, neuroscience and other scientific disciplines spend a lot of time spotting and tracing trends, patterns of exploration that say, "Hey, here is what's hot right now." Audiences appreciate trend stories about science because they offer a Big Picture, a frame in which to put any future discovery stories that come along. Without such frames, science can appear fragmented and incoherent. With them, the work researchers do takes on meaning and heightened interest.

But trends within scientific disciplines aren't the only changes science writers track for their audiences. They are also quick to spot changes within the larger culture as science, technology and society intersect: the growing popularity of high school courses in forensic science, for example, or a change in military postmortems that helps to keep soldiers safe. Such stories not only provide audiences with the Big Picture, they also connect science and technology to everyday life and concerns.

In his book "The Art and Craft of Feature Writing," former Wall Street Journal writing coach William E. Blundell lists six things that journalists would do well to explore when covering trends. The six are:

- **History** behind the development (where it came from)
- **Scope** of the development (how widespread, intense and varied it is)
- **Reasons for the development** (why it's happening *now*)

- **Impact** (the consequences of the trend–who is being helped/hurt, especially)

- **Countermoves** (what people are saying or doing to deflect the impacts)

- **Future** (where the development is headed)[1]

Two of the trend stories in this chapter, the story on the bat die-off and the story on monster waves, attend to most of these things. Others, like the story on scientists' growing interest in mirror neurons, emphasize one over others (scope, in this case). Not all of these elements need to be addressed in any one story, and different stories may focus on different ones, but it's helpful to at least consider them all when making your reporting plans.

Many of the elements Blundell has identified for trend stories can also be useful to consider when writing stories about issues, matters or disputes involving science that are of special public importance. And indeed, many of these elements are integral to two issue stories in this chapter, one on the nuisance that once-endangered beavers now pose for a New England community, and the other on the influence of pharmaceutical companies on the education students receive at Harvard's august medical school.

In addition to trend and issue stories, two other kinds of stories appear in this chapter—one a traditional anniversary story that reviews the history of the gene, and the other a classic detective story about astronomers' search for new planets, a piece that dwells in the future. Stories that zoom in on past and future are harder to write than stories that capture people and organizations acting in the here and now. But they lengthen the public's time horizon, which is a good thing for those of us who seek to appreciate and learn from the richness of the past and to give thoughtful consideration to the future. Such stories can be made to work if you can find a hook, as the gene story does, and if, as in the space exploration piece, you can find compelling ways to propel readers forward.

 STORY**SCAN**

Selection 5.1

Tina Kelley's engaging story on the demise of bats was one of the most read science/technology stories on The Times Web site in 2008. It is annotated here to highlight elements that make up many good trend stories. In a podcast accompanying the online story, the writer—speaking over the sounds of bats—vividly describes some of what she saw.

Bats Perish, and No One Knows Why

By TINA KELLEY

Al Hicks was standing outside an old mine in the Adirondacks, the largest bat hibernaculum, or winter resting place, in New York State.

It was broad daylight in the middle of winter, and bats flew out of the mine about one a minute. Some had fallen to the ground where they flailed around on the snow like tiny wind-broken umbrellas, using the thumbs at the top joint of their wings to gain their balance.

All would be dead by nightfall. Mr. Hicks, a mammal specialist with the state's Environmental Conservation Department, said: "Bats don't fly in the daytime, and bats don't fly in the winter. Every bat you see out here is a 'dead bat flying,' so to speak."

They have plenty of company. In what is one of the worst calamities to hit bat populations in the United States, on average 90 percent of the hibernating bats in four caves and mines in New York have died since last winter.

Wildlife biologists fear a significant die-off in about 15 caves and mines in New York, as well as at sites in Massachusetts and Vermont. Whatever is killing the bats leaves them unusually thin and, in some cases, dotted with a white fungus. Bat experts fear that what they call White Nose Syndrome may spell doom for several species that keep insect pests under control.

Researchers have yet to determine whether the bats are being killed by a virus, bacteria, toxin, environmental hazard, metabolic disorder or fungus. Some have been found with pneumonia, but that and the fungus are believed to be secondary symptoms.

"This is probably one of the strangest and most puzzling problems we have had with bats," said Paul Cryan, a bat ecologist with the United States Geological Survey. "It's really startling that we've not come up with a smoking gun yet."

This "establishing shot" shows the growing demise of bats, with heartbreaking particularity. Notice how bats flail on the snow "like tiny wind-broken umbrellas." This evocative detail— along with the fact that these bats will be dead by nightfall—says it all.

The story pulls back from the establishing shot to reveal the larger context: Most of the hibernating bats in some areas have already died (scope) and biologists fear the demise of several species (impact). Both scope and impact will be elaborated on later.

There are likely reasons for this trend, as there are for all patterns of change, but in this case the reasons aren't clear. That's O.K. If it's a puzzle, just say so. Quotes from experts can help you.

Published: March 25, 2008. Podcast available at: http://www.nytimes.com/2008/03/25/science/25bats.html

Merlin Tuttle, the president of Bat Conservation International, an education and research group in Austin, Tex., said: "So far as we can tell at this point, this may be the most serious threat to North American bats we've experienced in recorded history. It definitely warrants immediate and careful attention."

This part of the story segues back to the opening, at the same time offering more information. Hawks circling overhead complete the return to gritty reality. The way this story alternates abstract and concrete information is one of its strengths.

This month, Mr. Hicks took a team from the Environmental Conservation Department into the hibernaculum that has sheltered 200,000 bats in past years, mostly little brown bats (Myotis lucifugus) and federally endangered Indiana bats (Myotis sodalis), with the world's second largest concentration of small-footed bats (Myotis leibii).

He asked that the mine location not be published, for fear that visitors could spread the syndrome or harm the bats or themselves.

Other visitors do not need directions. The day before, Mr. Hicks saw eight hawks circling the parking lot of another mine, waiting to kill and eat the bats that flew out.

In a dank galley of the mine, Mr. Hicks asked everyone to count how many out of 100 bats had white noses. About half the bats in one galley did. They would be dead by April, he said.

Mr. Hicks, who was the first person to begin studying the deaths, said more than 10 laboratories were trying to solve the mystery.

Here we begin to get the known history of the development. Also elaborations on scope, which are continued in subsequent paragraphs.

In January 2007, a cave explorer reported an unusual number of bats flying near the entrance of a cavern near Albany. In March and April, thousands of dead bats were found in three other mines and caves. In one case, half the dead or living bats had the fungus.

One cave had 15,584 bats in 2005, 6,735 in 2007 and an estimated 1,500 this winter. Another went from 1,329 bats in 2006 to 38 this winter. Some biologists fear that 250,000 bats could die this year.

Since September, when hibernation began, dead or dying bats have been found at 15 sites in New York. Most of them had been visited by people who had been at the original four sites last winter, leading researchers to suspect that humans could transmit the problem.

Details on the problem in neighboring states are sketchier. "In the Berkshires in Massachusetts, we are getting reports of dying/dead bats in areas where we do not have known bat hibernacula, so we may have more sites than we will ever be able to identify," said Susi von Oettingen, an endangered species biologist with the United States Fish and Wildlife Service.

In Vermont, Scott Darling, a wildlife biologist with the Fish and Wildlife Department, said: "The last tally that I have is approximately 20 sites in New York, 4 in Vermont and 2 in Massachusetts. We only have estimates of the numbers of bats in the affected sites—more or less 500,000. It is impossible for us to count the dead bats, as many have flown away from the caves and died—we have over 90 reports from citizens across Vermont—as well as many are still dying."

People are not believed to be susceptible to the affliction. But New Jersey, New York and Vermont have advised everyone to stay out of all caverns that might have bats. Visitors to affected caves and mines are asked to decontaminate all clothing, boots, ropes and other gear, as well as the car trunks that transport them.

One affected mine is the winter home to a third of the Indiana bats between Virginia and Maine. These pink-nosed bats, two inches long and weighing a quarter-ounce, are particularly social and cluster together as tightly as 300 a square foot.

By zeroing in on one affected mine, the writer makes it easier to grasp the more abstract information.

"It's ironic, until last year most of my time was spent trying to delist it," or take it off the endangered species list, Mr. Hicks said, after the state's Indiana bat population grew, to 52,000 from 1,500 in the 1960s.

"It's very scary and a little overwhelming from a biologist's perspective," Ms. von Oettingen said. "If we can't contain it, we're going to see extinctions of listed species, and some of species that are not even listed."

Statements from biologists, named and unnamed, add to the growing sense of urgency. Much of it is speculation, but it's informed speculation.

Neighbors of mines and caves in the region have notified state wildlife officials of many affected sites when they have noticed bats dead in the snow, latched onto houses or even flying in a recent snowstorm.

Biologists are concerned that if the bats are being killed by something contagious either in the caves or elsewhere, it could spread rapidly, because bats can migrate hundreds of miles in any direction to their summer homes, known as maternity roosts. At those sites, females usually give birth to one pup a year, an added challenge for dropping populations.

Nursing females can eat up to half their weight in insects a day, Mr. Hicks said.

Researchers from institutions like the Centers for Disease Control and Prevention, the United States Geological Survey's National Wildlife Health Center, Boston University, the New York State Health Department and even Disney's Animal World are addressing the problem. Some are considering trying to feed underweight wild bats to help them survive the remaining weeks before spring. Some are putting temperature sensors on bats to monitor how often they wake up, and others are making thermal images of hibernating bats.

Other researchers want to know whether recently introduced pesticides, including those released to stop West Nile virus, may be contributing to the problem, either through a toxin or by greatly reducing the bat's food source.

Dr. Thomas H. Kunz, a biology professor at Boston University, said the body composition of the bats would also be studied, partly to determine the ratio of white to brown fat. Of particular interest is the brown fat between the shoulder blades, known to assist the bats in warming up when they begin to leave deep hibernation in April.

"It appears the white nose bats do not have enough fat, either brown or white, to arouse," Dr. Kunz said. "They're dying in situ and do not have the ability to arouse from their deep torpor."

His researchers' cameras have shown that bats in the caves that do wake up when disturbed take hours longer to do so, as was the case in the Adirondack mine. He also notes that if females become too emaciated, they will not have the hormonal reactions necessary to ovulate and reproduce.

It's always good to know when people and institutions are working to deflect the impacts of a trend (the countermoves). If you can, focus more on what people are actually doing than on what they are thinking about doing. Talk is cheap.

In searching for a cause of the syndrome, researchers are hampered by the lack of baseline knowledge about habits like how much bats should weigh in the fall, where they hibernate and even how many bats live in the region.

"We're going to learn an awful lot about bats in a comprehensive way that very few animal species have been looked at," said Dr. Elizabeth Buckles, an assistant professor at Cornell who coordinates bat research efforts. "That's good. But it's unfortunate it has to be under these circumstances."

The die-offs are big enough that they may have economic effects. A study of Brazilian free-tailed bats in southwestern Texas found that their presence saved cotton farmers a sixth to an eighth of the cash value of their crops by consuming insect pests.

Another impact—this one on people. When writing about any trend, try to think about who—or what—could possibly be affected. In this case, it is not just the bats, but farmers and the rest of us.

"Logic dictates when you are potentially losing as many as a half a million bats in this region, there are going to be ramifications for insect abundance in the coming summer," Mr. Darling, the Vermont wildlife biologist, said.

As Mr. Hicks traveled deeper in the cave, the concentrations of bats hanging from the ceiling increased. They hung like fruit, generally so still that they appeared dead. In some tightly packed groups, just individual noses or elbows peeked through. A few bats had a wing around their nearest cavemates. Their white bellies mostly faced downhill. When they awoke, they made high squeaks, like someone sucking a tooth.

We end where we began. Notice the sympathetic descriptions of the bats. The final quote, from the bat expert who has been our companion throughout the piece, points to the future. It is a poignant clincher.

The mine floors were not covered with carcasses, Mr. Hicks said, because raccoons come in and feed on them. Raccoon scat dotted the rocks along the trail left by their footprints.

In the six hours in the cave taking samples, nose counts and photographs, Mr. Hicks said that for him trying for the perfect picture was a form of therapy. "It's just that I know I'm never going to see these guys again," he said. "We're the last to see this concentration of bats in our lifetime."

Selection 5.2

Like the last feature, this one on oceanographers' growing interest in giant waves was one of the most read science/technology stories on The Times Web site the year it was written. Writer William Broad opens the piece with a vivid anecdote that shows the force of huge waves that once were believed to be as rare as mermaids and sea monsters. His fifth paragraph serves as a "nut graf," summing up the story's focus on scientists' developing interest in these killer waves, while the sixth paragraph sums up the practical significance of that interest. The remainder of the story dips into some of the historical reasons for the research, the impact of the findings on shipbuilders, and future directions for study. Along the way, we're fed a wealth of particulars about these giants—their frequency, size, range and ferocity. The result is a story in which we learn as much about these colossal waves as we do about scientists' growing interest in them.

Rogue Giants at Sea
By WILLIAM J. BROAD

The storm was nothing special. Its waves rocked the Norwegian Dawn just enough so that bartenders on the cruise ship turned to the usual palliative—free drinks.

Then, off the coast of Georgia, early on Saturday, April 16, 2005, a giant, seven-story wave appeared out of nowhere. It crashed into the bow, sent deck chairs flying, smashed windows, raced as high as the 10th deck, flooded 62 cabins, injured 4 passengers and sowed widespread fear and panic.

"The ship was like a cork in a bathtub," recalled Celestine Mcelhatton, a passenger who, along with 2,000 others, eventually made it back to Pier 88 on the Hudson River in Manhattan. Some vowed never to sail again.

Enormous waves that sweep the ocean are traditionally called rogue waves, implying that they have a kind of freakish rarity. Over the decades, skeptical oceanographers have doubted their existence and tended to lump them together with sightings of mermaids and sea monsters.

But scientists are now finding that these giants of the sea are far more common and destructive than once imagined, prompting a rush of new studies and research projects. The goals are to better tally them, understand why they form, explore the possibility of forecasts, and learn how to better protect ships, oil platforms and people.

Published: July 11, 2006.

The stakes are high. In the past two decades, freak waves are suspected of sinking dozens of big ships and taking hundreds of lives. The upshot is that the scientists feel a sense of urgency about the work and growing awe at their subjects.

"I never met, and hope I never will meet, such a monster," said Wolfgang Rosenthal, a German scientist who helped the European Space Agency pioneer the study of rogue waves by radar satellite. "They are more frequent than we expected."

Drawing on recent tallies and making tentative extrapolations, Dr. Rosenthal estimated that at any given moment 10 of the giants are churning through the world's oceans.

In size and reach these waves are quite different from earthquake-induced tsunamis, which form low, almost invisible mounds at sea before gaining height while crashing ashore. Rogue waves seldom, if ever, prowl close to land.

"We know these big waves cannot get into shallow water," said David W. Wang of the Naval Research Laboratory, the science arm of the Navy and Marine Corps. "That's a physical limitation."

By one definition, the titans of the sea rise to heights of at least 25 meters, or 82 feet, about the size of an eight-story building. Scientists have calculated their theoretical maximum at 198 feet—higher than the Statue of Liberty or the Capitol rotunda in Washington. So far, however, they have documented nothing that big. Large rogues seem to average around 100 feet.

Most waves, big and small alike, form when the wind blows across open water. The wind's force, duration and sweep determine the size of the swells, with big storms building their height. Waves of about 6 feet are common, though ones up to 30 or even 50 feet are considered unexceptional (though terrifying to people in even fairly large boats). As waves gain energy from the wind, they become steeper and the crests can break into whitecaps.

The trough preceding a rogue wave can be quite deep, what nautical lore calls a "hole in the sea." For anyone on a ship, it is a roller coaster plunge that can be disastrous.

Over the centuries, many accounts have told of monster waves that battered and sank ships. In 1933 in the North Pacific, the Navy oiler Ramapo encountered a huge wave. The crew, calm enough to triangulate from the ship's superstructure, estimated its height at 112 feet.

In 1966, the Italian cruise ship Michelangelo was steaming toward New York when a giant wave tore a hole in its superstructure, smashed heavy glass 80 feet above the waterline, and killed a crewman and two passengers. In 1978, the München, a German barge carrier, sank in the Atlantic. Surviving bits of twisted wreckage suggested that it surrendered to a wave of great force.

Despite such accounts, many oceanographers were skeptical. The human imagination tended to embellish, they said.

Moreover, bobbing ships were terrible reference points for trying to determine the size of onrushing objects with any kind of accuracy. Their mathematical models predicted that giant waves were statistical improbabilities that should arise once every 10,000 years or so.

That began to change on New Year's Day in 1995, when a rock-steady oil platform in the North Sea produced what was considered the first hard evidence of a rogue wave. The platform bore a laser designed to measure wave height.

During a furious storm, it registered an 84-foot giant.

Then, in February 2000, a British oceanographic research vessel fighting its way through a gale west of Scotland measured titans of up to 95 feet, "the largest waves ever recorded by scientific instruments," seven researchers wrote in the journal Geophysical Research Letters.

Once-skeptical scientists were soon holding conferences to discuss the findings and to design research strategies. A large meeting in Brest, France, in November 2000 attracted researchers from around the world.

It quickly became apparent that the big waves formed with some regularity in regions swept by powerful currents: the Agulhas off South Africa, the Kuroshio off Japan, and the Gulf Stream off the eastern United States, where the Norwegian Dawn got into trouble off Georgia. The Gulf Stream also flows through the Bermuda Triangle, famous for allegedly devouring large numbers of ships.

Dr. Bengt Fornberg, a mathematician at the University of Colorado who studies the giants, said the strong ocean currents appeared to focus waves "like a magnifying glass concentrates sunlight."

"It's the same idea," he said. "There are a few places in the world where there is a regular current, like a steady magnifying glass. In other places, the eddies come and go, and that makes the waves less predictable."

One way that rogue waves apparently form is when the strong currents meet winds and waves moving in the opposite direction, he said. The currents focus and concentrate sets of waves, shortening the distance between them and sending individual peaks higher. "That," Dr. Fornberg said in an interview, "makes for hot spots in a fairly predictable area."

A particularly threatening spot, he said, turned out to be where big oil tankers coming from the Middle East ride the Agulhas current around South Africa. There, the westward-flowing current meets prevailing easterly winds, at times disastrously.

"Three or four tankers a year there get badly damaged," Dr. Fornberg said. "That's one of the few places in the world where the phenomena is regular."

"With a big storm, you get lots of big waves," he added. "You have regular waves and then one or two giants. Then it's back to regular again."

The scientists who met at Brest in 2000, eager to track the phenomenon globally, laid plans to use radar satellites to conduct a census, calling it MaxWave.

They worked with the European Space Agency, which had lofted radar satellites in 1991 and 1995, as well as the German Aerospace Center and several other European research bodies. The radar beams were seen as potentially ideal for measuring the height of individual waves, based on the time it took the beams to bounce from orbit to the sea and back to space.

The MaxWave team, led by Dr. Rosenthal, examined three weeks of radar data and to its amazement discovered 10 giants, each at least 82 feet high. "We were quite successful," he said.

The team even tracked monster waves in a region of the South Atlantic where two cruise ships, the Bremen and the Caledonian Star, had come under assault.

Further confirmation with a different set of instruments came in September 2004 when Hurricane Ivan swept through the Gulf of Mexico.

It passed directly over six wave-tide gauges that the Naval Research Laboratory had deployed about 50 miles east of the Mississippi Delta. Dr. Wang and his colleagues analyzed the data and found to their surprise waves measuring more than 90 feet from trough to crest.

"We had no idea," Dr. Wang recalled. "It was the right time and the right place."

Already, the scientists said, naval architects and shipbuilders are discussing precautions. Some of the easiest are seen as increasing the strength of windows and hatch covers. But even the best physical protections may fail under assault by tons of roiling water, so the best precaution of all will be learning how to avoid the monsters in the first place.

Increasingly, scientists are focusing on better understanding how the big waves form and whether that knowledge can lead to accurate forecasts—a feat that, if achieved, may save hundreds of lives and many billions of dollars in lost commerce.

A suspected culprit, in addition to wind-current interactions, is the amplification that occurs when disparate trains of waves (perhaps emanating from different storms) come together. Such intersections are seen as sometimes canceling out waves, and other times making them higher and steeper.

Another birth ground is seen as choppy seas where several waves moving independently merge by chance. But scientists say a giant of that sort would live for no more than a few seconds or minutes, whereas some are suspected of lasting for hours and traveling long distances.

As for forecasts, oceanographers are focusing on the interplay of exceptionally strong winds and currents, especially in the Agulhas off South Africa.

Dr. Fornberg said that several years ago South African authorities began issuing predictions. "That's the only place the theory has succeeded," he said.

Dr. Rosenthal said that in the future the continued proliferation of radar satellites should create an opportunity to better understand not only the habitats of the giants but in theory also individual threats, bringing about a safer relationship between people and the sea.

"There will be warnings, maybe in 10 years," he said. "It should be possible."

Selection 5.3

A counterpoint to the years of celebrated attempts to bring species back from the brink of extinction, this issue story focuses on a running battle between people and other critters in their environment. Like the trend story on bats, it nicely alternates abstract information with on-the-scene storytelling. Environment writer Cornelia Dean begins with a meeting where local officials in one New England town have gathered with state wildlife experts to address the nuisance that beavers have become in their community. Dean puts the concerns into historical perspective, places the recovery of the beavers in the town within the larger context of species recoveries nationwide, then returns to the meeting where a state biologist tries to convince the locals of the rodents' benefits. When the meeting ends, Dean accompanies the biologist into the field to see where beavers live. This nicely descriptive scene drives home the advantages of beavers to the health of other wildlife and to the richness of the soil on which humans depend. (In environmental coverage, interdependence is foundational.) But notice how the story ends, with a quote of begrudging admiration for beavers from the town engineer—a man who, like those in the opening scene, appears not yet convinced that humans need to find a way to coexist with them. If you like this feature, remember it: Beginning journalists sent to public meetings all too often write listless stories that few want to read. Now you know you don't have to.

Return of the Once-Rare Beaver? Not in My Yard

By CORNELIA DEAN

CONCORD, Mass.—The dozens of public works officials, municipal engineers, conservation agents and others who crowded into a meeting room here one recent morning needed help. Property in their towns was flooding, they said. Culverts were clogged. Septic tanks were being overwhelmed.

"We have a huge problem," said David Pavlik, an engineer for the town of Lexington, where dams built by beavers have sent water flooding into the town's sanitary sewers. "We trapped them," he said. "We breached their dam. Nothing works. We are looking for long-term solutions."

Mary Hansen, a conservation agent from Maynard, said it starkly: "There are beavers everywhere."

Laura Hajduk, a biologist with the state's Division of Fisheries and Wildlife, had little to offer them. When beavers are trapped, others move in to replace them. And, she said, you can breach a beaver dam, but "I guarantee you that within 24 hours if the beavers are still there it will be repaired. Beavers are the ultimate ecosystem engineers."

That was not what Mr. Pavlik was hoping to hear.

He is not alone in his dismay, and it is not just beavers. Around the nation, decades of environmental regulation, conservation efforts and changing land use have brought many species, like beavers, so far back from the brink that they are viewed as nuisances. As Stuart Pimm, a conservation ecologist at Duke University, put it, "We are finding they are inconvenient."

In Florida, alligators were once nearly wiped out by hunters; today the state maintains a roster of trappers who remove thousands of nuisance gators each year. The pesticide DDT once left the Pelican State, Louisiana, bereft of the birds; today wildlife organizations say fishermen must guard their bait and catches from the birds. In California, warnings about marauding mountain lions are posted on hiking trails.

There were tens and maybe hundreds of millions of beavers in North America before it was settled by Europeans, whose craze for beaver hats is often cited as motivating much of the exploration of the continent. But by 1900 their numbers had been reduced to about 100,000, almost all of them in Canada. As farming faded and the forests reclaimed much of their lost ground, Castor canadensis made a spectacular comeback. Today there are believed to be 10 million to 15 million of the animals in North America, and they are regarded as pests in much of their range.

Published: June 9, 2009.

In 1999, for example, a colony moved into the Tidal Basin in Washington, where they cut down a number of cherry trees before being trapped and removed. According to the Department of Agriculture, states like Mississippi, North Carolina and Wisconsin lose tens of millions of dollars each year from beaver damage to buildings, roads, timber, crops and trout streams.

In Massachusetts, beavers had vanished by the early 19th century, killed by trappers and dispossessed by farmers who turned woods into pastures. But they have had a particularly strong comeback here as farmland has returned to woodland. The change has also brought an unwelcome abundance of coyotes, black bears, moose and other species. Wild turkeys, once extirpated, now go one-on-one with suburban pedestrians in what biologists call misguided efforts to establish their dominance in a pecking order.

The advice from the experts on beavers is to find a way to live with them and reduce the damage. As Ms. Hajduk said during the Concord meeting, chicken-wire fencing can keep beavers out of culverts or away from prized trees. Companies market water flow devices called "beaver deceivers" or "beaver bafflers" that can be installed in dams to lower the water level of beaver ponds. Some people even coat prized trees with paint and sand in the hope that the grit will discourage gnawing beavers. If people want to live in a more natural environment, they must adjust to animals, even inconvenient animals, Dr. Pimm said in a telephone interview. "You have to accept Mother Nature as she is," he said.

John Livsey, Mr. Pavlik's boss and the town engineer in Lexington, has firsthand experience with the beaver problem. The animals are building dams in wooded areas traversed by the town's sewer lines, he said, and as water rises, it seeps through manholes into the sewer pipes.

The town must pay for the treatment of this extra "inflow." Though Mr. Livsey said he could not put a dollar figure on it, "it's a lot of money."

The town periodically obtains permits to breach dams and trap and kill the animals, but destroying a beaver dam can have unintended consequences downstream, from flooding a neighbor's property to destroying habitat crucial for rare amphibians or silting up streams where endangered Atlantic salmon spawn. Some people date the beaver's return to Massachusetts to 1928, when beavers were observed in West Stockbridge and "greeted with enthusiasm," according to the Web site of the Division of Fisheries and Wildlife. By 1946, there were an estimated 300 beavers, all west of the Connecticut River.

Today, Ms. Hajduk said, there are at least 30,000 beavers, all over the state.

In her presentation in Concord, Ms. Hajduk said that beavers, which can reach 60 pounds and are the largest rodents in North America, are monogamous animals that mate for life and like to eat plants that grow underwater. They look for places to build a dam and create a pond. Their webbed feet are adapted for life in the water, and their front teeth, four giant incisors, are useful for cutting the trees they use as raw materials for their dams and lodges. (They also eat the bark, particularly in the winter.)

Typically, she said, they work at night, building a stick-and-mud lodge in the pond or at its edge, with its entrance underwater for safety. A pair of beavers typically live 10 years, producing a litter of two or more kits each spring. The kits stay with their parents until they are 2 years old, then disperse in search of their own territories.

Though the people at the meeting found it hard to believe—or irrelevant—the beavers have produced many benefits for the state's environment, Ms. Hajduk said. She pointed to some of them after the meeting, wthen she and Mary B. Griffin, the state's commissioner of fish and game, met at the Boxborough Station Wildlife Management Area, a state reserve northwest of here.

At first glance it hardly seemed like an ideal spot for beavers. Route 2, a major east-west highway, runs along one edge; a much-used rail line runs along another. "You are really surrounded by a lot of suburbia and roadways," Ms. Hajduk said.

But trees had reclaimed the land between the ancient stone walls. Beavers have taken full advantage of the site, damming a small stream with mud and branches to impound a 45-acre pond perhaps five or six feet deep, with a lodge in the middle.

As she and Dr. Griffin neared the pond, a group of wood ducks, alarmed by their approach, went squawking into the air. It was good to see them, Dr. Griffin said—they are among the species favored by hunters that the state is trying to encourage. She pointed to an osprey sitting on a dead tree. Ospreys were almost wiped out by DDT but are now back in Massachusetts, and this one was taking advantage of beaver-created habitat. Just then, a great blue heron glided to a landing in the pond, another guest of the beavers.

Impoundments like this one absorb water, especially in the spring, when streams swell with rain and snow runoff, Dr. Griffin said. And when the impoundment eventually silts up and the beavers move on, their dam will decay and the pond will drain, leaving unusually rich soil behind.

"These beaver meadows stand out like rich little oases," Ms. Hajduk said.

Dr. Griffin said she and her colleagues emphasized these advantages in urging people to adopt "tolerance and coexistence as a first line of defense."

Mr. Livsey can embrace this concept, up to a point, perhaps because he admires the animals' engineering ability.

"They're amazingly skilled creatures, actually," he said. "They seem to be able to put things where they want them. I wish they worked for us."

Selection 5.4

Fueled by programs like "Law and Order" and "C.S.I.," forensics is the hot new science in American high schools. With her usual high-spirited prose, Natalie Angier takes us into one science classroom where she shows us the excitement and impact of this growing branch of science education. Notice how she captures the scene with strong sensory language, and how skillfully she uses an anecdote to convey the development's history. The piece, in Angier's biweekly column, "Basics," ran as part of an entire issue of Science Times devoted to forensic science. It was accompanied by a four-minute video. (But viewers beware: The video you are about to see shows close-ups of maggots.)

Basics: A Hit in School, Maggots and All
By NATALIE ANGIER

NEW ROCHELLE, N.Y.—It's a sight that might make your skin crawl—if the chicken weren't already doing it for you.

Projected onto the classroom screen was live-action footage of putrefying poultry, the image blown up to festively pulsating proportions by way of a digital microscope. And lively the action was: maggots of all ages and body-mass indexes wriggled across the slick carnal landscape, some newly hatched and ravenous, other older ones on the verge of pupating, looking as plump and pompous as earthworms.

But did the students in Scott Rubins's advanced forensic science class at New Rochelle High School shriek or go "Ewww gross" or even so much as wrinkle their noses with revulsion? Not over their dead bodies. For one thing, Mr. Rubins doesn't tolerate squeamish outbursts in the classroom. "No one is allowed to react," he said. "If you're reacting, you won't be able to learn."

For another, the students were too busy furiously waving their hands in the air, begging to be chosen as the day's evidence collectors.

Published: May 12, 2009. Video available at: http://www.nytimes.com/2009/05/12/science/12angi .html

Far from being disgusted by the maggot-cam feed, they were desperate for the chance to snap on a pair of disposable rubber gloves and retrieve the rest of the decomposing chicken that Mr. Rubins had deposited outside a few days earlier. They wanted to pick up the slimy three-and-a-half-pound ex-bird and flip it this way and that, to lift the wings and the legs and find the dark, warm crevices where flies in training like to hide.

Nothing could keep the students from systematically probing the fetid fare. Quinton Witherspoon, a 16-year-old junior, had recently broken his foot playing baseball, but he hopped over on crutches to scrape a stick along the chicken's skin for samples. Ryan Lefkowitz, a 17-year-old senior, exulted: "I love this class! Where else do you get the chance to hold maggots?"

Many people fret these days about the supposedly feeble state of science education in America and how kids just don't like science and we'd better do something quick or we'll be flattened by the rising technocracies in Asia and Europe. Yet here at New Rochelle, among the largest and most ethnically and economically diverse high schools in New York if not the nation, one phylum of science class has proved a runaway success: forensic science, the application of science to solving crimes. Since the program was started 15 years ago, demand has waxed so strong that today the school offers seven different forensic classes, three of them so advanced that the students receive college credits from Syracuse University. "Forensic science is our most popular elective hands down," said Joyce Kent, head of the school's science department.

And though the forensic menu at New Rochelle is unusually extensive, schools everywhere are capitalizing on the subject's sex appeal to inspire respect for the power of the scientific mind-set generally. According to an informal survey of 285 high school and middle school teachers conducted in 2007 by the National Science Teachers Association, 75 percent replied yes when asked, "Do you or other teachers in your district use forensic investigation in the science classroom?" A third of the respondents said the subject was woven into the regular science curriculum, a quarter listed forensics as a stand-alone course at their school, and one-fifth replied, we do both. Bring out your dead!

Francis Eberle, executive director of the association, said that the thanato mania showed no sign of abating. At the organization's annual conference in 2006, 61 teachers gave presentations on the value of forensic science in the classroom; for last year's meeting, that figure rose to 98.

Forensic science wasn't always an easy sell. When Ms. Kent started the New Rochelle program, nobody knew what it was. "I went around trying to enlist students, saying, 'Quincy,' how many of you have ever watched 'Quincy'?" she said, referring to the television series about a medical examiner played by Jack Klugman. Now it's impossible to escape airwave forensics, and student interest has soared accordingly.

"I went through one week's worth of TV listings and found 35 to 40 shows on forensic science," Mr. Rubins said. " 'Law and Order,' 'C.S.I.,' the reality shows—the media is insane with it."

Yet one of the first things that Mr. Rubins points out in his classes is how boneheaded a lot of those hit shows can be. Three students in the advanced course excitedly rattled off to me the many gaffes and sloppy techniques they had seen on TV: failing to use gloves, improper bagging of evidence, letting the neighbors stampede through the crime scene and, worst of all, solving crimes tidily in a matter of hours or days while using techniques that would take weeks or months. "It's like magic," Mr. Rubins said. "The kids come in as a raw product, not knowing or noticing anything, and then one day, they watch something on the news, and they come in and tell me, I think the police in the background were doing it wrong. All of a sudden, they get it."

They also end up getting a lot of serious science without necessarily realizing it. "We do chemistry while studying soil composition, toxicology, all the different tests for drugs," said Andrea Schwach, who teaches two of the New Rochelle forensic classes. There are forays into biology and anatomy: the biology of blood, hair and skin, how fingerprints form, and how DNA can be extracted from the tiniest personal remains. Students learn how to distinguish a healthy liver and set of lungs from the organs of an alcoholic or a smoker, and how to analyze stomach contents and figure out what a victim ate and how long ago. Let's not forget forensic entomology, those magnificent maggots, and how a sampling of detritus recyclers can help estimate the breadth of a victim's p.m.I.—post mortem interval. Physics comes up in studying ballistics and explosives, or when students must reconstruct a car crash or make sense of blood spatters. "They have to understand how force affects spray angle," Ms. Schwach said. "There's a lot of math involved in that as well."

Forensic science also emphasizes what scientists complain is too often lacking in standard science education: hands-on lab work. The hands may be gloved, but they're out in the world, gathering and annotating evidence, disinterring fish bones, setting fire to different fabrics to see exactly how they burn, tracing bullet grooves, making casts of shoe imprints using dental stone, studying teeth from the victims of the World Trade Center attack and realizing, with a shock of sadness, that the ivory relics in their hands belonged to mouths that talked and smiled and violently died.

For the final exam, the students have an hour to make sense of a crime scene mocked up in the woods with the help of the New

Rochelle police. Here the core message of the semester is brutally distilled: that science, like life and its end, can be messy and uncertain, that you must notice what others overlook, and that if you collect and bag your evidence but fail to seal it, your teacher will dump your hard work in the trash. Remember, you're a forensic scientist. You're not just playing one on TV.

Selection 5.5

Writer Denise Grady stumbled on this particular story while investigating a new development in medicine—the growing use of computed tomography (CT) scans to determine the cause of death. A source told her that doctors were making the most of the technique in the military. "I called to ask about it," she says, "and found that with the wars in Afghanistan and Iraq, the government was performing autopsies on all the troops who were killed. This had never been done before—there were some autopsies, but not on all who were killed. In addition, all the dead are being put through CT scanners, and this had never been done before." Although a news magazine had mentioned the military's use of "virtual autopsies," no one had focused on it. Grady decided to, and the resulting story ran on Page 1 of The Times. As newsworthy as this story was, it revealed many of the qualities of fine feature writing, including a powerful account of how a military radiologist got the idea to do these scans and equally powerful descriptions of the impact of the new autopsy reports on families left behind. On the Web, the piece was accompanied by an arresting, if grim, Web feature—a scan that shows the path a lethal ball bearing took in one soldier's brain. The story prompted a blog post from Times health writer Tara Parker-Pope and nearly 50 comments from readers, including some doctors.

Autopsies of War Dead Reveal Ways to Save Others
By DENISE GRADY

Within an hour after the bodies arrive in their flag-draped coffins at Dover Air Force Base, they go through a process that has never been used on the dead from any other war.

Under Capt. Craig T. Mallak, pathologists from the Armed Forces Medical Examiner System conduct autopsies and CT scans on all service members killed in Iraq and Afghanistan.

Since 2004, every service man and woman killed in Iraq or Afghanistan has been given a CT scan, and since 2001, when the

Published: May 25, 2009. Web feature available at: http://www.nytimes.com/2009/05/26/health/26autopsy.html.

fighting began in Afghanistan, all have had autopsies, performed by pathologists in the Armed Forces Medical Examiner System. In previous wars, autopsies on people killed in combat were uncommon, and scans were never done.

The combined procedures have yielded a wealth of details about injuries from bullets, blasts, shrapnel and burns—information that has revealed deficiencies in body armor and vehicle shielding and led to improvements in helmets and medical equipment used on the battlefield.

The military world initially doubted the usefulness of scanning corpses but now eagerly seeks data from the scans, medical examiners say, noting that on a single day in April, they received six requests for information from the Defense Department and its contractors.

"We've created a huge database that's never existed before," said Capt. Craig T. Mallak, 48, a Navy pathologist and lawyer who is chief of the Armed Forces Medical Examiner System, a division of the Armed Forces Institute of Pathology.

The medical examiners have scanned about 3,000 corpses, more than any other institution in the world, creating a minutely detailed and permanent three-dimensional record of combat injuries. Although the scans are sometimes called "virtual autopsies," they do not replace old-fashioned autopsies. Rather, they add information and can help guide autopsies and speed them by showing pathologists where to look for bullets or shrapnel, and by revealing fractures and tissue damage so clearly that the need for lengthy dissection is sometimes eliminated. The examiners try to remove as many metal fragments as possible, because the pieces can yield information about enemy weapons.

One discovery led to an important change in the medical gear used to stabilize injured troops on the battlefield.

Col. Howard T. Harcke, a 71-year-old Army Reserve radiologist who delayed retirement to read CT scans at Dover, noticed something peculiar in late 2005. The emergency treatment for a collapsed lung involves inserting a needle and tube into the chest cavity to relieve pressure and allow the lung to reinflate. But in one case, Colonel Harcke could see from a scan that the tube was too short to reach the chest cavity. Then he saw another case, and another, and half a dozen more.

In an interview, Colonel Harcke said it was impossible to tell whether anyone had died because the tubes were too short; all had other severe injuries. But a collapsed lung can be life-threatening, so proper treatment is essential.

Colonel Harcke pulled 100 scans from the archives and used them to calculate the average thickness of the chest wall in American troops; he found that the standard tubing, five centimeters long, was too short for 50 percent of the troops. If the tubing was lengthened to eight centimeters, it would be long enough for 99 percent.

"Soldiers are bigger and stronger now," Colonel Harcke said.

The findings were presented to the Army Surgeon General, who in August 2006 ordered that the kits given to combat medics be changed to include only the longer tubing.

"I was thrilled," Colonel Harcke said.

The medical examiners also discovered that troops were dying from wounds to the upper body that could have been prevented by body armor that covered more of the torso and shoulders. The information, which became public in 2006, led the military to scramble to ship more armor plates to Iraq.

It was Captain Mallak who decided that autopsies should be performed on all troops killed in Afghanistan or Iraq. Federal law gives him that authority.

"Families want a full accounting," he said. During World War II and the Vietnam War, he explained, families were told simply that their loved one had died in service of their country.

"Personally, I felt that families would no longer just accept that," Captain Mallak said.

The examiner's office has not publicized the autopsy policy and has not often discussed it. Families are informed that autopsies are being performed and that they can request a copy of the report. Occasionally, families object, but the autopsy is done anyway. About 85 percent to 90 percent of families request the reports, and 10 percent also ask for photographs from the autopsy, said Paul Stone, a spokesman for the medical examiner system. Relatives are also told they can call or e-mail the medical examiners with questions.

"Every day, families come back for more information," Captain Mallak said. "The No. 1 question they want to know is, 'Did my loved one suffer?' If we can say, 'No, it was instantaneous, he or she never knew what happened,' they do get a great sense of relief out of that. But we don't lie."

Indeed, the reports are sent with cover letters urging the families not to read them alone.

The possibility that a relative burned to death is a particular source of anguish for families, and one area in which CT can outperform an autopsy. In a body damaged by flames, CT can help pathologists figure out whether the burns occurred before or after death. The scans can also tell whether a person found in water died from drowning. Families who request the autopsy reports often put off reading them, said Ami Neiberger-Miller, a spokeswoman for the Tragedy

Assistance Program for Survivors, a nonprofit group for people who have lost relatives in war.

"I think people feel, 'We should request it; we may not want to read it today, but we may want to read it 10 years from now,' " Ms. Neiberger-Miller said. Her brother was killed in Baghdad in 2007, she said, and her family has never opened his autopsy report.

Liz Sweet, whose 23-year-old son, T. J., committed suicide in Iraq in 2003, requested his autopsy report and read it.

"For our family, we needed it," Mrs. Sweet said. "I just felt better knowing I had that report." T. J. Sweet's coffin was closed, so Mrs. Sweet asked Captain Mallak for a photograph taken before the autopsy, to prove to herself that it really was her son who had died.

"He was one of the most compassionate people throughout this whole process that I dealt with from the Department of Defense," Mrs. Sweet said of Captain Mallak.

The scans and autopsies are done in a 70,000-square-foot facility at the Dover base that is both a pathology laboratory and a mortuary. Journalists are not allowed inside. The CT scanning began in 2004, when it was suggested and paid for by the Defense Advanced Research Projects Agency, or Darpa, part of the Defense Department. Darpa got the idea of using CT scanners to perform virtual autopsies from Switzerland, where it started about 10 years ago.

Now the idea of virtual autopsies has begun to catch on with medical examiners in this country, who are eager to use it in murder cases but also to learn the cause of death in people from religious groups that forbid traditional autopsies. Scans can also help pathologists plan limited autopsies if a family finds a complete one too invasive.

John Getz, the program manager for the Armed Forces medical examiners, said mobile CT scanners could also be used to screen mass casualties during disasters like Hurricane Katrina, to help with identification and also to determine if any of the dead were the victims of crimes rather than accidents.

The Armed Forces CT scanner, specially designed to scan entire corpses one after another, is the envy of medical examiners and crime laboratories around the country, and several states have asked Captain Mallak and his colleagues for advice on setting up scanners.

Colonel Harcke said he hoped the technology would help to increase the autopsy rates at civilian hospitals, which now perform them only 5 percent to 10 percent of the time.

"We hope to return to a time where we were 50 years ago," he said, "when autopsies were an important part of the medical model, and we continued to learn after death."

Selection 5.6

The lede of this story vividly reproduces a moment of discovery that, in the words of writer Sandra Blakeslee, "is shaking up numerous scientific disciplines, shifting the understanding of culture, empathy, philosophy, language, imitation, autism and psychotherapy." The discovery—of mirror neurons—is not only shifting scientific thought, she writes, but also making us look at everyday experiences in a new way, revealing "how children learn, why people respond to certain types of sports, dance, music and art, why watching media violence may be harmful and why many men like pornography." Determined to show the scope of emerging research on these neurons, Blakeslee mentions them all. While there are those who have argued that Blakeslee, along with other science writers, has made too much of this discovery,² there's no denying that mirror neurons have generated excitement across scientific disciplines. The story was one of the most read science/technology stories on The Times Web site in 2006.

Cells That Read Minds
By SANDRA BLAKESLEE

On a hot summer day 15 years ago in Parma, Italy, a monkey sat in a special laboratory chair waiting for researchers to return from lunch. Thin wires had been implanted in the region of its brain involved in planning and carrying out movements.

Every time the monkey grasped and moved an object, some cells in that brain region would fire, and a monitor would register a sound: *brrrrrip, brrrrrip, brrrrrip.*

A graduate student entered the lab with an ice cream cone in his hand. The monkey stared at him. Then, something amazing happened: when the student raised the cone to his lips, the monitor sounded— brrrrrip, brrrrrip, brrrrrip—even though the monkey had not moved but had simply observed the student grasping the cone and moving it to his mouth.

The researchers, led by Giacomo Rizzolatti, a neuroscientist at the University of Parma, had earlier noticed the same strange phenomenon with peanuts. The same brain cells fired when the monkey watched humans or other monkeys bring peanuts to their mouths as when the monkey itself brought a peanut to its mouth.

Later, the scientists found cells that fired when the monkey broke open a peanut or heard someone break a peanut. The same thing happened with bananas, raisins and all kinds of other objects.

Published: January 10, 2006.

"It took us several years to believe what we were seeing," Dr. Rizzolatti said in a recent interview. The monkey brain contains a special class of cells, called mirror neurons, that fire when the animal sees or hears an action and when the animal carries out the same action on its own.

But if the findings, published in 1996, surprised most scientists, recent research has left them flabbergasted. Humans, it turns out, have mirror neurons that are far smarter, more flexible and more highly evolved than any of those found in monkeys, a fact that scientists say reflects the evolution of humans' sophisticated social abilities.

The human brain has multiple mirror neuron systems that specialize in carrying out and understanding not just the actions of others but their intentions, the social meaning of their behavior and their emotions.

"We are exquisitely social creatures," Dr. Rizzolatti said. "Our survival depends on understanding the actions, intentions and emotions of others."

He continued, "Mirror neurons allow us to grasp the minds of others not through conceptual reasoning but through direct simulation. By feeling, not by thinking."

The discovery is shaking up numerous scientific disciplines, shifting the understanding of culture, empathy, philosophy, language, imitation, autism and psychotherapy.

Everyday experiences are also being viewed in a new light. Mirror neurons reveal how children learn, why people respond to certain types of sports, dance, music and art, why watching media violence may be harmful and why many men like pornography.

How can a single mirror neuron or system of mirror neurons be so incredibly smart?

Most nerve cells in the brain are comparatively pedestrian. Many specialize in detecting ordinary features of the outside world. Some fire when they encounter a horizontal line while others are dedicated to vertical lines. Others detect a single frequency of sound or a direction of movement.

Moving to higher levels of the brain, scientists find groups of neurons that detect far more complex features like faces, hands or expressive body language. Still other neurons help the body plan movements and assume complex postures.

Mirror neurons make these complex cells look like numbskulls. Found in several areas of the brain—including the premotor cortex, the posterior parietal lobe, the superior temporal sulcus and the insula—they fire in response to chains of actions linked to intentions.

Studies show that some mirror neurons fire when a person reaches for a glass or watches someone else reach for a glass; others fire when the person puts the glass down and still others fire when the person reaches for a toothbrush and so on. They respond when someone kicks a ball, sees a ball being kicked, hears a ball being kicked and says or hears the word "kick."

"When you see me perform an action—such as picking up a baseball—you automatically simulate the action in your own brain," said Dr. Marco Iacoboni, a neuroscientist at the University of California, Los Angeles, who studies mirror neurons. "Circuits in your brain, which we do not yet entirely understand, inhibit you from moving while you simulate," he said. "But you understand my action because you have in your brain a template for that action based on your own movements.

"When you see me pull my arm back, as if to throw the ball, you also have in your brain a copy of what I am doing and it helps you understand my goal. Because of mirror neurons, you can read my intentions. You know what I am going to do next."

He continued: "And if you see me choke up, in emotional distress from striking out at home plate, mirror neurons in your brain simulate my distress. You automatically have empathy for me. You know how I feel because you literally feel what I am feeling."

Mirror neurons seem to analyze scenes and to read minds. If you see someone reach toward a bookshelf and his hand is out of sight, you have little doubt that he is going to pick up a book because your mirror neurons tell you so.

In a study published in March 2005 in Public Library of Science, Dr. Iacoboni and his colleagues reported that mirror neurons could discern if another person who was picking up a cup of tea planned to drink from it or clear it from the table. "Mirror neurons provide a powerful biological foundation for the evolution of culture," said Patricia Greenfield, a psychologist at the U.C.L.A. who studies human development.

Until now, scholars have treated culture as fundamentally separate from biology, she said. "But now we see that mirror neurons absorb culture directly, with each generation teaching the next by social sharing, imitation and observation."

Other animals—monkeys, probably apes and possibly elephants, dolphins and dogs—have rudimentary mirror neurons, several mirror neuron experts said. But humans, with their huge working memory, carry out far more sophisticated imitations.

Language is based on mirror neurons, according to Michael Arbib, a neuroscientist at the University of Southern California. One such system, found in the front of the brain, contains overlapping circuitry for spoken language and sign language.

In an article published in Trends in Neuroscience in March 1998, Dr. Arbib described how complex hand gestures and the complex tongue and lip movements used in making sentences use the same machinery. Autism, some researchers believe, may involve broken mirror neurons. A study published in the Jan. 6 issue of Nature Neuroscience by Mirella Dapretto, a neuroscientist at U.C.L.A., found that while many people with autism can identify an emotional expression, like sadness, on another person's face, or imitate sad looks with their own faces, they do not feel the emotional significance of the imitated emotion. From observing other people, they do not know what it feels like to be sad, angry, disgusted or surprised.

Mirror neurons provide clues to how children learn: they kick in at birth. Dr. Andrew Meltzoff at the University of Washington has published studies showing that infants a few minutes old will stick out their tongues at adults doing the same thing. More than other primates, human children are hard-wired for imitation, he said, their mirror neurons involved in observing what others do and practicing doing the same things.

Still, there is one caveat, Dr. Iacoboni said. Mirror neurons work best in real life, when people are face to face. Virtual reality and videos are shadowy substitutes.

Nevertheless, a study in the January 2006 issue of Media Psychology found that when children watched violent television programs, mirror neurons, as well as several brain regions involved in aggression were activated, increasing the probability that the children would behave violently.

The ability to share the emotions of others appears to be intimately linked to the functioning of mirror neurons, said Dr. Christian Keysers, who studies the neural basis of empathy at the University of Groningen in the Netherlands and who has published several recent articles on the topic in Neuron.

When you see someone touched in a painful way, your own pain areas are activated, he said. When you see a spider crawl up someone's leg, you feel a creepy sensation because your mirror neurons are firing.

People who rank high on a scale measuring empathy have particularly active mirror neurons systems, Dr. Keysers said.

Social emotions like guilt, shame, pride, embarrassment, disgust and lust are based on a uniquely human mirror neuron system found in a part of the brain called the insula, Dr. Keysers said. In a study not yet published, he found that when people watched a hand go forward to caress someone and then saw another hand push it away rudely, the insula registered the social pain of rejection. Humiliation appears to be mapped in the brain by the same mechanisms that encode real physical pain, he said.

Psychotherapists are understandably enthralled by the discovery of mirror neurons, said Dr. Daniel Siegel, the director of the Center for Human Development in Los Angeles and the author of "Parenting From the Inside Out," because they provide a possible neurobiological basis for the psychological mechanisms known as transference and countertransference.

In transference, clients "transfer" feelings about important figures in their lives onto a therapist. Similarly, in countertransference, a

therapist's reactions to a client are shaped by the therapist's own earlier relationships.

Therapists can use their own mirror system to understand a client's problems and to generate empathy, he said. And they can help
clients understand that many of their experiences stem from what
other people have said or done to them in the past.

Art exploits mirror neurons, said Dr. Vittorio Gallese, a neuroscientist at Parma University. When you see the Baroque sculptor
Gian Lorenzo Bernini's hand of divinity grasping marble, you see the
hand as if it were grasping flesh, he said. Experiments show that when
you read a novel, you memorize positions of objects from the narrator's point of view.

Professional athletes and coaches, who often use mental practice
and imagery, have long exploited the brain's mirror properties perhaps
without knowing their biological basis, Dr. Iacoboni said. Observation directly improves muscle performance via mirror neurons.

Similarly, millions of fans who watch their favorite sports on
television are hooked by mirror neuron activation. In someone who
has never played a sport—say tennis—the mirror neurons involved in
running, swaying and swinging the arms will be activated, Dr. Iacoboni said.

But in someone who plays tennis, the mirror systems will be
highly activated when an overhead smash is observed. Watching a
game, that person will be better able to predict what will happen next,
he said.

In yet another realm, mirror neurons are powerfully activated by
pornography, several scientists said. For example, when a man watches
another man have sexual intercourse with a woman, the observer's
mirror neurons spring into action. The vicarious thrill of watching sex,
it turns out, is not so vicarious after all.

Selection 5.7

*This issue story, about the growing influence of pharmaceutical companies on
the education of students at Harvard Medical School, begins with an account
of one student who was outraged when he realized he wasn't getting the whole
truth about cholesterol drugs. Writer Duff Wilson, who covers the pharmaceutical and tobacco industries for The Times, gives both sides of the debate on
Pharma's influence their say. However, the first and last words go to those
students and faculty who seek to jettison the influence of industry on what students learn. Given that Harvard had just received an "F" from a national group
that evaluates how well medical schools monitor and control such influence,
and given that peer institutions had received much higher grades, Wilson's
choice to emphasize the protestors' perspective over others made journalistic
sense.*

Harvard Medical School in Ethics Quandary

By DUFF WILSON

BOSTON—In a first-year pharmacology class at Harvard Medical School, Matt Zerden grew wary as the professor promoted the benefits of cholesterol drugs and seemed to belittle a student who asked about side effects.

Mr. Zerden later discovered something by searching online that he began sharing with his classmates. The professor was not only a full-time member of the Harvard Medical faculty, but a paid consultant to 10 drug companies, including five makers of cholesterol treatments.

"I felt really violated," Mr. Zerden, now a fourth-year student, recently recalled. "Here we have 160 open minds trying to learn the basics in a protected space, and the information he was giving wasn't as pure as I think it should be."

Mr. Zerden's minor stir four years ago has lately grown into a full-blown movement by more than 200 Harvard Medical School students and sympathetic faculty, intent on exposing and curtailing the industry influence in their classrooms and laboratories, as well as in Harvard's 17 affiliated teaching hospitals and institutes.

They say they are concerned that the same money that helped build the school's world-class status may in fact be hurting its reputation and affecting its teaching.

The students argue, for example, that Harvard should be embarrassed by the F grade it recently received from the American Medical Student Association, a national group that rates how well medical schools monitor and control drug industry money.

Harvard Medical School's peers received much higher grades, ranging from the A for the University of Pennsylvania, to B's received by Stanford, Columbia and New York University, to the C for Yale.

Harvard has fallen behind, some faculty and administrators say, because its teaching hospitals are not owned by the university, complicating reform; because the dean is fairly new and his predecessor was such an industry booster that he served on a pharmaceutical company board; and because a crackdown, simply put, could cost it money or faculty.

Further, the potential embarrassments—a Senate investigation of several medical professors, the F grade, a new state law effective July 1 requiring Massachusetts doctors to disclose corporate gifts over $50—are only now adding to pressure for change.

The dean, Dr. Jeffrey S. Flier, who says he wants Harvard to catch up with the best practices at other leading medical schools,

Published: March 2, 2009.

recently announced a 19-member committee to re-examine his school's conflict-of-interest policies. The group, which includes three students, is to meet in private on Thursday.

Advising the group will be Dr. David Korn, a former dean of the Stanford Medical School who started work at Harvard about four months ago as vice provost for research. Last year he helped the Association of American Medical Colleges draft a model conflict-of-interest policy for medical schools.

The Harvard students have already secured a requirement that all professors and lecturers disclose their industry ties in class—a blanket policy that has been adopted by no other leading medical school. (One Harvard professor's disclosure in class listed 47 company affiliations.)

"Harvard needs to live up to its name," said Kirsten Austad, 24, a first-year Harvard Medical student who is one of the movement's leaders. "We are really being indoctrinated into a field of medicine that is becoming more and more commercialized."

David Tian, 24, a first-year Harvard Medical student, said: "Before coming here, I had no idea how much influence companies had on medical education. And it's something that's purposely meant to be under the table, providing information under the guise of education when that information is also presented for marketing purposes."

The students say they worry that pharmaceutical industry scandals in recent years—including some criminal convictions, billions of dollars in fines, proof of bias in research and publishing and false marketing claims—have cast a bad light on the medical profession. And they criticize Harvard as being less vigilant than other leading medical schools in monitoring potential financial conflicts by faculty members.

Dr. Flier says that the Harvard Medical faculty may lead the nation in receiving money from industry, as well as government and charities, and he does not want to tighten the spigot. "One entirely appropriate source, if done properly, is industrial funds," Dr. Flier said in an interview.

And school officials see corporate support for their faculty as all the more crucial, as the university endowment has lost 22 percent of its value since last July and the recession has caused philanthropic contributors to retrench. The school said it was unable to provide annual measures of the money flow to its faculty, beyond the $8.6 million that pharmaceutical companies contributed last year for basic science research and the $3 million for continuing education classes on campus. Most of the money goes to professors at the Harvard-affiliated teaching hospitals, and the dean's office does not keep track of the total.

But no one disputes that many individual Harvard Medical faculty members receive tens or even hundreds of thousands of dollars a year through industry consulting and speaking fees. Under the school's disclosure rules, about 1,600 of 8,900 professors and lecturers have reported to the dean that they or a family member had a financial interest in a business related to their teaching, research or clinical care. The reports show 149 with financial ties to Pfizer and 130 with Merck.

The rules, though, do not require them to report specific amounts received for speaking or consulting, other than broad indications like "more than $30,000." Some faculty who conduct research have limits of $30,000 in stock and $20,000 a year in fees. But there are no limits on companies' making outright gifts to faculty—free meals, tickets, trips or the like.

Other blandishments include industry-endowed chairs like the three Harvard created with $8 million from sleep research companies; faculty prizes like the $50,000 award named after Bristol-Myers Squibb, and sponsorships like Pfizer's $1 million annual subsidy for 20 new M.D.'s in a two-year program to learn clinical investigation and pursue Harvard Master of Medical Science degrees, including classes taught by Pfizer scientists.

Dr. Flier, who became dean 17 months ago, previously received a $500,000 research grant from Bristol-Myers Squibb. He also consulted for three Cambridge biotechnology companies, but says that those relationships have ended and that he has accepted no new industry affiliations.

That is in contrast to his predecessor as dean, Dr. Joseph B. Martin. Harvard's rules allowed Dr. Martin to sit on the board of the medical products company Baxter International for 5 of the 10 years he led the medical school, supplementing his university salary with up to $197,000 a year from Baxter, according to company filings.

Dr. Martin is still on the medical faculty and is founder and co-chairman of the Harvard NeuroDiscovery Center, which researches degenerative diseases, and actively solicits industry money to do so. Dr. Martin declined any comment.

A smaller rival faction among Harvard's 750 medical students has circulated a petition signed by about 100 people that calls for "continued interaction between medicine and industry at Harvard Medical School."

A leader of the group, Vijay Yanamadala, 22, said, "To say that because these industry sources are inherently biased, physicians should never listen to them, is wrong."

Encouraging them is Dr. Thomas P. Stossel, a Harvard Medical professor who has served on advisory boards for Merck, Biogen Idec and Dyax, and has written widely on academic-industry ties. "I think if you look at it with intellectual honesty, you see industry interaction has produced far more good than harm," Dr. Stossel said. "Harvard absolutely could get more from industry but I think they're very skittish. There's a huge opportunity we ought to mine."

Brian Fuchs, 26, a second-year student from Queens, credited drug companies with great medical discoveries. "It's not a problem," he said, pointing out a classroom window to a 12-story building nearby. "In fact, Merck is right there."

Merck built a corporate research center in 2004 across the street from Harvard's own big new medical research and class building. And Merck underwrites plenty of work on the Harvard campus, including the immunology lab run by Dr. Laurie H. Glimcher—a professor who also sits on the board of the drug maker Bristol-Myers Squibb, which paid her nearly $270,000 in 2007.

Dr. Glimcher says industry money is not only appropriate but necessary. "Without the support of the private sector, we would not have been able to develop what I call our 'bone team' in our lab," she said at a recent student and faculty forum to discuss industry relationships. Merck is counting on her team to help come up with a successor to Fosamax, the formerly $3 billion-a-year bone drug that went generic last year. But Dr. Marcia Angell, a faculty member and former editor in chief of The New England Journal of Medicine, is among the professors who argue that industry profit motives do not correspond to the scientific aims of academic medicine and that much of the financing needs to be not only disclosed, but banned. Too many medical schools, she says, have struck a "Faustian bargain" with pharmaceutical companies.

"If a school like Harvard can't behave itself," Dr. Angell said, "who can?"

Selection 5.8

Written on the eve of the 100th anniversary of the discovery of the gene, this story by Carl Zimmer puts a strong emphasis on history: It reviews the many discoveries since 1909 that have led from primitive definitions of the gene to today's much more complex understandings. Historical features can be hard to make interesting to readers, but Zimmer opens the piece with a story about a scientist who spent a day without uttering the word gene. *This anecdotal hook not only humanizes the story but also reinforces its focus:* Gene *no longer describes the complex reality that scientists have uncovered over the last century. The story was part of a special edition of Science Times devoted to the gene's discovery. On the Web site, it was accompanied by two explanatory graphics, one of them a huge visual map of the epigenome.*

Now: The Rest of the Genome
By CARL ZIMMER

Over the summer, Sonja Prohaska decided to try an experiment. She would spend a day without ever saying the word "gene." Dr. Prohaska is a bioinformatician at the University of Leipzig in Germany. In other words, she spends most of her time gathering, organizing and analyzing information about genes. "It was like having someone tie your hand behind your back," she said.

But Dr. Prohaska decided this awkward experiment was worth the trouble, because new large-scale studies of DNA are causing her and many of her colleagues to rethink the very nature of genes. They no longer conceive of a typical gene as a single chunk of DNA encoding a single protein. "It cannot work that way," Dr. Prohaska said. There are simply too many exceptions to the conventional rules for genes.

It turns out, for example, that several different proteins may be produced from a single stretch of DNA. Most of the molecules produced from DNA may not even be proteins, but another chemical known as RNA. The familiar double helix of DNA no longer has a monopoly on heredity. Other molecules clinging to DNA can produce striking differences between two organisms with the same genes. And those molecules can be inherited along with DNA.

The gene, in other words, is in an identity crisis.

This crisis comes on the eve of the gene's 100th birthday. The word was coined by the Danish geneticist Wilhelm Johanssen in 1909, to describe whatever it was that parents passed down to their offspring so that they developed the same traits. Johanssen, like other biologists of his generation, had no idea what that invisible factor was. But he thought it would be useful to have a way to describe it.

"The word 'gene' is completely free from any hypothesis," Johanssen declared, calling it "a very applicable little word."

Over the next six decades, scientists transformed that little word from an abstraction to concrete reality. They ran experiments on bread mold and bacteria, on fruit flies and corn. They discovered how to alter flowers and eyes and other traits by tinkering with molecules inside cells. They figured out that DNA was a pair of strands twisted around each other. And by the 1960s, they had a compelling definition of the gene.

A gene, they argued, was a specific stretch of DNA containing the instructions to make a protein molecule. To make a protein from a gene, a cell had to read it and build a single-stranded copy known as a transcript out of RNA. This RNA was then grabbed by a cluster

Published: November 10, 2008. Graphics available at: http://www.nytimes.com/2008/11/11/science/11gene.html

of molecules called a ribosome, which used it as a template to build a protein.

A gene was also the fundamental unit of heredity. Every time a cell divided, it replicated its genes, and parents passed down some of their genes to their offspring. If you inherited red hair—or a predisposition for breast cancer—from your mother, chances were that you inherited a gene that helped produce that trait.

This definition of the gene worked spectacularly well—so well, in fact, that in 1968 the molecular biologist Gunther Stent declared that future generations of scientists would have to content themselves with "a few details to iron out."

The Details

Stent and his contemporaries knew very well that some of those details were pretty important. They knew that genes could be shut off and switched on when proteins clamped onto nearby bits of DNA. They also knew that a few genes encoded RNA molecules that never became proteins. Instead, they had other jobs, like helping build proteins in the ribosome.

But these exceptions did not seem important enough to cause scientists to question their definitions. "The way biology works is different from mathematics," said Mark Gerstein, a bioinformatician at Yale. "If you find one counterexample in mathematics, you go back and rethink the definitions. Biology is not like that. One or two counterexamples—people are willing to deal with that."

More complications emerged in the 1980s and 1990s, though. Scientists discovered that when a cell produces an RNA transcript, it cuts out huge chunks and saves only a few small remnants. (The parts of DNA that the cell copies are called exons; the parts cast aside are introns.) Vast stretches of noncoding DNA also lie between these protein-coding regions. The 21,000 protein-coding genes in the human genome make up just 1.2 percent of that genome.

The Genome

In 2000, an international team of scientists finished the first rough draft of that genome—all of the genetic material in a human cell. They identified the location of many of the protein-coding genes, but they left the other 98.8 percent of the human genome largely unexplored.

Since then, scientists have begun to wade into that genomic jungle, mapping it in fine detail.

One of the biggest of these projects is an effort called the Encyclopedia of DNA Elements, or Encode for short. Hundreds of scientists are carrying out a coordinated set of experiments to determine the function of every piece of DNA in the human genome. Last summer they published their results on 1 percent of the genome—some 30 million "letters" of DNA. The genetic code is written in letters, like the title of the movie "Gattaca," with each letter standing for a molecule called a base: guanine (G), adenine (A), thymine (T), cytosine (C). The Encode team expects to have initial results on the other 99 percent by next year.

Encode's results reveal the genome to be full of genes that are deeply weird, at least by the traditional standard of what a gene is supposed to be. "These are not oddities—these are the rule," said Thomas R. Gingeras of Cold Spring Harbor Laboratory and one of the leaders of Encode.

A single so-called gene, for example, can make more than one protein. In a process known as alternative splicing, a cell can select different combinations of exons to make different transcripts. Scientists identified the first cases of alternative splicing almost 30 years ago, but they were not sure how common it was. Several studies now show that almost all genes are being spliced. The Encode team estimates that the average protein-coding region produces 5.7 different transcripts. Different kinds of cells appear to produce different transcripts from the same gene.

Even weirder, cells often toss exons into transcripts from other genes. Those exons may come from distant locations, even from different chromosomes.

So, Dr. Gingeras argues, we can no longer think of genes as being single stretches of DNA at one physical location.

"I think it's a paradigm shift in how we think the genome is organized," Dr. Gingeras said.

The Epigenome

But it turns out that the genome is also organized in another way, one that brings into question how important genes are in heredity. Our DNA is studded with millions of proteins and other molecules, which determine which genes can produce transcripts and which cannot. New cells inherit those molecules along with DNA. In other words, heredity can flow through a second channel.

One of the most striking examples of this second channel is a common flower called toadflax. Most toadflax plants grow white petals arranged in a mirror-like symmetry. But some have yellow five-pointed stars. These two forms of toadflax pass down their flower to their offspring. Yet the difference between their flowers does not come down to a difference in their DNA.

Instead, the difference comes down to the pattern of caps that are attached to their DNA. These caps, made of carbon and hydrogen, are known as methyl groups. The star-shaped toadflax have a distinct pattern of caps on one gene involved in the development of flowers.

DNA is not just capped with methyl groups; it is also wrapped around spool-like proteins called histones that can wind up a stretch of DNA so that the cell cannot make transcripts from it. All of the molecules that hang onto DNA, collectively known as epigenetic marks, are essential for cells to take their final form in the body. As an embryo matures, epigenetic marks in different cells are altered, and as a result they develop into different tissues. Once the final pattern of epigenetic marks is laid down, it clings stubbornly to cells. When cells divide, their descendants carry the same set of marks. "They help cells remember what genes to keep on, and what genes can never be turned on," said Bradley Bernstein of Harvard University.

Scientists know much less about this "epigenome" than the genome. In September, the National Institutes of Health began a $190 million program to start mapping epigenetic marks on DNA in different tissues. "Now we can chart all these changes beyond the gene," said Eric Richards of Cornell University.

This survey may provide clues to the origins of cancer and other diseases. It has long been known that when DNA mutates, a cell may become prone to turning cancerous. Some studies now suggest that when epigenetic marks are disturbed, cells may also be made more vulnerable to cancer, because essential genes are shut off and genes that should be shut off are turned on. What makes both kinds of changes particularly dangerous is that they are passed down from a cell to all its descendants.

When an embryo begins to develop, the epigenetic marks that have accumulated on both parents' DNA are stripped away. The cells add a fresh set of epigenetic marks in the same pattern that its parents had when they were embryos.

This process turns out to be very delicate. If an embryo experiences certain kinds of stress, it may fail to lay down the right epigenetic marks.

In 1944, for example, the Netherlands suffered a brutal famine. Scientists at the University of Leiden recently studied 60 people who were conceived during that time. In October, the researchers reported that today they still have fewer epigenetic marks than their siblings. They suggest that during the 1944 famine, pregnant mothers could not supply their children with the raw ingredients for epigenetic marks.

In at least some cases, these new epigenetic patterns may be passed down to future generations. Scientists are debating just how often this happens. In a paper to be published next year in The Quarterly Review of Biology, Eva Jablonski and Gal Raz of Tel Aviv University in Israel assemble a list of 101 cases in which a trait linked to an epigenetic change was passed down through three generations.

For example, Matthew Anway of Washington State University and his colleagues found that exposing pregnant rats to a chemical for killing fungus disrupted the epigenetic marks in the sperm of male embryos. The embryos developed into adult rats that suffered from defective sperm and other disorders, like cancer. The males passed down their altered epigenetic marks to their own offspring, which passed them down to yet another generation.

Last year Dr. Anway and his colleagues documented an even more surprising effect of the chemical. Female rats exposed in the womb avoided mating with exposed male rats. The scientists found this preference lasted at least three generations.

While these experiments are eye-opening, scientists are divided about how important these generation-spanning changes are. "There's a lot of disagreement about whether it matters," Dr. Richards said.

RNA in the Spotlight

Epigenetic marks are intriguing not just for their effects, but also for how they are created in the first place. To place a cap of methyl groups on DNA, for example, a cluster of proteins must be guided to the right spot. It turns out they must be led there by an RNA molecule that can find it.

These RNA guides, like the RNA molecules in ribosomes, do not fit the classical concept of the gene. Instead of giving rise to a protein, these RNA molecules immediately start to carry out their own task in the cell. Over the last decade, scientists have uncovered a number of new kinds of RNA molecules that never become proteins. (Scientists call them noncoding RNA.) In 2006, for example, Craig Mello of the University of Massachusetts and Andrew Fire of Stanford University won the Nobel Prize for establishing that small RNA molecules could silence genes by interfering with their transcription.

These discoveries left scientists wondering just how much noncoding RNA our cells make. The early results of Encode suggest the answer is a lot. Although only 1.2 percent of the human genome encodes proteins, the Encode scientists estimate that a staggering 93 percent of the genome produces RNA transcripts.

John Mattick, an Encode team member at the University of Queensland in Australia, is confident that a lot of those transcripts do important things that scientists have yet to understand. "My bet is the vast majority of it—I don't know whether that's 80 or 90 percent," he said.

"When you cross the Rubicon and look back, you see the protein-centric view as being quite primitive," he said.

Certain versions of those RNA-coding genes may raise the risk of certain diseases. As part of the Encode project, scientists identified the location of variations in DNA that have been linked to common diseases like cancer. A third of those variations were far from any protein-coding gene. Understanding how noncoding RNA works may help scientists figure out how to use drugs to counteract genetic risks for diseases. "This is going to be a huge topic of research this coming decade," said Ewan Birney, one of the leaders of the Encode project at the European Bioinformatics Institute.

Despite the importance of noncoding RNA, Dr. Birney suspects that most of the transcripts discovered by the Encode project do not actually do much of anything. "I think it's a hypothesis that has to be on the table," he said.

David Haussler, another Encode team member at the University of California, Santa Cruz, agrees with Dr. Birney. "The cell will make RNA and simply throw it away," he said.

Dr. Haussler bases his argument on evolution. If a segment of DNA encodes some essential molecule, mutations will tend to produce catastrophic damage. Natural selection will weed out most mutants. If a segment of DNA does not do much, however, it can mutate without causing any harm. Over millions of years, an essential piece of DNA will gather few mutations compared with less important ones.

Only about 4 percent of the noncoding DNA in the human genome shows signs of having experienced strong natural selection. Some of those segments may encode RNA molecules that have an important job in the cell. Some of them may contain stretches of DNA that control neighboring genes. Dr. Haussler suspects that most of the rest serve no function.

"Most of it is baggage being dragged along," he said.

But the line between the useless baggage and the useful DNA is hard to draw. Mutations can make it impossible for a cell to make a protein from a gene. Scientists refer to such a disabled piece of DNA as a pseudogene. Dr. Gerstein and his colleagues estimate that there are 10,000 to 20,000 pseudogenes in the human genome. Most of them are effectively dead, but a few of them may still make RNA molecules that serve an important function. Dr. Gerstein nicknames these functioning pseudogenes "the undead."

Alien DNA

Much of the baggage in the genome comes not from dead genes, however, but from invading viruses. Viruses repeatedly infected our distant ancestors, adding their DNA to the genetic material passed down from generation to generation. Once these viruses invaded our genomes, they sometimes made new copies of themselves, and the copies were pasted in other spots in the genome. Over many generations, they mutated and lost their ability to move.

"Our genome is littered with the rotting carcasses of these little viruses that have made their home in our genome for millions of years," Dr. Haussler said.

As these chunks of viral DNA hop around, they can cause a lot of harm. They can disrupt the genome, causing it to stop making essential proteins. Hundreds of genetic disorders have been linked to their leaps. One of the most important jobs that noncoding RNA serves in the genome is preventing this virus DNA from spreading quickly.

Yet some of these invaders have evolved into useful forms. Some stretches of virus DNA have evolved to make RNA genes that our cells use. Other stretches have evolved into sites where our proteins can attach and switch on nearby genes. "They provide the raw material for innovation," Dr. Haussler said.

In this jungle of invading viruses, undead pseudogenes, shuffled exons and epigenetic marks, can the classical concept of the gene survive? It is an open question, one that Dr. Prohaska hopes to address at a meeting she is organizing at the Santa Fe Institute in New Mexico next March.

In the current issue of American Scientist, Dr. Gerstein and his former graduate student Michael Seringhaus argue that in order to define a gene, scientists must start with the RNA transcript and trace it back to the DNA. Whatever exons are used to make that transcript would constitute a gene. Dr. Prohaska argues that a gene should be the smallest unit underlying inherited traits. It may include not just a collection of exons, but the epigenetic marks on them that are inherited as well.

These new concepts are moving the gene away from a physical snippet of DNA and back to a more abstract definition. "It's almost a recapture of what the term was originally meant to convey," Dr. Gingeras said.

A hundred years after it was born, the gene is coming home.

Selection 5.9

Any story that focuses on the future poses challenges, especially given humanity's notorious inability to predict with any specificity what lies ahead. But Dennis Overbye meets the challenge in this description of probes for new planets planned for the unmanned spacecraft Kepler. His arresting prose connects to our wistful longings (in this case, for "not-too-cold, not-too-hot Goldilocks zones around stars where liquid water can exist") and to our innate curiosity ("The point is not to find any particular planet—hold off on the covered-wagon spaceships—but to find out just how rare planets like Earth are in the cosmos"). By the end, Overbye can contain his own enthusiasm no longer, departing from "journalistic objectivity to venture a hope that other Earths are out there." An interactive graphic of this spacecraft accompanies the story on the Web site. It is simple and clean, offering a good sense of scale. As a former science writing student and artist put it, "It's almost like something you'd see in a science book for a younger-level audience, which is good. It makes it easy to want to look at and understand."

In a Lonely Cosmos, a Hunt for Worlds like Ours
By DENNIS OVERBYE

Someday it might be said that this was the beginning of the end of cosmic loneliness.

Presently perched on a Delta 2 rocket at Cape Canaveral is a one-ton spacecraft called Kepler. If all goes well, the rocket will lift off about 10:50 Friday evening on a journey that will eventually propel Kepler into orbit around the Sun. There the spacecraft's mission will be to discover Earth-like planets in Earth-like places—that is to say, in the not-too-cold, not-too-hot, Goldilocks zones around stars where liquid water can exist.

The job, in short, is to find places where life as we know it is possible.

"It's not E.T., but it's E.T.'s home," said William Borucki, an astronomer at NASA's Ames Research Center at Moffett Field in California, who is the lead scientist on the project. Kepler, named after the German astronomer who in 1609 published laws of planetary motion that now bear his name, will look for tiny variations in star-light caused by planets passing in front of their stars. Dr. Borucki and his colleagues say that Kepler could find dozens of such planets—if they exist. The point is not to find any particular planet—hold off on the covered-wagon spaceships—but to find out just how rare planets like Earth are in the cosmos.

Jon Morse, director for astrophysics at NASA headquarters, calls Kepler the first planetary census taker.

Kepler's strategy is, in effect, to search for the shadows of planets. The core of the spacecraft, which carries a 55-inch-diameter tele-scope, is a 95-million-pixel digital camera. For three and a half years, the telescope will stare at the same patch of sky about 10 degrees, or 20 full moons, wide, in the constellations Cygnus and Lyra. It will read out the brightnesses of 100,000 stars every half-hour, looking for the telltale blips when a planet crosses in front of its star, a phenom-enon known as a transit.

To detect something as small as the Earth, the measurements need to be done with a precision available only in space, away from the atmospheric turbulence that makes stars twinkle, and far from Earth so that our home world does not intrude on the view of shadow worlds in that patch of sky. It will take three or more years—until the end of Barack Obama's current term in office—before astronomers know whether Kepler has found any distant Earths.

Published: March 3, 2009. Graphic available at: http://www.nytimes.com/2009/03/03/health/03 iht-03kepl.20549229.html

If Kepler finds the planets, Dr. Borucki explained, life could be common in the universe. The results will point the way for future missions aimed at getting pictures of what Carl Sagan, the late Cornell astronomer and science popularizer, called "pale blue dots" out in the universe, and the search for life and perhaps intelligence.

But the results will be profound either way. If Kepler doesn't come through, that means Earth is really rare and we might be the only extant life in the universe and our loneliness is just beginning. "It would mean there might not be 'Star Trek,' " Dr. Borucki said during a recent news conference.

The need, indeed even the possibility, of a planetary census is a recent development in cosmic history. It was only in 1995 that the first planet was detected orbiting another Sun-like star, by Michel Mayor and his colleagues at Geneva Observatory. In the years since then there has been a torrent of discoveries, 340 and counting, that has bewildered astronomers and captured the popular imagination.

"What exists is an incredibly random, chaotic, wild range of planets," said Debra Fischer of San Francisco State University, also a veteran planet hunter who is not a member of the Kepler team. So far none of them qualify as prime real estate for life, and few of them reside in systems that resemble our own solar system. Many of the first planets discovered were so-called hot Jupiters, gas giants zipping around their stars in a few days in tight, blisteringly hot orbits.

Most of the planets have been found by what is called the wobble method, in which the presence of a planet is deduced by observing the to-and-fro gravitational tug it gives its star as it orbits. The closer a planet is to its star, the bigger the tug and the easier it is to detect.

The smallest exoplanet discovered is about three times as massive as the Earth. It is known as MOA-2007-BLG-192-L b, but astronomers don't know yet whether its home star is a real star or a failed star called a brown dwarf.

Last summer Dr. Mayor announced that his team had found three so-called warm super-Earths—roughly four, seven and nine times the mass of the Earth—orbiting within frying distance of a star known as HD 40307 in the constellation Pictor. Indeed, Dr. Mayor proclaimed that according to their data, about a third of all Sun-like stars host such super-Earths or super-Neptunes in tight orbits.

But all this is prelude. Astronomers agree that these planets are oddballs according to any reasonable theory of planet formation. But as Alan Boss of the Carnegie Institution of Washington pointed out, they are easy to detect by the wobble method. The fact that they are there suggests that there are many more modest-size planets to be found in larger, more habitable orbits.

The Kepler mission is a tribute to the perseverance of
Dr. Borucki, who began proposing it to NASA in the 1980s, before
any exoplanets had been discovered, and kept campaigning for it.
"He had the true faith," Dr. Boss said.

Many technical hurdles had be overcome before Kepler became
practical. In particular it required very accurate and sensitive digital detectors, said James Fanson, of the Jet Propulsion Laboratory,
Kepler's project manager. As seen from outside the solar system,
the Earth blocks only about 0.008 percent of the Sun's light when it
passes in front, or "transits." Kepler has been built to detect changes
in brightness as small as 0.002 percent, equivalent to a flea crawling
across a car headlight.

By measuring the diminution of a star's light during an exoplanet transit, astronomers in principle will be able to determine the
size of the exoplanet. From the intervals between eclipses, astronomers will be able to determine its orbit. By combining this with other
data, from, say, wobble measurements, they will be able to zero in on
important properties like mass and density.

However, natural variations in the star's output, caused by something like starspots, could interfere with the data and obscure the signals from small planets. That is a problem, Dr. Fanson said, with the
Corot satellite, which was launched by the European Space Agency
at the end of 2006 and also carries a telescope and camera to look for
small changes in starlight. To weed out the noisy stars, Kepler will
keep track of 170,000 stars for the first year and then narrow its attention to a mere 100,000.

Corot, which stands for convection, rotation and planetary transits, is smaller than Kepler and is designed to investigate the structure
of stars by detecting vibrations and tremors within them that cause
them to periodically brighten and fade. Corot, which Dr. Borucki
called "a complementary mission," also looks at a given patch of stars
for only a few months and so would miss the successive transits of an
Earth-like planet, which, to be habitable, would have to take about a
year to orbit a Sun-like star.

Not all 100,000 stars in the field of Kepler's view would
have their planetary systems oriented to provide eclipses from our
particular point of view, of course. Dr. Borucki and his colleagues
estimate that for an Earth-like star in its habitable zone, the stars
would align to produce a blot out in half of 1 percent of cases,
yielding a few dozen to a few hundred new Earths out there.
For planets that are closer in, however, the odds rise to about
10 percent, so there are ample reasons to expect a bumper crop of
new planets.

Dr. Borucki said the astronomers had set the goal of observing
at least three such transits, to confirm the period and rule out interfer-
ence from starspots, and then obtaining backup observations from

other telescopes—of wobble measurements, say—before announcing they have found a planet.

"When we make a discovery we want it to be bulletproof," Dr. Borucki said.

That means that the first planets to be discovered and announced will be the biggest planets with the shortest orbits, the so-called hot Jupiters. Four stars with such planets are in the search area and thus will be an early test of Kepler's acuity.

"In the first six months, hot Jupiters are going to roll off the Kepler assembly line," Dr. Fischer said, adding, "These are bizarre planets, we don't understand how they form."

The hardest and most exciting part of the mission, detecting bona fide Earths, will also take the longest. Such a planet should take about a year to circle a Sun-like star, producing only one blip a year in its starlight. So it would take more than three years to produce the requisite three blips and subsequent confirmation by ground-based telescopes before the epochal discovery is announced.

Dr. Borucki said, "We're not going to be able to tell you very quickly."

But they will eventually tell us.

Dr. Boss, a high-ranking member of the Kepler science team, said: "It really is going to count many Earths. About four years from now we will have a really good estimate of how many Earths there are."

If the history of exoplanet astronomy is any guide, there are likely to be surprises that geologists had not imagined—water worlds, for example. And then, if all keeps going well, it will be time to confront the next series of questions: whether anywhere else in this galaxy the dust that once spewed from stars has come alive and conscious.

"In my 25 years of working with NASA this is the most exciting mission I've worked on, said Dr. Fanson, who will step down as project manager after the launching. "We are going to be able to answer for the first time a question that has been pondered since the time of the ancient Greeks. Are there other worlds like ours? The question has come down to us from 100 generations. We get to answer it. I find that tremendously exciting."

When a reporter departed from journalistic objectivity to venture a hope that other Earths are out there, Dr. Fanson happily joined in. "I hope the answer is yes," he said. "I hope the universe is teeming with planets like Earth."

MAKING**CONNECTIONS**

①

Consider This. Choose two stories from this chapter and study them for:

- *Focus and significance: Where and how do the writers signal the focus or theme of the story? And where and how do they convey the story's significance? What similarities and differences do you notice?*

- *The reporting: How deep is the reporting that fleshes out the focus of each story? Consider especially the details gathered by observation and interview. Any tips you will take away for your own reporting?*

Try This. Scan the front section of the journals Science and Nature, and identify a trend or issue in science. Alternatively, identify a social trend or issue that has some connection to science or technology. Do background research to see what has already been done in national media and what if anything has been done in local media. Making use of what you find, propose a trend or issue story for media in your community. Your proposal should convey the significance of the trend or issue, and a range of national and local sources you could tap for the story. If there are places you could visit where people are likely to be engaged in actions relevant to the story, mention those. If you have ideas for conveying the story in visual ways—say, with an interactive graphic like the one of retreating ice in the story on page 40)—include them.

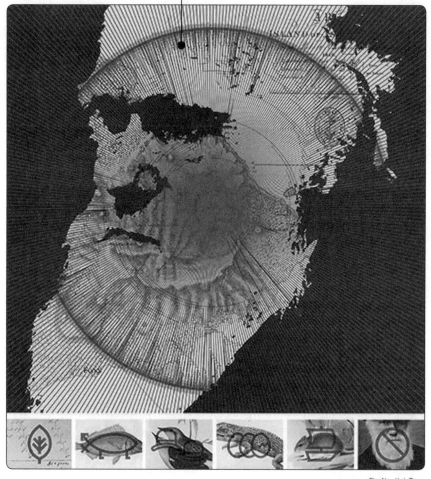

extended narratives

YOU'VE HEARD IT BEFORE: News consumers are insanely busy. Few have the patience to sit with long stories that unfold across multiple screens. If they want the stories that journalists write at all, they want them short—as in new bites, as in tweets, as in (give it a few months) nano-news. At least that is the conventional wisdom.

But there are holdouts. In a movement that's come to be known as "creative nonfiction," hundreds of writers do battle with such thinking every day. These journalists believe audiences *will* engage with longer stories. You just need to find the right stories and tell them in the right way.

To these journalists, the right stories are ones that convey the timeless drama in the most intimate and ordinary parts of people's lives—in classrooms where belief systems clash, in conflict-riven courtrooms and in the fear-fogged waiting rooms of hospitals. And the right way to tell these tales is to use scenes, dialogue, character details and other narrative elements we normally associate with fiction writing. These journalists are convinced that if you find the good stories and you tell them well, readers will come—and they will be moved, even changed.

Not all fans of the narrative form believe narratives have to be long. In fact, after Twitter was launched, at least one imaginative writer wondered if even tweets couldn't tell some stories well.[1] Still, most fans of the narrative form believe such tales require a whole lot more than 140 characters. They require space to involve readers in the tale. They also require time to report and write.

Since you can't make anything up, you have to spend the time it takes to find the best subject, ideally a sympathetic person who is trying to overcome a complication that readers can relate to. Then you have to build up trust—talking, listening, watching and eavesdropping to dig up the kinds of details that will convey character, motivation and action. This can take weeks, even months, depending on the story. It can take almost as long to rifle through stacks of collected material to find the "arc" of the story—which scenes best establish the character as someone we care about, set up the complication or obstacle, show the character's efforts to resolve their problem, and, if there is a resolution to be had, resolves it. Then there's the outline. Then the writing.

The process is arduous. But the legions of writers who take up such stories, despite the challenges, are testament to the narrative form's abiding ability to fascinate ambitious writers, as well as its perceived power. The extended narrative is "the most painful kind of story to write," says Times writer Amy Harmon. "It's nevertheless my favorite."

At The Times, Harmon immerses herself for what is sometimes months to produce extended narratives about how science and technology penetrate the lives of ordinary people. This section contains two of her narratives, the first a feature on a teacher's efforts to teach evolutionary biology to students whose religious faith creates obstacles to their learning, the second a dramatic story of a young woman determined to learn about her genetic inheritance, even if it means knowing how she will die. Both stories unroll, as all engrossing narratives do, in scenes. The second story, in addition, builds suspense, very much in the manner of the best literary narratives, and was part of a package that won Harmon a Pulitzer Prize, her second. Harmon discusses both of these selections in a conversation at the end of the chapter.

The third story is an excerpt from another Pulitzer Prize–winning story, this one by the late Times writer Nan Robertson, who wrote about how she came close to losing her life to toxic shock syndrome in the early 1980s. When this story ran in The New York Times Magazine, extended narratives were more of a novelty at the newspaper. It is included to reveal some of the changes that have taken place in narrative writing since the start of the Internet, but more importantly, to provide an exercise in editing narrative stories for the Web.

Selection 6.1

When a high school biology teacher confronts the challenges of teaching evolutionary theory to a class of students who believe none of it, writer Amy Harmon records the tensions. A shorter, more conventional feature would have conveyed these tensions through anecdotes and quotes. Instead, this story takes us into the classroom to witness the tensions for ourselves. We hear the dialogue that ensues between teacher and students. But we also go behind the eyes of the teacher, to read his thoughts as he surveys the students before him: his appreciation of the smallest of victories, and his determination to choose his words carefully. Harmon could not have known these particulars of the teacher's inner world. So she did what good journalistic storytellers always do: She asked what he was thinking. Then, confident of the man's thoughts and feelings, she inserted them into her story. Alongside the online version of this story, editors reserved a place for readers' comments. More than 340 readers responded, one an Australian reader who wrote, "How sad that so many Americans are so backwards that they need to be gently coaxed to accept the scientific truth." The majority of comments, though, came from readers who wanted to express their appreciation for the teacher—not unexpected, given the scientifically attentive readership of The Times.

A Teacher on the Front Line as Faith and Science Clash

By AMY HARMON

ORANGE PARK, Fla.—David Campbell switched on the over-head projector and wrote "Evolution" in the rectangle of light on the screen.

He scanned the faces of the sophomores in his Biology I class. Many of them, he knew from years of teaching high school in this Jacksonville suburb, had been raised to take the biblical creation story as fact. His gaze rested for a moment on Bryce Haas, a football player who attended the 6 a.m. prayer meetings of the Fellowship of Christian Athletes in the school gymnasium.

"If I do this wrong," Mr. Campbell remembers thinking on that humid spring morning, "I'll lose him."

In February, the Florida Department of Education modified its standards to explicitly require, for the first time, the state's public schools to teach evolution, calling it "the organizing principle of life science." Spurred in part by legal rulings against school districts seeking to favor religious versions of natural history, over a dozen other states have also given more emphasis in recent years to what has long been the scientific consensus: that all of the diverse life forms on Earth descended from a common ancestor, through a process of mutation and natural selection, over billions of years.

But in a nation where evangelical Protestantism and other religious traditions stress a literal reading of the biblical description of God's individually creating each species, students often arrive at school fearing that evolution, and perhaps science itself, is hostile to their faith.

Some come armed with "Ten questions to ask your biology teacher about evolution," a document circulated on the Internet that highlights supposed weaknesses in evolutionary theory. Others scrawl their opposition on homework assignments. Many just tune out.

With a mandate to teach evolution but little guidance as to how, science teachers are contriving their own ways to turn a culture war into a lesson plan. How they fare may bear on whether a new generation of Americans embraces scientific evidence alongside religious belief.

"If you see something you don't understand, you have to ask 'why?' or 'how?' " Mr. Campbell often admonished his students at Ridgeview High School.

Yet their abiding mistrust in evolution, he feared, jeopardized their belief in the basic power of science to explain the natural world—and their ability to make sense of it themselves.

Published: August 24, 2008.

Passionate on the subject, Mr. Campbell had helped to devise the state's new evolution standards, which will be phased in starting this fall. A former Navy flight instructor not used to pulling his punches, he fought hard for their passage. But with his students this spring, he found himself treading carefully, as he tried to bridge an ideological divide that stretches well beyond his classroom.

A Cartoon and a Challenge

He started with Mickey Mouse.

On the projector, Mr. Campbell placed slides of the cartoon icon: one at his skinny genesis in 1928; one from his 1940 turn as the impish Sorcerer's Apprentice; and another of the rounded, ingratiating charmer of Mouse Club fame.

"How," he asked his students, "has Mickey changed?"

Natives of Disney World's home state, they waved their hands and called out answers.

"His tail gets shorter," Bryce volunteered.

"Bigger eyes!" someone else shouted.

"He looks happier," one girl observed. "And cuter."

Mr. Campbell smiled. "Mickey evolved," he said. "And Mickey gets cuter because Walt Disney makes more money that way. That is 'selection.' "

Later, he would get to the touchier part, about how the minute changes in organisms that drive biological change arise spontaneously, without direction. And how a struggle for existence among naturally varying individuals has helped to generate every species, living and extinct, on the planet.

For now, it was enough that they were listening.

He strode back to the projector, past his menagerie of snakes and baby turtles, and pointed to the word he had written in the beginning of class.

"Evolution has been the focus of a lot of debate in our state this year," he said. "If you read the newspapers, everyone is arguing, 'is it a theory, is it not a theory?' The answer is, we can observe it. We can see it happen, just like you can see it in Mickey."

Some students were nodding. As the bell rang, Mr. Campbell stood by the door, satisfied. But Bryce, heavyset with blond curls, left with a stage whisper as he slung his knapsack over his shoulder.

"I can see something else, too," he said. "I can see that there's no way I came from an ape."

Fighting for a Mandate

As recently as three years ago, the guidelines that govern science education in more than a third of American public schools gave exceedingly short shrift to evolution, according to reviews by education experts. Some still do, science advocates contend. Just this summer, religious advocates lobbied successfully for a Louisiana law that protects the right of local schools to teach alternative theories for the origin of species, even though there are none that scientists recognize as valid. The Florida Legislature is expected to reopen debate on a similar bill this fall.

Even states that require teachers to cover the basics of evolution, like natural selection, rarely ask them to explain in any detail how humans, in particular, evolved from earlier life forms. That subject can be especially fraught for young people taught to believe that the basis for moral conduct lies in God's having created man uniquely in his own image.

The poor treatment of evolution in some state education standards may reflect the public's widely held creationist beliefs. In Gallup polls over the last 25 years, nearly half of American adults have consistently said they believe God created all living things in their present form, sometime in the last 10,000 years. But a 2005 defeat in federal court for a school board in Dover, Pa., that sought to cast doubt on evolution gave legal ammunition to evolution proponents on school boards and in statehouses across the country.

In its wake, Ohio removed a requirement that biology classes include "critical analysis" of evolution. Efforts to pass bills that implicitly condone the teaching of religious theories for life's origins have failed in at least five states. And as science standards come up for regular review, other states have added material on evolution to student achievement tests, and required teachers to spend more time covering it.

When Florida's last set of science standards came out in 1996, soon after Mr. Campbell took the teaching job at Ridgeview, he studied them in disbelief. Though they included the concept that biological "changes over time" occur, the word evolution was not mentioned.

He called his district science supervisor. "Is this really what they want us to teach for the next 10 years?" he demanded.

In 2000, when the independent Thomas B. Fordham Foundation evaluated the evolution education standards of all 50 states, Florida was among 12 to receive a grade of F. (Kansas, which drew international attention in 1999 for deleting all mention of evolution and later embracing supernatural theories, received an F-minus.)

Mr. Campbell, 52, who majored in biology while putting himself through Cornell University on a Reserve Officers Training Corps scholarship, taught evolution anyway. But like nearly a third of biology teachers across the country, and more in his politically conservative district, he regularly heard from parents voicing complaints.

With no school policy to back him up, he spent less time on the subject than he would have liked. And he bit back his irritation at Teresa Yancey, a biology teacher down the hall who taught a unit she called "Evolution or NOT."

Animals do adapt to their environments, Ms. Yancey tells her students, but evolution alone can hardly account for the appearance of wholly different life forms. She leaves it up to them to draw their own conclusions. But when pressed, she tells them, "I think God did it."

Mr. Campbell was well aware of her opinion. "I don't think we have this great massive change over time where we go from fish to amphibians, from monkeys to man," she once told him. "We see lizards with different-shaped tails, we don't see blizzards—the lizard bird."

With some approximation of courtesy, Mr. Campbell reminded her that only a tiny fraction of organisms that ever lived had been preserved in fossils. Even so, he informed his own students, scientists have discovered thousands of fossils that provide evidence of one species transitioning into another—including feathered dinosaurs.

But at the inaugural meeting of the Florida Citizens for Science, which he co-founded in 2005, he vented his frustration. "The kids are getting hurt," Mr. Campbell told teachers and parents. "We need to do something."

The Dover decision in December of that year dealt a blow to "intelligent design," which posits that life is too complex to be explained by evolution alone, and has been widely promoted by religious advocates since the Supreme Court's 1987 ban on creationism in public schools. The federal judge in the case called the doctrine "creationism re-labeled," and found the Dover school board had violated the constitutional separation of church and state by requiring teachers to mention it. The school district paid $1 million in legal costs.

Inspired, the Florida citizens group soon contacted similar groups in other states advocating better teaching of evolution. And in June 2007, when his supervisor invited Mr. Campbell to help draft Florida's new standards, he quickly accepted.

During the next six months, he made the drive to three-day meetings in Orlando and Tallahassee six times. By January 2008 the Board of Education budget had run out. But the 30 teachers on the standards committee paid for their own gasoline to attend their last meeting.

Mr. Campbell quietly rejoiced in their final draft. Under the proposed new standards, high school students could be tested on how fossils and DNA provide evidence for evolution. Florida students would even be expected to learn how their own species fits into the tree of life.

Whether the state's board of education would adopt them, however, was unclear. There were heated objections from some religious organizations and local school boards. In a stormy public comment session, Mr. Campbell defended his fellow writers against complaints that they had not included alternative explanations for life's diversity, like intelligent design.

His attempt at humor came with an edge:

"We also failed to include astrology, alchemy and the concept of the moon being made of green cheese," he said. "Because those aren't science, either."

The evening of the vote, Mr. Campbell learned by e-mail message from an education official that the words "scientific theory of" had been inserted in front of "evolution" to appease opponents on the board. Even so, the standards passed by only a 4-to-3 vote.

Mr. Campbell cringed at the wording, which seemed to suggest evolution was a kind of hunch instead of the only accepted scientific explanation for the great variety of life on Earth. But he turned off his computer without scrolling through all of the frustrated replies from other writers. The standards, he thought, were finally in place.

Now he just had to teach.

The Limits of Science

The morning after his Mickey Mouse gambit, he bounced a pink rubber Spalding ball on the classroom's hard linoleum floor.

"Gravity," he said. "I can do this until the end of the semester, and I can only assume that it will work the same way each time."

He looked around the room. "Bryce, what is it called when natural laws are suspended—what do you call it when water changes into wine?"

"Miracle?" Bryce supplied.

Mr. Campbell nodded. The ball hit the floor again.

"Science explores nature by testing and gathering data," he said. "It can't tell you what's right and wrong. It doesn't address ethics. But it is not anti-religion. Science and religion just ask different questions."

He grabbed the ball and held it still.

"Can anybody think of a question science can't answer?"

"Is there a God?" shot back a boy near the window.

"Good," said Mr. Campbell, an Anglican who attends church most Sundays. "Can't test it. Can't prove it, can't disprove it. It's not a question for science."

Bryce raised his hand.

"But there is scientific proof that there is a God," he said. "Over in Turkey there's a piece of wood from Noah's ark that came out of a glacier."

Mr. Campbell chose his words carefully.

"If I could prove, tomorrow, that that chunk of wood is not from the ark, is not even 500 years old and not even from the right kind of tree—would that damage your religious faith at all?"

Bryce thought for a moment.

"No," he said.

The room was unusually quiet.

"Faith is not based on science," Mr. Campbell said. "And science is not based on faith. I don't expect you to 'believe' the scientific explanation of evolution that we're going to talk about over the next few weeks."

"But I do," he added, "expect you to understand it."

The Lure of T. Rex

Over the next weeks, Mr. Campbell regaled his students with the array of evidence on which evolutionary theory is based. To see how diverse species are related, they studied the embryos of chickens and fish, and the anatomy of horses, cats, seals and bats.

To simulate natural selection, they pretended to be birds picking light-colored moths off tree bark newly darkened by soot.

But the dearth of questions made him uneasy.

"I still don't have a good feeling on how well any of them are internalizing any of this," he worried aloud.

When he was 5, Mr. Campbell's aunt took him on a trip from his home in Connecticut to the American Museum of Natural History in New York City. At the end of the day, she had to pry him away from the Tyrannosaurus rex.

If this didn't hook them, he thought one Wednesday morning, admiring the cast of a T. rex brain case he set on one of the classroom's long, black laboratory tables, nothing would. Carefully, he distributed several other fossils, including two he had collected himself.

He placed particular hope in the jaw of a 34-million-year-old horse ancestor. Through chance, selection and extinction, he had told his class, today's powerfully muscled, shoulder-high horses had evolved from squat dog-sized creatures.

The diminutive jaw, from an early horse that stood about two feet tall, offered proof of how the species had changed over time. And maybe, if they accepted the evolution of Equus caballus, they could begin to contemplate the origin of Homo sapiens.

Mr. Campbell instructed the students to spend three minutes at each station. He watched Bryce and his partner, Allie Farris, look at the illustration of a modern horse jaw he had posted next to the fossil of its Mesohippus ancestor. Hovering, he kicked himself for not acquiring a real one to make the comparison more tangible. But they lingered, well past their time limit. Bryce pointed to the jaw in the picture and held the fossil up to his own mouth.

"It's maybe the size of a dog's jaw or a cat's," he said, measuring.

He looked at Allie. "That's pretty cool, don't you think?"

After class, Mr. Campbell fed the turtles. It was time for a test, he thought.

'I Don't Believe in This'

Bryce came to Ridgeview as a freshman from a Christian private school where he attended junior high.

At 16, Bryce, whose parents had made sure he read the Bible for an hour each Sunday as a child, no longer went to church. But he did make it to the predawn meetings of the Fellowship of Christian Athletes, a national Christian sports organization whose mission statement defines the Bible as the "authoritative Word of God." Life had been dark after his father died a year ago, he told the group, but things had been going better recently, and he attributed that to God's help.

When the subject of evolution came up at a recent fellowship meeting, several of the students rolled their eyes.

"I think a big reason evolutionists believe what they believe is they don't want to have to be ruled by God," said Josh Rou, 17.

"Evolution is telling you that you're like an animal," Bryce agreed. "That's why people stand strong with Christianity, because it teaches people to lead a good life and not do wrong."

Doug Daugherty, 17, allowed that he liked science.

"I'll watch the Discovery Channel and say 'Ooh, that's interesting,' " he said. "But there's a difference between thinking something is interesting and believing it."

The last question on the test Mr. Campbell passed out a week later asked students to explain two forms of evidence supporting evolutionary change and natural selection.

"I refuse to answer," Bryce wrote. "I don't believe in this."

Losing Heart

Mr. Campbell looked at the calendar. Perhaps this semester, he thought, he would skip over the touchy subject of human origins. The new standards, after all, had not gone into effect. "Maybe I'll just give them the fetal pig dissection," he said with a sigh.

It wasn't just Bryce. Many of the students, Mr. Campbell sensed, were not grasping the basic principles of biological evolution. If he forced them to look at themselves in the evolutionary mirror, he risked alienating them entirely.

The discovery that a copy of "Evolution Exposed," published by the creationist organization Answers in Genesis, was circulating among the class did not raise his flagging spirits. The book lists each reference to evolution in the biology textbook Mr. Campbell uses and offers an explanation for why it is wrong.

Where the textbook states, for example, that "Homo sapiens appeared in Africa 200,000 years ago based on fossil and DNA evidence," "Exposed" counters that "The fossil evidence of hominids (alleged human ancestors) is extremely limited." A pastor at a local church, Mr. Campbell learned, had given a copy of "Exposed" to every graduating senior the previous year.

But the next week, at a meeting in Tallahassee where he sorted the new science standards into course descriptions for other teachers, the words he had helped write reverberated in his head.

"Evolution," the standards said, "is the fundamental concept underlying all biology."

When he got home, he dug out his slide illustrating the nearly exact match between human and chimpanzee chromosomes, and prepared for a contentious class.

Facing the Challenge

"True or false?" he barked the following week, wearing a tie emblazoned with the DNA double helix. "Humans evolved from chimpanzees."

The students stared at him, unsure. "True," some called out.

"False," he said, correcting a common misconception. "But we do share a common ancestor."

More gently now, he started into the story of how, five or six million years ago, a group of primates in Africa split. Some stayed in the forest and evolved into chimps; others—our ancestors—migrated to the grasslands.

On the projector, he placed a picture of the hand of a gibbon, another human cousin. "There's the opposable thumb," he said, wiggling his own. "But theirs is a longer hand because they live in trees, and their arms are very long."

Mr. Campbell bent over, walking on the outer part of his foot. He had intended to mimic how arms became shorter and legs became longer. He planned to tell the class how our upright gait, built on a body plan inherited from tree-dwelling primates, made us prone to lower back pain. And how, over the last two million years, our jaws have grown shorter, which is why wisdom teeth so often need to be removed.

But too many hands had gone up.

He answered as fast as he could, his pulse quickening as it had rarely done since his days on his high school debate team.

"If that really happened," Allie wanted to know, "wouldn't you still see things evolving?"

"We do," he said. "But this is happening over millions of years. With humans, if I'm lucky I might see four generations in my lifetime."

Caitlin Johnson, 15, was next.

"If we had to have evolved from something," she wanted to know, "then whatever we evolved from, where did IT evolve from?"

"It came from earlier primates," Mr. Campbell replied.

"And where did those come from?"

"You can trace mammals back 250 million years," he said. The first ones, he reminded them, were small, mouselike creatures that lived in the shadow of dinosaurs.

Other students were jumping in.

"Even if we did split off from chimps," someone asked, "how come they stayed the same but we changed?"

"They didn't stay the same," Mr. Campbell answered. "They were smaller, more slender—they've changed a lot."

Bryce had been listening, studying the hand of the monkey on the screen.

"How does our hand go from being that long to just a smaller hand?" he said. "I don't see how that happens."

"If a smaller hand is beneficial," Mr. Campbell said, "individuals with small hands will have more children, while those with bigger hands will disappear."

"But if we came from them, why are they still around?"

"Just because a new population evolves doesn't mean the old one dies out," Mr. Campbell said.

Bryce spoke again. This time it wasn't a question.

"So it just doesn't stop," he said.

"No," said Mr. Campbell. "If the environment is suitable, a species can go on for a long time."

"What about us," Bryce pursued. "Are we going to evolve?"

Mr. Campbell stopped, and took a breath.

"Yes," he said. "Unless we go extinct."

When the bell rang, he knew that he had not convinced Bryce, and perhaps many of the others. But that week, he gave the students an opportunity to answer the questions they had missed on the last test. Grading Bryce's paper later in the quiet of his empty classroom, he saw that this time, the question that asked for evidence of evolutionary change had been answered.

MAKING**CONNECTIONS**

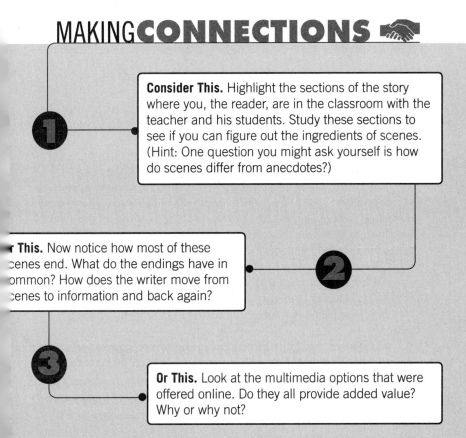

Consider This. Highlight the sections of the story where you, the reader, are in the classroom with the teacher and his students. Study these sections to see if you can figure out the ingredients of scenes. (Hint: One question you might ask yourself is how do scenes differ from anecdotes?)

This. Now notice how most of these scenes end. What do the endings have in common? How does the writer move from scenes to information and back again?

Or This. Look at the multimedia options that were offered online. Do they all provide added value? Why or why not?

Selection 6.2

This narrative was the lead story in "The Best American Science Writing 2008.² It closely follows principles laid out by Jon Franklin in his guide to narrative journalism, "Writing for Story: Craft Secrets of Dramatic Nonfiction."³ It features a sympathetic protagonist who faces a complication in her life and searches for a resolution, in this case by seeking information about her genetic inheritance. Along the way she encounters obstacles, including her mother's resistance. Like a good piece of fiction, the story contains suspense, a climax and a resolution that comes about by the character's own hand. (No deus ex machina *here.) The ending may not be exactly happy, as Franklin recommends (at least for writers who are new to the form), but it is at least emotionally satisfying. On the Web site, the story is accompanied by many additional features. In a video called "Reporter's Notebook," the writer interviews a scientist who studies the disease and is herself at risk for it; she also discusses her own fascination with the wider issues this particular story raises. In another video, Katharine Moser, the principal character of the story, discusses her reasons for getting tested, how she lives with knowing she has tested positive and her plans for the future. In addition, a slide show and photos offer close-ups of Katharine and others featured in the narrative, while an explanatory graphic shows how Huntington's disease travels in families and how it has travelled in this young woman's family in particular. Finally, in a comment section, readers are urged to respond to a question about whether or not they, if carrying a gene for a fatal genetic illness, would want to know.*

THE DNA AGE
Facing Life With a Lethal Gene
By AMY HARMON

The test, the counselor said, had come back positive.

Katharine Moser inhaled sharply. She thought she was as ready as anyone could be to face her genetic destiny. She had attended a genetic counseling session and visited a psychiatrist, as required by the clinic. She had undergone the recommended neurological exam. And yet, she realized in that moment, she had never expected to hear those words.

"What do I do now?" Ms. Moser asked.

"What do you want to do?" the counselor replied.

"Cry," she said quietly.

Her best friend, Colleen Elio, seated next to her, had already begun.

Ms. Moser was 23. It had taken her months to convince the clinic at New York-Presbyterian Hospital/Columbia University

Published: March 18, 2007. Features available at: http://www.nytimes.com/2007/03/18/health/18huntington.html.

Medical Center in Manhattan that she wanted, at such a young age, to find out whether she carried the gene for Huntington's disease.

Huntington's, the incurable brain disorder that possessed her grandfather's body and ravaged his mind for three decades, typically strikes in middle age. But most young adults who know the disease runs in their family have avoided the DNA test that can tell whether they will get it, preferring the torture—and hope—of not knowing.

Ms. Moser is part of a vanguard of people at risk for Huntington's who are choosing to learn early what their future holds. Facing their genetic heritage, they say, will help them decide how to live their lives.

Yet even as a raft of new DNA tests are revealing predispositions to all kinds of conditions, including breast cancer, depression and dementia, little is known about what it is like to live with such knowledge.

"What runs in your own family, and would you want to know?" said Nancy Wexler, a neuropsychologist at Columbia and the president of the Hereditary Disease Foundation, which has pioneered Huntington's research. "Soon everyone is going to have an option like this. You make the decision to test, you have to live with the consequences."

On that drizzly spring morning two years ago, Ms. Moser was feeling her way, with perhaps the most definitive and disturbing verdict genetic testing has to offer. Anyone who carries the gene will inevitably develop Huntington's.

She fought her tears. She tried for humor.

Don't let yourself get too thin, said the clinic's social worker. Not a problem, Ms. Moser responded, gesturing to her curvy frame. No more than two drinks at a time. Perhaps, Ms. Moser suggested to Ms. Elio, she meant one in each hand.

Then came anger.

"Why me?" she remembers thinking, in a refrain she found hard to shake in the coming months. "I'm the good one. It's not like I'm sick because I have emphysema from smoking or I did something dangerous."

The gene that will kill Ms. Moser sits on the short arm of everyone's fourth chromosome, where the letters of the genetic alphabet normally repeat C-A-G as many as 35 times in a row. In people who develop Huntington's, however, there are more than 35 repeats.

No one quite knows why this DNA hiccup causes cell death in the brain, leading Huntington's patients to jerk and twitch uncontrollably and rendering them progressively unable to walk, talk, think and swallow. But the greater the number of repeats, the earlier symptoms tend to appear and the faster they progress.

Ms. Moser's "CAG number" was 45, the counselor said. She had more repeats than her grandfather, whose first symptoms—loss of short-term memory, mood swings and a constant ticking noise he made with his mouth—surfaced when he turned 50. But it was another year before Ms. Moser would realize that she could have less than 12 years until she showed symptoms.

Immediately after getting her results, Ms. Moser was too busy making plans.

"I'm going to become super-strong and super-balanced," she vowed over lunch with Ms. Elio, her straight brown hair pulled into a determined bun. "So when I start to lose it I'll be a little closer to normal."

In the tumultuous months that followed, Ms. Moser often found herself unable to remember what normal had once been. She forced herself to renounce the crush she had long nursed on a certain fire-fighter, sure that marriage was no longer an option for her. She threw herself into fund-raising in the hopes that someone would find a cure. Sometimes, she raged.

She never, she said, regretted being tested. But at night, crying herself to sleep in the dark of her lavender bedroom, she would go over and over it. She was the same, but she was also different. And there was nothing she could do.

A Lesson in Stigma

Ms. Moser grew up in Connecticut, part of a large Irish Catholic family. Like many families affected by Huntington's, Ms. Moser's regarded the disease as a curse, not to be mentioned even as it dominated their lives in the form of her grandfather's writhing body and unpredictable rages.

Once, staying in Ms. Moser's room on a visit, he broke her trundle bed with his violent, involuntary jerking. Another time, he came into the kitchen naked, his underpants on his head. When the children giggled, Ms. Moser's mother defended her father: "If you don't like it, get out of my house and go."

But no one explained what had happened to their grandfather, Thomas Dowd, a former New York City police officer who once had dreams of retiring to Florida.

In 1990, Mr. Dowd's older brother, living in a veteran's hospital in an advanced stage of the disease, was strangled in his own restraints. But a year or so later, when Ms. Moser wanted to do her sixth-grade science project on Huntington's, her mother recoiled.

"Why," she demanded, "would you want to do it on this disease that is killing your grandfather?"

Ms. Moser was left to confirm for herself, through library books and a CD-ROM encyclopedia, that she and her brothers, her mother, her aunts, an uncle and cousins could all face the same fate.

Any child who has a parent with Huntington's has a 50 percent chance of having inherited the gene that causes it, Ms. Moser learned.

Her mother, who asked not to be identified by name for fear of discrimination, had not always been so guarded. At one point, she drove around with a "Cure HD" sign in the window of her van. She told people that her father had "Woody Guthrie's disease," invoking the folk icon who died of Huntington's in 1967.

But her efforts to raise awareness soon foundered. Huntington's is a rare genetic disease, affecting about 30,000 people in the United States, with about 250,000 more at risk. Few people know what it is. Strangers assumed her father's unsteady walk, a frequent early symptom, meant he was drunk.

"Nobody has compassion," Ms. Moser's mother concluded. "People look at you like you're strange, and 'What's wrong with you?'"

Shortly after a simple DNA test became available for Huntington's in 1993, one of Ms. Moser's aunts tested positive. Another, driven to find out if her own medical problems were related to Huntington's, tested negative. But when Ms. Moser announced as a teenager that she wanted to get tested one day, her mother insisted that she should not. If her daughter carried the gene, that meant she did, too. And she did not want to know.

"You don't want to know stuff like that," Ms. Moser's mother said in an interview. "You want to enjoy life."

Ms. Moser's father, who met and married his wife six years before Ms. Moser's grandfather received his Huntington's diagnosis, said he had managed not to think much about her at-risk status.

"So she was at risk," he said. "Everyone's at risk for everything."

The test, Ms. Moser remembers her mother suggesting, would cost thousands of dollars. Still, in college, Ms. Moser often trolled the Web for information about it. Mostly, she imagined how sweet it would be to know she did not have the gene. But increasingly she was haunted, too, by the suspicion that her mother did.

As awful as it was, she admitted to Ms. Elio, her freshman-year neighbor at Elizabethtown College in Pennsylvania, she almost hoped it was true. It would explain her mother's strokes of meanness, her unpredictable flashes of anger.

Ms. Moser's mother said she had never considered the conflicts with her daughter out of the ordinary. "All my friends who had daughters said that was all normal, and when she's 25 she'll be your best friend," she said. "I was waiting for that to happen, but I guess it's not happening."

When Ms. Moser graduated in 2003 with a degree in occupational therapy, their relationship, never peaceful, was getting worse. She moved to Queens without giving her mother her new address.

Wanting to Know

Out of school, Ms. Moser soon spotted a listing for a job at Terence Cardinal Cooke Health Care Center, a nursing home on the Upper East Side of Manhattan. She knew it was meant for her.

Her grandfather had died there in 2002 after living for a decade at the home, one of only a handful in the country with a unit devoted entirely to Huntington's.

"I hated visiting him growing up," Ms. Moser said. "It was scary."

Now, though, she was drawn to see the disease up close.

On breaks from her duties elsewhere, she visited her cousin James Dowd, the son of her grandfather's brother who had come to live in the Huntington's unit several years earlier. It was there, in a conversation with another staff member, that she learned she could be tested for only a few hundred dollars at the Columbia clinic across town. She scheduled an appointment for the next week.

The staff at Columbia urged Ms. Moser to consider the downside of genetic testing. Some people battle depression after they test positive. And the information, she was cautioned, could make it harder for her to get a job or health insurance.

But Ms. Moser bristled at the idea that she should have to remain ignorant about her genetic status to avoid discrimination. "I didn't do anything wrong," she said. "It's not like telling people I'm a drug addict."

She also recalls rejecting a counselor's suggestion that she might have asked to be tested as a way of crying for help.

"I'm like, 'No,'" Ms. Moser recalls replying. "'I've come to be tested because I want to know.'"

No one routinely collects demographic information about who gets tested for Huntington's. At the Huntington's Disease Center at Columbia, staff members say they have seen few young people taking the test.

Ms. Moser is still part of a distinct minority. But some researchers say her attitude is increasingly common among young people who know they may develop Huntington's.

More informed about the genetics of the disease than any previous generation, they are convinced that they would rather know how many healthy years they have left than wake up one day to find the illness upon them. They are confident that new reproductive technologies can allow them to have children without transmitting the disease and are eager to be first in line should a treatment become available.

"We're seeing a shift," said Dr. Michael Hayden, a professor of human genetics at the University of British Columbia in Vancouver who has been providing various tests for Huntington's for 20 years. "Younger people are coming for testing now, people in their 20s and early 30s; before, that was very rare. I've counseled some of them. They feel it is part of their heritage and that it is possible to lead a life that's not defined by this gene."

Before the test, Ms. Moser made two lists of life goals. Under "if negative," she wrote married, children and Ireland. Under "if positive" was exercise, vitamins and ballroom dancing. Balance, in that

case, would be important. Opening a bed-and-breakfast, a goal since
childhood, made both lists.

In the weeks before getting the test results, Ms. Moser gave
Ms. Elio explicit instructions about acceptable responses. If she was
negative, flowers were O.K. If positive, they were not. In either case,
drinking was acceptable. Crying was not.

But it was Ms. Elio's husband, Chris Elio, who first broached
the subject of taking care of Ms. Moser, whom their young children
called "my Katie," as in "this is my mom, this is my dad, this is my
Katie." They should address it before the results were in, Mr. Elio told
his wife, so that she would not feel, later, that they had done it out of a
sense of obligation.

The next day, in an e-mail note that was unusually formal for
friends who sent text messages constantly and watched "Desperate
Housewives" while on the phone together, Ms. Elio told Ms. Moser
that she and her husband wanted her to move in with them if she got
sick. Ms. Moser set the note aside. She did not expect to need it.

'It's Too Hard to Look'

The results had come a week early, and Ms. Moser assured her friends
that the "Sex and the City" trivia party she had planned for that night
was still on. After all, she was not sick, not dying. And she had already
made the dips.

"I'm the same person I've always been," she insisted that night
as her guests gamely dipped strawberries in her chocolate fountain.
"It's been in me from the beginning."

But when she went to work the next day, she lingered outside
the door of the occupational therapy gym, not wanting to face her
colleagues. She avoided the Huntington's floor entirely, choosing to
attend to patients ailing of just about anything else. "It's too hard to
look at them," she told her friends.

In those first months, Ms. Moser summoned all her strength to
pretend that nothing cataclysmic had happened. At times, it seemed
easy enough. In the mirror, the same green eyes looked back at her.
She was still tall, a devoted Julia Roberts fan, a prolific baker.

She dropped the news of her genetic status into some conversations like small talk, but kept it from her family. She made light of her
newfound fate, though often friends were not sure how to take the
jokes.

"That's my Huntington's kicking in," she told Rachel Markan, a
co-worker, after knocking a patient's folder on the floor.

Other times, Ms. Moser abruptly dropped any pretense of
routine banter. On a trip to Florida, she and Ms. Elio saw a man in a
wheelchair being tube-fed, a method often used to keep Huntington's
patients alive for years after they can no longer swallow.

"I don't want a feeding tube," she announced flatly.

In those early days, she calculated that she had at least until 50 before symptoms set in. That was enough time to open a bed-and-breakfast, if she acted fast. Enough time to repay $70,000 in student loans under her 30-year term.

Doing the math on the loans, though, could send her into a tailspin.

"I'll be repaying them and then I'll start getting sick," she said. "I mean, there's no time in there."

Finding New Purpose

At the end of the summer, as the weather grew colder, Ms. Moser forced herself to return to the Huntington's unit.

In each patient, she saw her future: the biophysicist slumped in his wheelchair, the refrigerator repairman inert in his bed, the onetime professional tennis player who floated through the common room, arms undulating in the startlingly graceful movements that had earned the disease its original name, "Huntington's chorea," from the Greek "to dance."

Then there was her cousin Jimmy, who had wrapped papers for The New York Post for 19 years until suddenly he could no longer tie the knots. When she greeted him, his bright blue eyes darted to her face, then away. If he knew her, it was impossible to tell.

She did what she could for them. She customized their wheelchairs with padding to fit each one's unique tics. She doled out special silverware, oversized or bent in just the right angles to prolong their ability to feed themselves.

Fending off despair, Ms. Moser was also filled with new purpose. Someone, somewhere, she told friends, had to find a cure.

It has been over a century since the disease was identified by George Huntington, a doctor in Amagansett, N.Y., and over a decade since researchers first found the gene responsible for it.

To raise money for research, Ms. Moser volunteered for walks and dinners and golf outings sponsored by the Huntington's Disease Society of America. She organized a Hula-Hoop-a-thon on the roof of Cardinal Cooke, then a bowl-a-thon at the Port Authority. But at many of the events, attendance was sparse.

It is hard to get people to turn out for Huntington's benefits, she learned from the society's professional fund-raisers. Even families affected by the disease, the most obvious constituents, often will not help publicize events.

"They don't want people to know they're connected to Huntington's," Ms. Moser said, with a mix of anger and recognition. "It's like in my family—it's not a good thing."

Her first session with a therapist brought a chilling glimpse of how the disorder is viewed even by some who know plenty about it. "She told me it was my moral and ethical obligation not to have children," Ms. Moser told Ms. Elio by cellphone as soon as she left the office, her voice breaking.

In lulls between fund-raisers, Ms. Moser raced to educate her own world about Huntington's. She added links about the disease to her MySpace page. She plastered her desk at work with "Cure HD" stickers and starred in a video about the Huntington's unit for her union's Web site.

Ms. Moser gave blood for one study and spoke into a microphone for researchers trying to detect subtle speech differences in people who have extra CAG repeats before more noticeable disease symptoms emerge.

When researchers found a way to cure mice bred to replicate features of the disease in humans, Ms. Moser sent the news to friends and acquaintances.

But it was hard to celebrate. "Thank God," the joke went around on the Huntington's National Youth Alliance e-mail list Ms. Moser subscribed to, "at least there won't be any more poor mice wandering around with Huntington's disease."

In October, one of Ms. Moser's aunts lost her balance while walking and broke her nose. It was the latest in a series of falls. "The cure needs to be soon for me," Ms. Moser said. "Sooner for everybody else."

A Confrontation in Court

In the waiting room of the Dutchess County family courthouse on a crisp morning in the fall of 2005, Ms. Moser approached her mother, who turned away.

"I need to tell her something important," Ms. Moser told a family member who had accompanied her mother to the hearing.

He conveyed the message and brought one in return: Unless she was dying, her mother did not have anything to say to her.

That Ms. Moser had tested positive meant that her mother would develop Huntington's, if she had not already. A year earlier, Ms. Moser's mother had convinced a judge that her sister, Nora Maldonado, was neglecting her daughter. She was given guardianship of the daughter, 4-year-old Jillian.

Ms. Moser had been skeptical of her mother's accusations that Ms. Maldonado was not feeding or bathing Jillian properly, and she wondered whether her effort to claim Jillian had been induced by the psychological symptoms of the disease.

Her testimony about her mother's genetic status, Ms. Moser knew, could help persuade the judge to return Jillian. Ms. Maldonado had found out years earlier that she did not have the Huntington's gene.

Ms. Moser did not believe that someone in the early stages of Huntington's should automatically be disqualified from taking care of a child. But her own rocky childhood had convinced her that Jillian would be better off with Ms. Maldonado.

She told her aunt's lawyer about her test results and agreed to testify.

In the courtroom, Ms. Moser took the witness stand. Her mother's lawyer jumped up as soon as the topic of Huntington's arose. It was irrelevant, he said. But by the time the judge had sustained his objections, Ms. Moser's mother, stricken, had understood.

The next day, in the bathroom, Ms. Maldonado approached Ms. Moser's mother.

"I'm sorry," she said. Ms. Moser's mother said nothing.

The court has continued to let Ms. Moser's mother retain guardianship of Jillian. But she has not spoken to her daughter again.

"It's a horrible illness," Ms. Moser's mother said, months later, gesturing to her husband. "Now he has a wife who has it. Did she think of him? Did she think of me? Who's going to marry her?"

Facing the Future

Before the test, it was as if Ms. Moser had been balanced between parallel universes, one in which she would never get the disease and one in which she would. The test had made her whole.

She began to prepare the Elio children and Jillian for her illness, determined that they would not be scared, as she had been with her grandfather. When Jillian wanted to know how people got Huntington's disease "in their pants," Ms. Moser wrote the text of a children's book that explained what these other kinds of "genes" were and why they would make her sick.

But over the winter, Ms. Elio complained gently that her friend had become "Ms. H.D." And an impromptu note that arrived for the children in the early spring convinced her that Ms. Moser was dwelling too much on her own death.

"You all make me so happy, and I am so proud of who you are and who you will be," read the note, on rainbow scratch-and-write paper. "I will always remember the fun things we do together."

Taking matters into her own hands, Ms. Elio created a profile for Ms. Moser on an online dating service. Ms. Moser was skeptical but supplied a picture. Dating, she said, was the worst thing about knowing she had the Huntington's gene. It was hard to imagine someone falling enough in love with her to take on Huntington's knowingly, or asking it of someone she loved. At the same time, she said, knowing her status could help her find the right person, if he was out there.

"Either way, I was going to get sick," she said. "And I'd want someone who could handle it. If, by some twist of fate, I do get married and have children, at least we know what we're getting into."

After much debate, the friends settled on the third date as the right time to mention Huntington's. But when the first date came, Ms. Moser wished she could just blurt it out.

"It kind of just lingers there," she said. "I really just want to be able to tell people, 'Someday, I'm going to have Huntington's disease.'"

'A Part of My Life'

Last May 6, a year to the day after she had received her test results, the subject line "CAG Count" caught Ms. Moser's attention as she was scrolling through the online discussion forums of the Huntington's Disease Advocacy Center. She knew she had 45 CAG repeats, but she had never investigated it further.

She clicked on the message.

"My mother's CAG was 43," it read. "She started forgetting the punch line to jokes at 39/40." Another woman whose husband's CAG count was 47 had just sold his car. "He's 39 years old," she wrote. "It was time for him to quit driving."

Quickly, Ms. Moser scanned a chart that accompanied the messages for her number, 45. The median age of onset to which it corresponded was 37.

Ms. Elio got drunk with her husband the night Ms. Moser finally told her.

"That's 12 years away," Ms. Moser said.

The statistic, they knew, meant that half of those with her CAG number started showing symptoms after age 37. But it also meant that the other half started showing symptoms earlier.

Ms. Moser, meanwhile, flew to the annual convention of the Huntington's Disease Society, which she had decided at the last minute to attend.

"Mother or father?" one woman, 23, from Chicago, asked a few minutes after meeting Ms. Moser in the elevator of the Milwaukee Hilton. "Have you tested? What's your CAG?"

She was close to getting herself tested, the woman confided. How did it feel to know?

"It's hard to think the other way anymore of not knowing," Ms. Moser replied. "It's become a part of my life."

After years of trying to wring conversation from her family about Huntington's, Ms. Moser suddenly found herself bathing in it. But for the first time in a long time, her mind was on other things. At a youth support group meeting in the hotel hallway, she took her place in the misshapen circle. Later, on the dance floor, the spasms of the symptomatic seemed as natural as the gyrations of the normal.

"I'm not alone in this," Ms. Moser remembers thinking. "This affects other people, too, and we all just have to live our lives."

Seizing the Day

July 15, the day of Ms. Moser's 25th birthday party, was sunny, with a hint of moisture in the air. At her aunt's house in Long Beach, N.Y.,

Ms. Moser wore a dress with pictures of cocktails on it. It was, she and Ms. Elio told anyone who would listen, her "cocktail dress." They drew the quotation marks in the air.

A bowl of "Cure HD" pins sat on the table. Over burgers from the barbecue, Ms. Moser mentioned to family members from her father's side that she had tested positive for the Huntington's gene.

"What's that?" one cousin asked.

"It will affect my ability to walk, talk and think," Ms. Moser said. "Sometime before I'm 50."

"That's soon," an uncle said matter-of-factly.

"So do you have to take medication?" her cousin asked.

"There's nothing really to take," Ms. Moser said.

She and the Elios put on bathing suits, loaded the children in a wagon and walked to the beach.

More than anything now, Ms. Moser said, she is filled with a sense of urgency.

"I have a lot to do," she said. "And I don't have a lot of time."

Over the next months, Ms. Moser took tennis lessons every Sunday morning and went to church in the evening.

When a planned vacation with the Elio family fell through at the last minute, she went anyway, packing Disney World, Universal Studios, Wet 'n Wild and Sea World into 36 hours with a high school friend who lives in Orlando. She was honored at a dinner by the New York chapter of the Huntington's society for her outreach efforts and managed a brief thank-you speech despite her discomfort with public speaking.

Having made a New Year's resolution to learn to ride a unicycle, she bought a used one. "My legs are tired, my arms are tired, and I definitely need protection," she reported to Ms. Elio. On Super Bowl Sunday, she waded into the freezing Atlantic Ocean for a Polar Bear swim to raise money for the Make-a-Wish Foundation.

Ms. Elio complained that she hardly got to see her friend. But one recent weekend, they packed up the Elio children and drove to the house the Elios were renovating in eastern Pennsylvania. The kitchen floor needed grouting, and, rejecting the home improvement gospel that calls for a special tool designed for the purpose, Ms. Moser and Ms. Elio had decided to use pastry bags.

As they turned into the driveway, Ms. Moser studied the semi-attached house next door. Maybe she would move in one day, as the Elios had proposed. Then, when she could no longer care for herself, they could put in a door.

First, though, she wanted to travel. She had heard of a job that would place her in different occupational therapy positions across the country every few months and was planning to apply.

"I'm thinking Hawaii first," she said.

Then they donned gloves, mixed grout in a large bucket of water and began the job.

MAKING**CONNECTIONS**

Consider This. This story contains two kinds of scenes—scenes the writer witnessed and scenes that were reconstructed from her subject's memory. In the scene that opens the story, the author recreates dialogue from two years before. If you weren't there and you don't have a tape recording of the scene, is it ethical to do this? And if it is, how do you go about making sure you've got it right?

Or This. Three additional scenes flesh out the resolution of this story: one at a convention, one at a family barbeque and one at a home that friends were renovating. What do these scenes, especially the last one, communicate, and what kinds of reporting do you imagine the writer had to do in order to be able to write them?

Or This. Do the multimedia options on the Web site provide added value? Compare and contrast these multimedia options with those that accompany both the previous narrative, about a science teacher, and the firefly story in Chapter 5. What have you learned that will be of help to you as you consider multimedia options for your own work?

Selection 6.3

This first-person account, by Times writer Nan Robertson, who came down with a sometimes fatal illness and lived to tell about it, won the Pulitzer Prize for feature writing in 1983. The story contains both Robertson's personal narrative and blocks of information about the illness. Most students who read this story today find the narrative portion of the tale compelling, if a little long. But the piece also contains information that a 21st-century journalist would be tempted to delete or pull out into sidebars or online features. As you read this excerpt, think about what you could pare away to streamline the story. Also notice information you could rework to create added features for the Web.

New York Times Magazine
Toxic Shock

By NAN ROBERTSON

I went dancing the night before in a black velvet Paris gown, on one of those evenings that was the glamour of New York epitomized. I was blissfully asleep at 3 a.m.

Twenty-four hours later, I lay dying, my fingers and legs darkening with gangrene. I was in shock, had no pulse and my blood pressure was lethally low. The doctors in the Rockford, Ill., emergency room where I had been taken did not know what was wrong with me. They thought at first that I might have consumed some poison that had formed in my food. My sister and brother-in-law, whom I had been visiting, could see them through the open emergency-room door: "They were scurrying around and telephoning, calling for help, because they knew they had something they couldn't handle, that they weren't familiar with," was the instinctive reaction of my brother-in-law, Warren Paetz.

I was awake and aware, although confused and disoriented. The pain in my muscles was excruciating. I could hear the people bent over me, blinding lights behind them, asking me how old I was, when I had stopped menstruating, and, over and over, what I had eaten for Thanksgiving dinner the previous afternoon, Thursday, Nov. 26, 1981, and what I had had the day before.

The identical, delicious restaurant meal my mother, Eve, and I had consumed on Thursday centered on roast turkey with the classic Middle Western bread stuffing seasoned with sage that I had loved since childhood. I had eaten slowly, prudently, because I had had only three hours' sleep the night before, catching an early plane to Chicago to connect with a bus to Rockford, a city of 140,000 in north-central Illinois where all my family lives. Immediately after finishing my

Published: September 19, 1982. Article available at: http://www.nytimes.com/1982/09/19/magazine/toxic-shock.html.

Thanksgiving dinner, I threw it up. It was 4 p.m. at the Clock Tower Inn in Rockford. I thought excitement and fatigue had made me ill. Neither I nor my mother, a gutsy 90-year-old, was overly concerned.

That was how it began: almost discreetly. I felt drained; my legs were slightly numb. The manager, apologizing all the way, drove us back to my sister's house in the hotel van. I was put to bed in the downstairs den.

I awoke, trancelike, in the middle of the night to find myself crawling and crashing up the stairs to the bathroom. The vomiting and diarrhea were cataclysmic. My only thought was to get to the bathtub to clean myself. I sat transfixed in my filthy nightgown in the empty tub, too weak to turn on the water. Warren and my sister, Jane, awakened by the noise of my passage, carried me back downstairs, with exclamations of horror and disgust at the mess I had created. Warren, an engineer who is strong on detail, remembers it as five minutes before 3 a.m.

As I lay in the darkened den, I could hear their voices, wrangling. Jane said it must be the 24-hour flu: "Let's wait until morning and see how she is." Warren said: "No, I can't find a pulse. It's serious. I'm calling an ambulance. Nan, do you want to go to the hospital now?'" "Yes,'" I said. His choice, of course, was Rockford Memorial—the status Protestant hospital in Rockford where my family's doctors practiced.

The ambulance came within a few minutes, in the wake of a sheriff's car and a fire truck. People in uniform spoke to me gently, gave me oxygen. Lying in the ambulance, I could feel it surging forward, then beginning to turn right, toward Rockford Memorial, 15 minutes across town. I heard an emergency medical technician, 18-year-old Anita Powell, cry out: "Left! Left! Go to St. Anthony! She has no pulse! Rockford Memorial is 15 minutes–away—she'll be D.O.A. [dead on arrival] if we go there! St. Anthony is three minutes from here—she'll have a chance.'"

"Do what she says," my sister told the driver. We turned left to St. Anthony Hospital, and my life may have been saved for the second time that night, following Warren's decision to call the ambulance.

In the early hours of Friday, Nov. 27, the baffled young medical staff on holiday emergency-room duty telephoned several physicians. One of them was Dr. Thomas E. Root, an infectious-diseases consultant for the Rockford community. He arrived at 7:30 a.m.

Dr. Root was informed about the vomiting, the diarrhea, the plummeting blood pressure. By then, a faint rash was also beginning to stipple my body. I did not develop the last of the disease's five classic acute symptoms—a fever of more than 102 degrees—until later. But Dr. Root is a brilliant diagnostician. And, incredibly, he and his colleagues had treated two similar cases within the previous year. "I think she has toxic shock syndrome," Dr. Root said to his colleagues. "Let's get going."

Most doctors have never seen, or have failed to recognize, a single case of this rare malady. Yet the St. Anthony doctors had treated two before me. The first, an 18-year-old who was hospitalized for six months in 1981, was left with total amnesia regarding the first weeks of her illness, but no other apparent damage. The second, a 17-year-old boy, who had a mild case, was out of the hospital within a week with no lasting damage.

"The most striking thing about you was your terribly ill appearance," Dr. Root recalled later. "Your whole legs and arms were blue—not just the fingers and toes. But the central part of your body, the trunk and your face, were more an ashen color. You were in profound shock. Your blood was not being pumped to your extremities. There was just almost no circulation at all. Your eyes were red, another important clue. But you were 55 years old and you had not worn tampons since the onset of your menopause 11 years before." Nevertheless, Dr. Root made the diagnostic leap to toxic shock syndrome.

This is the story of how, almost miraculously and with brilliant care, I survived and prevailed over that grisly and still mysterious disease. Almost every major organ of my body, including my heart, lungs and liver, was deeply poisoned. I narrowly escaped brain damage and kidney collapse. The enzyme released into my bloodstream that reflected muscle destruction showed almost inconceivable damage—an abnormally high reading would have been anything over 100 units; I showed 21,000 units. At first, the Rockford doctors thought they would have to amputate my right leg and the toes of my left foot. Because of the treatment, my legs were saved. But the dry gangrene on eight fingers persisted.

The end joints of my fingers were amputated. In all, three operations were performed. The first, at St. Anthony on Jan. 14, 1982, was delayed in a successful effort to save more of each digit. The other operations, involving corrective surgery, took place at University Hospital in New York at the end of April and again in May. The Illinois doctors theorized that gangrene had not affected my thumbs because the blood vessels in them were larger and nearer to a major artery.

This is also the story of how—with luck and expertise—this life threatening disease can be avoided or detected, monitored, treated and destroyed before it reaches the acute stage. Yet few physicians know how to test for it or what to do about it once the strain of a common bacterium, Staphylococcus aureus, releases its toxins. Toxic shock syndrome strikes healthy people like a tidal wave, without warning. Only two weeks before in New York, my internist of 25 years had said, after my annual physical checkup, which included a gynecological examination: "If you didn't smoke, Nan, you'd be perfect." Later, other doctors told me that smoking constricts blood vessels, further impeding circulation and thereby worsening gangrene when it occurs.

But, "Nobody should die of toxic shock syndrome," says Don Berreth, a spokesman for the United States Public Health Service's Centers for Disease Control in Altanta, "provided one gets prompt treatment and appropriate supportive care." This view is shared by Dr. Kathryn N. Shands, the physician who until last June headed the Federal toxic shock syndrome task force at the C.D.C. and who has studied every case reported to it from January 1980 to last June.

Toxic shock is rooted in the public mind—and in the minds of many doctors as well—as a tampon-related disease. It is true that of menstruating cases, about two-thirds occur in women under the age of 25, almost all of whom are using tampons when the disease strikes. They are at very high risk.

But about 15 percent of all cases are nonmenstruating women such as myself, men and children. In this group, there has been no recorded case of a recurrence of toxic shock.

Dr. Shands warns, however, that a tristate study—conducted by the Wisconsin, Minnesota and Iowa departments of health—"showed that menstruating women who have had toxic shock syndrome and who have not been treated with an antistaphylococcal antibiotic and who continue to wear tampons have possibly as high as a 70 percent–chance—horrifyingly high—of getting toxic shock again. Some people have had their second episode six months later; others as soon as one month later." The shockingly high rate of recurrence among menstruating women indicates that most doctors may misdiagnose toxic shock the first time around, or that sufferers may not seek medical aid if the case is relatively mild.

The disease was first given its present name in 1978 by Dr. James K. Todd, an associate professor of pediatrics at the University of Colorado and director of infectious diseases at Denver Children's Hospital. Writing in the British medical publication Lancet, Dr. Todd described several cases of the devastating malady he called toxic shock syndrome and suggested that staphylococcus bacteria might be the cause. His patients were seven children from 8 to 17 years old; three were boys and four were girls of menstrual age. One boy died with "irreversible shock" on the fourth day after being hospitalized. One girl, aged 15, suffered amputation of the end joints on two toes.

By June 1980, the national Centers for Disease Control had linked toxic shock with tampon use. The findings were based on a study it had conducted after surveys of victims of the disease by the Wisconsin state health department had suggested a correlation. Publicity about the disease ballooned, spreading alarm across the nation, particularly among the estimated 52 million American women who wear tampons.

Also that June, the CDC toxic shock task force invited the major tampon manufacturers to Atlanta to brief them on the results of the studies. Shortly thereafter, the Federal Food and Drug Administration (F.D.A.) issued a ruling requesting tampon manufacturers to include warnings about their products.

As part of its surveillance, the CDC began to take cultures of women patients at family-planning clinics for Staphylococcus aureus—a procedure as simple as obtaining a pap smear to test for cervical cancer. It was found that 10 percent of the menstruating patients carried the bacterium in their vaginas, a statistic that still holds. "But it is not necessarily the particular strain that causes toxic shock syndrome," Dr. Shands pointed out in a recent telephone interview. Only "about 1 percent of all menstruating women," she said, "carry the poison-producing strain of the bacterium in their vaginas during their menstrual periods." Infectious-disease experts say that approximately 2 percent of the general population carry the poison-producing strain of Staphylococcus aureus in the mucous membranes of their noses.

In September 1980, the C.D.C. reported that of 50 toxic shock victims contacted who had become ill during the previous two months, 71 percent had used superabsorbent Rely tampons. Of the control group of 150 healthy women, 26 percent used Rely. From January through August of 1980, 299 cases had been reported. The death rate was 25 persons, or 8.4 percent.

Late in September 1980, after the C.D.C. toxic shock task force had met with F.D.A. officials in Washington about the matter, Procter & Gamble announced it would withdraw its Rely tampons from the market. (Other superabsorbent tampons, however, are still being marketed.) The company is now facing about 400 lawsuits from the surviving victims, or the next of kin of those who died. The plantiffs have won every one of the half-dozen or so cases that have come to trial, and last month Procter & Gamble settled out of court with a woman whose original trial was the first against the company.

In October 1980, Procter & Gamble blitzed the country with advertisements encouraging women to stop using the superabsorbent Rely tampon. Then, both publicity and the number of reported cases among menstruating women fell precipitously in virtually all states. One of the few exceptions is Minnesota, where the health department has vigorously ridden hard on doctors and hospitals to count and report all toxic shock cases. There, the incidence has remained at about nine cases a year for every 100,000 menstruating women. The severity of the disease can range from mild to fatal: The death rate in cases *reported* in 1981 was 3.3 percent over all but the actual count is almost certainly higher, according to experts on the disease.

A National Academy of Sciences advisory panel also warned last June that toxic shock syndrome had not disappeared. (For further information on their report, see box on page 117.) Indeed, the academy's experts concluded, the disease is probably underreported by physicians who don't recognize the symptoms in victims or don't report the cases they do identify to state authorities. State health agencies, however, are still giving notice of about 30 to 50 cases a month to the Centers for Disease Control in Atlanta.

Between 1970 and April 30, 1982, the Centers for Disease Control received word of 1,660 toxic shock cases, including 88 deaths.

Although only 492 cases were reported in 1981, down from a high of 867 in 1980, the Institute of Medicine of the National Academy of Sciences estimated that the true number is about 10 times greater, or at least 4,500 a year. That estimate is based on figures from Minnesota.

Last month, the Journal of the American Medical Association carried an article by three doctors from the Yale University School of Medicine that said a review of five toxic shock studies found flaws that could lead to biased conclusions against tampons. However, an editorial in the same issue of the journal, while agreeing that there were deficiencies in the studies (the largest of which found tampon users were up to 18 times more likely than nonusers to develop the disease), said that "only substantial new research evidence evoking alternative explanations for the existing observations would be sufficient to negate the association betweenTSS in menstruating women and tampon use."

In the cases of nonmenstruating victims, Staphylococcus aureus can enter the body through a postsurgical wound or boil; is found inside women who have recently given birth; or anywhere on the skin. According to Dr. Root, there is no evidence that it can be sexually transmitted. In my case, among many theories, a tiny sore on the vaginal wall "may have favored the staphylococcus getting there from somewhere on your skin and then growing," according to Dr. Root. The staph was also found in my colon and urinary tract.

I was one of the dangerously ill cases. For at least four days after toxic shock struck me, the Rockford doctors did not believe I would live. Dr. Edward Sharp, a leading surgeon at St. Anthony, who would later perform the first amputation of the ends of my fingers, alternately bullied and coaxed me to fight on, and was "amazed" that I survived. "If ever anybody had a good reason to die, you did," he said later. "Your age alone! If you had been a 15- or 20-year-old, it wouldn't be so unusual. Of course, this just means you're as tough as nails."

It also meant the treatment was swift and superlative, once Dr. Root decided I had the syndrome. Afterward, Dr. Root recalled: "There are two aspects to the therapy. One is the right antibiotic to treat the staphylococcus germ. Almost all staph is resistant to penicillin now." So he prescribed beta-lactamase-resistant antibiotics to inhibit and wipe out Staphylococcus aureus and to prevent recurrences. Last June, the National Academy of Sciences' advisory panel on toxic shock emphasized, however, that, in the disease as it usually appears in menstruation, "evidence is not available to indicate that such treatment ameliorates symptoms or shortens the course of the acute illness."

The two-pronged attack on the disease in my case began, as it would in all others, with "vigorous therapy for the cardiovascular collapse, the shock. And what that involves," Dr. Root said, "is massive amounts of intravenous fluid. Your body has to have a certain amount of fluid within the blood vessels, the heart, to be able to pump effectively."

The amount of fluid that flowed from wide-open bottles and flushed through me in the first 24 hours "would stagger the imagination of many physicians," Dr. Root declared. "You got approximately 24 liters, or quarts, of fluid: I think it was because of that 24 liters, 10 of which replaced fluid lost from vomiting and diarrhea before coming to the hospital, that your kidneys managed to make it through without being terribly damaged. You gained, with those fluids, about 40 pounds in the first day. Your body blew up."

At one point, a nurse emerged from the intensive-care cubicle where I lay and blurted out to my sister and brother-in-law: "Your sister has become a conduit."

"But if we hadn't kept that adequate volume of fluid in your blood, then the kidneys would have gone and we would have lost the whole ball game because everything would have collapsed," Dr. Root explained. "The single most important thing in your therapy, in my opinion, was the incredible volume of fluid we put into you, keeping some measure of circulation going. And then, as the effects of the poison weakened, that circulation eventually picked up and was enough to restore you back to normal."

I was left, however, with eight partially dead and gangrenous fingers; bilateral foot-drop, a form of paralysis in both feet caused by lack of blood flow resulting in damaged nerves, which can leave the patient with a permanent limp, and severely poison-damaged muscles all over my body.

*   *   *

MAKING**CONNECTIONS**

1

Try This. "Toxic Shock" was an excellent story for its day, and it remains a good story now. But what would it look like in a more modern presentation? Edit this excerpt (or, if you have time, the complete piece on the publisher's Web site) to tighten the story and improve narrative flow. Reshape some of the facts into timelines or other online sidebars. See if you can also come up with ideas for graphics or other multimedia options.

© The New York Times

A Conversation with . . . **Amy Harmon**

NATIONAL CORRESPONDENT

Amy Harmon began her journalism career as many college students do, by writing for her college paper. After earning her B.A. in American Culture Studies from the University of Michigan in 1990, she worked as a researcher in the Detroit bureau of the Los Angeles Times. In 1993 she transferred to the L.A. office, where she eventually began writing about the Internet. In 1997 she moved to the "other" Times, to cover technology. She switched her focus to science and health in 2004. Today, as a national correspondent for The New York Times, she writes stories on how science and technology shape the lives of ordinary people.

Harmon is known for writing "long-form narratives" that often read like fiction. For these stories, she has won two Pulitzer Prizes. The first came in 2001 when she wrote a narrative about two Internet entrepreneurs—one black and one white—for a team-produced series on race, and the second arrived in 2008 for a 16-part series, on the social impacts of genetic testing. One story from the latter series, the narrative about genetic testing that appears in this chapter, was included in "The Best American Science Writing 2008."

Harmon lives in New York City with Scott Matthews, whom she describes as a "Web wonk," and their daughter, Sasha.

In a Q&A conducted in 2008 (see "Talk to the Newsroom" on The Times Web site), Harmon discussed her love of narrative, how she envisions her audience, how it felt to win a Pulitzer and more. The following conversation delves into her fascination with the impacts of science and technology, how she writes her extended narratives and the fun she takes in learning to tell multimedia stories. Along the way, Harmon discusses both of her stories that appear in this chapter. The interview, conducted by telephone, has been edited for length and flow.

You're obviously drawn to covering the social impacts of science and technology. What is it about these impacts that so fascinates you?

Well, maybe I'll start answering that by saying how I fell into doing what I do. I majored in American Culture Studies at the University of Michigan, and I thought I would go back to school into anthropology or sociology, but I happened to get a job as an intern in the Detroit bureau of the Los Angeles Times, where I ended up writing about the auto industry. That was pretty far removed from anything I cared about. But the Times eventually moved me to Los Angeles to write about other things for the business section.

Now this was the early days of e-mail and the Internet. At the University of Michigan, students had all been given e-mail accounts, but when I got to the newsroom in L.A., it was just reporters working at terminals connected to a mainframe, and I felt very deprived by my inability to communicate with my friends as I worked. So I borrowed a laptop, and I plugged it into the phone jack under my desk, so I could e-mail and use some early Web browsers. And my editors would come by my desk, and they were so fascinated by the technology, I started thinking maybe I could write some stories about this Internet thing.

I started to write about what it meant that people could communicate with each other over long distances in such an immediate way. And about some of the ethical, privacy and business issues, and eventually my parents were getting online, and I wrote about that. So I had a personal connection to the technology, but I'm not a technologist; I'm a classic liberal arts major. I just felt that that the human side of information technology wasn't being covered. We had a reporter in Silicon Valley who covered the business of new technology, and we had people who did reviews of new digital media products, but we didn't have anyone who was really trying to write about the anthropology or sociology of it.

I did that for the LA Times for a while, and then The New York Times recruited me to do the same thing, which I did for my first few years here. After covering the Internet essentially for ten years, though, I was ready for something new, and about five years ago, I had personal entrée to the subject of genetic technology.

I was pregnant and I got some genetic tests, which is pretty standard, but which I had never realized until then, that you are offered the chance to find out about what diseases you might be carrier for and what condition your fetus might be in. At the same time there were a bunch of news stories about how more consumer genetic tests were becoming available, and I could see that more people were going to experience the technology, not just when pregnant, but throughout their lives, learning about their personal history, ancestry and other things.

And so when I got back to work after maternity leave, I wanted to write about that. I had an amazing colleague from Science Times who was writing about new scientific discoveries in genetic testing and the scientists involved, and the business section was writing about the business of the science, but no one was really writing about how this technology affected ordinary lives. And that's what I wanted to do.

One criticism of science and technology reporting is that there's often a lot of hype . . .

Right. I agree that there's this kind of American predisposition to sort of say, "Hey, new technology, scientific progress, that's great." And to an extent, it *is* great. But often the pace of technological innovation outstrips the cultural debate about how a technology could be used or should be used. So I try to look at that in my stories, hopefully not in a didactic sort of way, but by observing in depth how individuals cope with new technologies.

For example, I wrote about this young woman who tested positive for a genetic mutation that causes Huntington's disease, which is a really devastating neurological disorder. She didn't have it now, but the test meant she would get it sometime in middle age, and the question at the heart of the story was how do you deal with that knowledge? And what I hoped for with that story was that it wouldn't just be relevant to people who tested positive for Huntington's disease; it's a pretty rare disease, and we're certainly not all going to learn so definitively how in fact we're going to die. But we all are going to have the ability to learn something about ourselves, so I hoped that by telling that story it would provoke people to think about what it might be like for them.

You write about science and technology, yet *you* don't consider yourself a science writer. So what if any interactions have you had with the writers on the science desk?
I run all of my stories by them, because they're so smart. And I ask them for advice, and I try to consult them to make sure that I'm getting the science part of my stories right.

You have said your favorite way to write about the social impacts of technology is through the long-form narrative. Why is that?
One of the things I've learned is that one person's story can illustrate a broader trend, often more powerfully than three or five people's stories or quoting a bunch of experts can. But you have to find the right person's story to tell.

And if people are going to care about your character, their story really does have to illustrate a more universal theme and a broader point about science or technology or whatever you're writing about. But if you can find it, and you can get inside someone's life and inside their head and tell a story about a conflict they are facing and how they resolve it (a story with a beginning, middle and end), these are the kinds of stories that we've been trained to absorb from childhood.

News analyses or profiles or just reporting information in a straightforward way can be great, obviously, and people need that and I wouldn't want a newspaper without those stories. But in terms of the kinds of stories that emotionally engage readers, I think those tend to be narrative stories.

So how did you learn how to write narratives? And how would you advise others to learn?
I have to give a lot of credit to my editors. The first story that I did that was like this was about that woman who tested positive for the Huntington's gene. I followed this woman for almost a year. I had written down everything that was in my notebook, and I turned it in at 10,000 or 11,000 words. I was lucky to have an editor who could look at it and say, "Here's why this is compelling. Keep this and cut out the rest."

It's a little easier with shorter time spans. I recently wrote about a high school biology teacher who was trying to teach evolution to a classroom of students who had been raised as creationists. That unit took place over about three months. But it still took a lot of drafts to figure out which were the most important moments to focus on.

I guess if I had any advice for people who are trying to do this it would be to just write chronologically. I try to go through my notes and say, "The story starts here, and it ends here." And then I organize my notes by chronology, and try to highlight the scenes that moved me and that show the character moving toward a resolution, and also illuminate the bigger theme that I'm trying to get at with this individual's story.

I'm also a real fan of outlining. It's a lot of up-front work, but it makes the writing so much easier if you know where you're going at the outset. When I get to the point where I have all this stuff and I'm panicking because I don't know what the story is, writing an outline often calms me down.

You're basically a print journalist who is being asked to produce other story options using new media. What's that like?
It's fun! I really find that having another outlet helps convey the full story to readers. I find it helpful to try to explain the story as I envision it in print to the videographer and to think about how it can translate to a video, and to maybe take some element of it that I can't go so in depth on in the print version and explode that into a video version.

We are now being asked to incorporate links to outside material that can add depth to our stories on the Web, too, which can be very useful. If I'm writing about the impact of some new technology on people, I try not to clutter my story with a lot of technical information. But I do want readers who want it to have access to it, so I often try to link to a scientific journal article or a Science Times article that explains the science behind what I'm writing about. So I see hyper-links as a great tool, especially for my kinds of stories.

What about blogs and Twitter?
I did a quick story on a Facebook trend that became my first blog post. There were people writing "25 random things about me," and it became almost like a virus on Facebook. And I kind of poked fun at it as an exercise in narcissism. And so it was a humorous piece, and there was really no place for it in the paper. So it ran on The Times blog, and I got tons of response and it was really fun.

I think that that's what The Times is trying to get reporters to do more and more [blog and use other new ways to reach audiences]. Not that we have to switch from the way we typically write stories, but just weave together what we already do with these new forms. Maybe I'm naive, but I don't see them as necessarily a threat. To some degree, I feel like I've mastered the basic print journalism forms, so I kind of welcome the idea of learning something new.

Since you write about the social impacts of new technologies, it's only natural to ask how new media have affected your own life. Have they affected your relationships with audiences? What about your family?

The best thing as a reporter is to get feedback from readers. That's what you write for. And e-mail has been great for that. But I also check blogs now to see if people are blogging about my stories. And it's really gratifying to see that other people pick them up and say whatever they want to say about them in public, so that's a new mechanism for feedback that I really appreciate. The other thing that has had a huge impact is The Times' "most-emailed" list. It's what every reporter at The Times reads now, probably more than the front page. We have a list of the 25 most e-mailed stories, and you're always happy when your story makes it onto that list.

As for my family, I'm always checking my e-mail. I was on vacation with my daughter recently, and I didn't check my e-mail for a little over four days. And it was such a pleasure, I have to say, because e-mail is both a blessing and a curse. It's great to be able to flex my time, which I take advantage of so I can work late at night from home, and be with my daughter in the early evening and afternoon. So it's great to be connected, but your work is definitely always there with you.

Part III

commentary

A lot of science writers tuck their opinions into their suit pockets. Like most of the scientists they cover, they prefer to "let the data decide." On occasion they may depart from third-person conventions to speak with an authoritative "I," but temperamentally they would rather report than opine.

Other science writers, though, have few such compunctions. They sally forth, science in hand, and boldly declare what's on their minds. A few of *these* writers produce editorials. Others fill weekly columns with analysis, reflection and opinion. Still others write long, interpretive analyses of the news, produce reviews of books and films and muse in essays about science and themselves. A growing number, at The Times and elsewhere, also sound off on daily blogs, jostling and communing with their readers.

This part of The Reader presents only a small selection of the many kinds of commentary in the media today. But it covers the kinds of pieces that you are most likely to produce for a science writing course and for campus publications: editorials, op-ed pieces and reviews of books and films. In addition, it includes a couple of essays, and for those of you with the platform, columns and blog posts.

Writing some of these pieces can be a nice change of pace. But be warned: Opinions and reflections that involve and persuade others do not just pop up like hands in a classroom. Writing authoritatively, as you must with commentary, demands knowledge. And knowledge demands thorough reporting. A great editorial, column or blog post may require you to read dozens of articles and interview half a dozen expert sources. A solid review may require you to familiarize yourself with a period of history or a field of science or other books and films on the same topic. And if you seek to write an evocative essay, you not only will need to know a lot about the subject that's captured your imagination, but you also will need to brave the cosmic bursts in the deep and expanding reaches of your own mind; to many, this is the hardest task of all—unless, of course, you happen to *like* to venture where no one else has gone before. In that case, as Captain Kirk used to say, "Engage!"

editorials and op-eds

ASPIRING SCIENCE WRITERS don't usually think about editorial writing as part of the job description. And in truth, it usually isn't. At most major newspapers and respectable online news sites, there is a huge divide between those who write the news and those who write the editorials, a divide intended to keep these functions separate. There's a huge divide at The Times too. In fact, writers on the science desk read the science editorials at the same time we do.

Philip M. Boffey, a former writer on the science desk who now works in the editorial department, writes the science editorials at The Times. Boffey makes it his business to track events in science and science policy, research them and write opinions about pressing public issues as diverse as stem cells and the safety of salmon. His unsigned editorials appear on the editorial page, straddling the letters to the editor.

Opposite the editorial page, in longer "op-ed" pieces, well-known scientists and accomplished freelance science writers speak their own minds on matters of public importance. These pieces offer Times readers a diversity of opinion about physics, crime, the influence of pharmaceuticals companies on doctors' prescriptions and many other timely topics involving science.

Editorials and op-ed pieces serve many purposes. Some work to broaden awareness and understanding. Some calm fears. Still others raise alarms or call for action. Whatever their purpose, the best present their arguments clearly and logically, and bolster them with a wealth of credible evidence, usually study results, statistics, case studies and expert testimony. Tight writing is also a must.

The selections in this chapter include two well-crafted editorials about science and technology. The first is a 340-word piece related to perceived risks of a huge international physics project that was gearing up to launch at the time, and the second, a more unusual 280-word reflection on how blasé the public has become to the findings of recent space probes.

A 720-word op-ed piece, written by a research scientist with a pet peeve, is included for those of you who are yourselves scientists or scientists-in-training. When a subject that you know a lot about is not getting a fair shake in the media or elsewhere, an op-ed can be a great way to set the record straight and garner a clip at the same time. Be aware, though, that if you want to wind up on the op-ed page of most big city papers, you have to be a widely recognized expert in your field, and even then, there is no guarantee. Campus papers and small city papers are another matter.

Selection 7.1

This editorial criticizes a lawsuit filed in 2008 to address concerns that the Large Hadron Collider could "gobble up the entire Earth or produce strange new forms of matter that would destroy the world as we know it." Its aim is to calm people's fears about what the writer clearly regards as a worthy scientific effort. In working to achieve that objective, it offers as evidence European efforts to review the safety issues, prior cases where the worry proved unfounded and nature's own bombardment of cosmic rays, which so far has proved benign. The combination of logic, evidence and strong writing works. Pay particular attention to how word choice, especially nouns and verbs, adds vigor to the critique. Notice too how the editorial lands with a knockout punch.

But It's Just a Small Black Hole
THE EDITORIAL DESK

If you thought you didn't have enough to worry about, consider this catastrophe projected in a lawsuit filed recently in Hawaii: The plaintiffs warn that a huge particle accelerator on the Swiss-French border could create a ravenous black hole that could gobble up the entire Earth or produce strange new forms of matter that would destroy the world as we know it.

It is not clear that a federal court in Honolulu could do much about a project in Europe even if it wanted to. The plaintiffs are hoping to block American agencies from assisting work at the Large Hadron Collider.

Probing realms at the frontiers of high-energy physics, scientists hope experiments with the accelerator will detect a long-sought particle that may explain how elementary particles acquire mass. They also yearn for other startling insights, perhaps even by creating microscopic black holes, a mini-version of the massive energy-sucking holes believed to exist at the centers of galaxies.

The European Center for Nuclear Research, which will operate the collider, has rightly pooh-poohed the dangers but is revisiting the safety issue in an effort to lay the concerns to rest. We draw comfort

Published: April 6, 2008.

from the fact that similar concerns were raised nine years ago by one of the plaintiffs, a former radiation safety officer for the federal government, about a collider at Brookhaven National Laboratory on Long Island. His suit was dismissed. The accelerator was turned on. We're still here.

We are further reassured that the Earth has been bombarded for billions of years by cosmic rays far more powerful than anything the collider will produce without, so far, being sucked into a black hole or turning into uninhabitable yuck.

More than once over the years we have felt as if we were transported to another universe listening to lawyers and judges wield the complexities and arcana of their trade. It would be fun to watch them struggle with theoretical physics. But if the courts have any sense, they will drop this suit into the nearest black hole.

Selection 7.2

The intention of this editorial appears to be a simple one: to deepen our appreciation of technological triumphs. The occasion, in this case, is new photographic evidence from Saturn. Notice the simple, conversational tone the writer uses to describe events that once inspired awe. Even while using the royal "we," the editorial conveys the voice of one person chatting amiably to another: "Most of us tend to lose track . . . what this brings to mind . . . this is the sort of thing that happens on Earth all the time."

Photos From Saturn
THE EDITORIAL DESK

Most of us tend to lose track of space missions, especially unmanned ones. Even a shuttle launch slips by almost unnoticed—a far cry from the old days when the whole planet paused to watch Gagarin or Shepard or Glenn jump skyward in what now look like pressurized tin cans. Such is the hectic gradualism of modern life. What brings this thought to mind is a new collection of photos from NASA's Cassini spacecraft, which has been orbiting Saturn since mid-2004.

What these photographs show is the planet, its moons and its alphabetical rings in many different orientations. Some photographs show Saturn's turbulent surface. Some show disturbances in the rings

Published: April 26, 2009.

(made of ice, dust and debris) caused by so-called shepherd moons, whose gravity helps define the edge of a ring.

Most of the photos were shot at a distance of several hundred thousand miles, but they have a serene and eerie clarity, as if they had been created by computer graphics software. And here is what's surprising: we find ourselves marveling simply at their beauty, not the technical difficulty of capturing the images.

After all, we have been looking at images from space for a long time now. We have seen video from the moon. We are accustomed to panoramic snapshots from Mars. Thanks to the Hubble telescope, we have looked back through a knothole in time, into a realm where galaxies are as thick as dust motes.

This is the sort of thing that happens on Earth all the time: humans growing used to what is completely extraordinary. The hard part is grasping the actual—understanding that Cassini is actually out there, orbiting Saturn some 700 million miles away.

Selection 7.3

The writer of this op-ed piece, a researcher on issues related to youth crime, is irked that teenagers get much of the blame for brainless behaviors that he claims are more the province of middle–aged baby boomers. Using recent reports on the teenage brain as a news peg, he invokes statistics and research studies to redirect criticism that he believes has been unfairly aimed at the kids he champions. Notice the use of bullets to break up the litany of statistics.

This Is Your (Father's) Brain on Drugs
By MIKE MALES

SANTA CRUZ, Calif.—A spate of news reports have breathlessly announced that science can explain why adults have such trouble dealing with teenagers: adolescents possess "immature," "undeveloped" brains that drive them to risky, obnoxious, parent-vexing behaviors. The latest example is a study out of Temple University that found that the "temporal gap between puberty, which impels adolescents toward thrill seeking, and the slow maturation of the cognitive-control system, which regulates these impulses, makes adolescence a time of heightened vulnerability for risky behavior."

Published: September 17, 2007.

We know the rest of the script: Commentators brand teenagers as stupid, crazy, reckless, immature, irrational and even alien, then advocate tough curbs on youthful freedoms. Jay Giedd, who heads the brain imaging project at the National Institutes of Health, argues that the voting and drinking ages should be raised to 25. Deborah Yurgelun-Todd, a psychologist at Harvard Medical School, asks whether we should allow teenagers to be lifeguards or to enlist in the military. And state legislators around the country have proposed raising driving ages.

But the handful of experts and officials making these claims are themselves guilty of reckless overstatement. More responsible brain researchers—like Daniel Siegel of the University of California at Los Angeles and Kurt Fischer at Harvard's Mind, Brain and Education Program—caution that scientists are just beginning to identify how systems in the brain work.

"People naturally want to use brain science to inform policy and practice, but our limited knowledge of the brain places extreme limits on that effort," Dr. Siegel told me. "There can be no 'brain-based education' or 'brain-based parenting' at this early point in the history of neuroscience."

Why, then, do many pundits and policy makers rush to denigrate adolescents as brainless? One troubling possibility: youths are being maligned to draw attention from the reality that it's actually middle-aged adults—the parents—whose behavior has worsened.

Our most reliable measures show Americans ages 35 to 54 are suffering ballooning crises:

- 18,249 deaths from overdoses of illicit drugs in 2004, up 550 percent per capita since 1975, according to data from the National Center for Health Statistics.

- 46,925 fatal accidents and suicides in 2004, leaving today's middle-agers 30 percent more at risk for such deaths than people aged 15 to 19, according to the national center.

- More than four million arrests in 2005, including one million for violent crimes, 500,000 for drugs and 650,000 for drinking-related offenses, according to the F.B.I. All told, this represented a 200 percent leap per capita in major index felonies since 1975.

- 630,000 middle-agers in prison in 2005, up 600 percent since 1977, according to the Bureau of Justice Statistics.

- 21 million binge drinkers (those downing five or more drinks on one occasion in the previous month), double the number among teenagers and college students combined, according to the government's National Household Survey on Drug Use and Health.

- 370,000 people treated in hospital emergency rooms for abusing illegal drugs in 2005, with overdose rates for heroin, cocaine, pharmaceuticals and drugs mixed with alcohol far higher than among teenagers.

- More than half of all new H.I.V./AIDS diagnoses in 2005 were given to middle-aged Americans, up from less than one-third a decade ago, according to the Centers for Disease Control.

What experts label "adolescent risk taking" is really baby boomer risk taking. It's true that 30 years ago, the riskiest age group for violent death was 15 to 24. But those same boomers continue to suffer high rates of addiction and other ills throughout middle age, while later generations of teenagers are better behaved. Today, the age group most at risk for violent death is 40 to 49, including illegal-drug death rates five times higher than for teenagers.

Strangely, the experts never mention even more damning new "discoveries" about the middle-aged brain, like the 2004 study of scans by Harvard researchers revealing declines in key memory and learning genes that become significant by age 40. In reality, human brains are highly adaptive. Both teenagers and adults display a wide variety of attitudes and behaviors derived from individual conditions and choices, not harsh biological determinism. There's no "typical teenager" any more than there's a "typical" 45-year-old.

Commentators slandering teenagers, scientists misrepresenting shaky claims about the brain as hard facts, 47-year-olds displaying far riskier behaviors than 17-year-olds, politicians refusing to face growing middle-aged crises . . . if grown-ups really have superior brains, why don't we act as if we do?

Correction: October 4, 2007. An Op-Ed article on Sept. 17, about teenagers' brains, incorrectly described the academic qualifications of a researcher at Harvard Medical School. Deborah Yurgelin-Todd is a psychologist, not a psychiatrist. The article also misstated the position taken by another researcher on voting and driving ages. The researcher, Dr. Jay Giedd of the National Institutes of Health, does not argue that those ages should be raised to 25.

MAKING**CONNECTIONS**

Consider This. The writer of the op-ed piece on youth crime made two mistakes that required correction. Does that affect the writer's credibility, in your mind? If you were The Times' editor responsible for selecting op-ed pieces, would you accept another op-ed piece from this person in the future? Why or why not? What if Times staffers have made similar errors (which, by the way, they have)? Should op-ed writers be judged by a different standard?

Try This. Find a new development in science or technology that has raised public fears; research the issue and decide whether or not the fears are warranted. Alternatively, find an issue in science or technology about which you have knowledge and a fresh opinion or perspective. Now write a 350-word piece for the editorial or op-ed page of your campus newspaper, using logic and evidence to persuade your audience of your opinion.

reviews

FEW LIKE TO ADMIT IT, but it's true: Many of us read book reviews just to keep up with what other people are thinking. We may read none of the books. But we will read every review in The New York Times Book Review because we know a knowledgeable writer will not only provide an evaluation of the book, but will summarize the contents and put them into a larger cultural context.

For busy readers, a good review is SparkNotes with the spark: It summarizes, analyzes and explains a book (or film or television program), but without neglecting the journalistic need to engage an audience. It provides an overview of the contents and their significance and explains the qualifications and intentions of the producers of the work. And in varying degrees, it analyzes how, both in style and content, the creators work to accomplish their goals. In addition, a helpful review puts its stamp of approval (or disapproval) on the work. With telling examples, it does all these things so that by the end, even if readers aren't persuaded to engage with the work on their own, at least they will have learned something.

For science writers, reviewing can be a great way to keep up with the competition for readers' attention in the hustle of today's multimedia environment. Knowing what's out there can help you to write your own pieces about science and technology. It can fill your head with new information, history and insights. And it's a nice way to break up your work so you don't begin to feel like you're huffing on an endless news-and-feature running wheel.

For science writers just starting out, reviewing can also be a great way to break into the field. At a conference on narrative writing some years ago, one science writer told how she broke into the big time by writing reviews about science books that no one else wanted to read. She proposed reviews to the book review editors of major metropolitan newspapers, and those editors, strapped for reviewers willing to tackle these books, were only too happy to consider her submissions. This writer also wrote for the alumni magazines of colleges and universities. Many alumni magazines run summaries or reviews of books that their alums have written, and if they accept freelance work, that's another source for clips.

In this chapter of The Reader, a freelance science writer and two Times writers offer their opinions on a book and two films that are intended to educate the public about science. Not all of these reviewers are kind. But then, critics have no obligation to be. Their duty is first and foremost to their audience—to inform and persuade them to read (or not), to view (or not) and to show how the book or film fits (or doesn't) into the larger cultural landscape.

Selection 8.1

This review appeared in the Sunday Book Review section of The Times. At 1,135 words, it is smart and tight. The writer, Steven Johnson, is himself an author of popular science and technology books.

THE NEW YORK TIMES BOOK REVIEW
Mind Matters
By STEVEN JOHNSON

Drawing on vivid examples from literature and the news, the reviewer draws us in and establishes why the topic is timely and significant.

Notice the reference to "Middlemarch." The reviewer will come back to this later.

Most great stories revolve around decisions: the snap brilliance of Captain Sullenberger choosing to land his plane in the Hudson, or Dorothea's prolonged, agonizing choice of whether to forsake her husband for true love in "Middlemarch," or your parents' oft-told account of the day they decided to marry. There is something powerfully human in the act of deliberately choosing a path; other animals have drives, emotions, problem-solving skills, but none rival our capacity for self-consciously weighing all the options, imagining potential outcomes and arriving at a choice. As George W. Bush might have put it, we are a species of deciders.

The reviewer wastes no time in introducing us to the book and what it's about. He also presents the author's qualifications and his intentions.

Jonah Lehrer's engaging new book, "How We Decide," puts our decision-making skills under the microscope. At 27, Lehrer is something of a popular science prodigy, having already published, in 2007, "Proust Was a Neuroscientist," which argued that great artists anticipated the insights of modern brain science. "How We Decide" tilts more decisively in the thinking-person's self-help direction, promising not only to explain how we decide, but also to help us do it better.

Published: March 22, 2009.

This is not exactly uncharted terrain. Early on, Lehrer introduces his main theme: "Sometimes we need to reason through our options and carefully analyze the possibilities. And sometimes we need to listen to our emotions." Most readers at this point, I suspect, will naturally think of Malcolm Gladwell's mega-best-seller "Blink," which explored a similar boundary between reason and intuition. But a key difference between the two books quickly emerges: Gladwell's book took an external vantage point on its subject, drawing largely on observations from psychology and sociology, while Lehrer's is an inside job, zooming in on the inner workings of the brain. We learn about the nucleus accumbens, spindle cells and the prefrontal cortex. Many of the experiments he recounts involve fMRI scans of brains in the process of making decisions (which, for the record, is a little like making a decision with your head stuck in a spinning clothes dryer).

In one swiftly moving paragraph, we learn the theme of the book and how the contents contrast with those of another work on the same topic. It's a wise move when a book might easily be confused with another.

Explaining decision-making on the scale of neurons makes for a challenging task, but Lehrer handles it with confidence and grace. As an introduction to the cognitive struggle between the brain's "executive" rational centers and its more intuitive regions, "How We Decide" succeeds with great panache, though readers of other popular books on this subject (Antonio Damasio's "Descartes' Error" and Daniel Goleman's "Emotional Intelligence," for example) will be familiar with a number of the classic experiments Lehrer describes.

Notice how the writer transitions from the previous informational paragraph to his overall evaluation. A summary judgment doesn't need to appear this high, but the fact that it does sets up the rest of the review nicely.

In part, the neuroscience medicine goes down so smoothly because Lehrer introduces each concept with an arresting anecdote from a diverse array of fields: Tom Brady making a memorable pass in the 2002 Super Bowl; a Stanford particle physicist nearly winning the World Series of Poker; Al Haynes, the Sully of 1989, making a remarkable crash landing of a jetliner whose hydraulic system had failed entirely. The anecdotes are, without exception, well chosen

Here's one reason the reviewer likes the book—its narrative style. Note the use of telling examples to make the point.

The reviewer pauses to mention a weakness in the narrative. He does not belabor it, though, but quickly moves on to more substantive matters.

and artfully told, but there is something in the structure of this kind of nonfiction writing that is starting to feel a little formulaic: startling mini-narrative, followed by an explanation of What the Science Can Teach Us, capped by a return to the original narrative with some crucial mystery unlocked. (I say this as someone who has used the device in my own books.) It may well be that this is simply the most effective way to convey these kinds of ideas to a lay audience. But part of me hopes that a writer as gifted as Lehrer will help push us into some new formal technique in future efforts.

A book that promises to improve our decision-making, however, should be judged on more than its narrative devices. The central question with one like "How We Decide" is, Do you get something out of it? It's fascinating to learn about the reward circuitry of the brain, but on some basic level, we know that we seek out rewards and feel depressed when we don't get them. Learning that this process is modulated by the neurochemical dopamine doesn't, on the face of it, help us in our pursuit of those rewards. But Lehrer's insights, fortunately, go well beyond the name-that-neurotransmitter trivia. He's insightful and engaging on "negativity bias" and "loss aversion": the propensity of the human brain to register bad news more strongly than good. (Negativity bias, for instance, explains why in the average marital relationship it takes five compliments to make up for a single cutting remark.) He has a wonderful section on creativity and working memory, which ends with the lovely epigram: "From the perspective of the brain, new ideas are merely several old thoughts that occur at the exact same time."

For this reader, though, the most provocative sections of "How We Decide" involve sociopolitical issues more than personal ones. A recurring theme is how certain innate bugs in our decision-making apparatus led to our current financial crisis. We may be heavily "loss

As the review turns from matters of style to the central question of content, note the use of supportive examples. If we never read the book, we at least learn something about decision making.

averse," but only in the short run: a long list of experiments have shown that completely distinct parts of the brain are activated if the potential loss lies in the mid- or long-term future, making us more susceptible to the siren song of the LCD TV or McMansion. So many of the financial schemes that led us astray over the past decade exploit precisely these defects in our decision-making tools. "Paying with plastic fundamentally changes the way we spend money, altering the calculus of our financial decisions," Lehrer writes. "When you buy something with cash, the purchase involves an actual loss—your wallet is literally lighter. Credit cards, however, make the transaction abstract." Proust may have been a neuroscientist, but so were the subprime mortgage lenders. These are scientific insights that should be instructive to us as individuals, of course, but they also have great import to us as a society, as we think about the new forms of regulation that are going to have to be invented in the coming years to prevent another crisis.

"How We Decide" has one odd omission. For a book that plumbs the mysteries of the emotional brain, it has almost nothing to say about the decisions that most of us would conventionally describe as "emotional." We hear about aviation heroism and poker strategies, and we hear numerous accounts of buying consumer goods. But there's barely a mention of a whole class of choices that are suffused with emotion: whether to break up with a longstanding partner, or to scold a disobedient child, or to let an old friend know that you feel betrayed by something he's said. For most of us, I suspect, these are the decisions that matter the most in our lives, and yet "How We Decide" is strangely silent about them. Perhaps Jonah Lehrer will use his considerable talents to tackle these most human of decisions in another volume. Until then, we've still got "Middlemarch."

Echoing what he did with narrative style earlier, Johnson identifies a weakness in the content and expresses the hope that this talented writer will rectify it in future works.

The end revisits the beginning. By circling back to the lede, the conclusion satisfies.

MAKING**CONNECTIONS**

1

Try This. Identify a new book about science written by a scientist or science writer for the general public, and write a 750-word review that conveys the subject of the book and its significance, the credentials of the author, his or her intentions, the contents of the book (with examples) and the value of the author's arguments, information and insights. If explanatory style and explanatory techniques are important to the success, or lack of success, of the book, consider them too. To the extent that you can, offer enough good information so that even if your readers don't read the book, they'll come away with some knowledge and understanding.

And This. When you finish your review, locate the alumni magazine of the author's college or university, and propose either a news item or a review of the book written to the specifications of the publication.

Section 8.2

Displaying knowledge of his subject, movie reviewer Stephen Holden zeros in on his main criticism of a science documentary: It sanctifies science. He doesn't ignore the strengths of the film; he simply focuses on what is its most telling weakness in his eyes. The review, nearly 800 words, contains many examples, enough to give a reader a sense of the film's contents. In fact, there are so many examples that even if you disagree with the reviewer's premise, you come away with enough information to decide whether this is a film you'd like to see, or not.

Film Review
Heroes of Science Through a Rose-Colored Lens
By STEPHEN HOLDEN

A warm and cuddly sage or a wild-eyed egomaniac demonically tinkering with the balance of nature? The image of the scientist in the popular imagination usually tilts toward one of these extremes. And in "Me and Isaac Newton," a glossy group portrait of seven noted scientists, the documentary filmmaker Michael Apted places his chips on the warm, cuddly side of the table.

Without going recklessly overboard, this handsomely photographed, meticulously edited film implies that the sort of world-class mind possessed by a scientist of Nobel Prize-winning caliber is likely to be accompanied by an equally refined moral sense. Well, maybe. But is the opportunity to play God automatically such a humbling experience? The film's gorgeous cinematography and mystically flavored world-music soundtrack underscore its sanctification of scientific pursuit as a potentially world-saving secular religion whose leading lights exude a priestly wisdom.

The movie's seven subjects, who represent a cross section of scientific endeavor, are interviewed sequentially in cinematic chapters that begin with chatty thumbnail biographies and broaden to include topics like "the work" and "the future." They offer a largely comforting vision of collective genius balanced by compassion, humor and judicious self-assessment.

The pharmaceutical chemist Gertrude Elion (who died last year at 81 shortly after participating in the film) is a stern but caring grandmotherly type you can imagine preparing and serving up the most delicious chicken soup. When the twinkling-eyed theoretical physicist Michio Kaku, shown gliding on an ice rink, remarks that here "it's just me and Isaac Newton," you practically want to hug him.

As anyone familiar with the world of science knows, of course, most scientists aren't this cuddlesome. Science, like every other elite field, is fraught with cutthroat politics, clashing egos and a certain amount of skulduggery. But none of that messy stuff makes it into this high-minded film. As the subjects reminisce about their lives and their work in polished paragraphs studded with homey anecdotes, you marvel at how carefully prepared and edited their remarks appear to be. When they contemplate the future and the role of science, they are not unaware of its perils (the development of nuclear power and the hydrogen bomb remains the ultimate cautionary event) but still express a guarded optimism.

Published: November 10, 2000.

A number of these biographies are personal stories of triumphing over difficult odds. Mr. Kaku, a Japanese-American whose parents were interned during World War II, recalls always feeling like an outsider. One of the founders of string theory—"the idea that vibrating strings are at the core of electrons, protons and neutrons"—he is now ardently pursuing Albert Einstein's goal of discovering a single theory to explain "everything."

Elion, the oldest of the seven, never finished her Ph.D. but still became one of the first women to break through the glass ceiling in her field. Among her many accomplishments was the discovery of an immune system suppressant that helps prevent the body's rejection of transplanted organs.

The environmental physicist Ashok Gadgil, who was born in Bombay, grew up surrounded by poverty and disease and has devoted his life to researching energy efficiency. He has developed a simple, inexpensive system of disinfecting polluted water with ultraviolet light. As the film follows him on his travels among the poor, it invests him with a saintly aura.

Among the other subjects are Maja Mataric, a Yugoslav emigrant who grew up in Kansas and works in robotics; Steven Pinker, a Canadian pioneer in the field of cognitive neuroscience; and Karol Sikora, a cancer researcher exploring how gene therapy can influence the molecular behavior of cancer cells.

Finally, we have Patricia Wright, a late-blooming primatologist and conservationist who was a social worker and housewife until her fascination with a pet owl monkey drew her into a new career. Ms. Wright subsequently spent many years in Madagascar studying the 32 varieties of lemurs indigenous to the island. She became an ardent conservationist when she realized that the slash-and-burn agriculture in Madagascar was endangering wildlife that existed nowhere else on earth. And she helped raise the money to establish a national preserve that is now operating.

Because she spends months at a time in the rain forest observing wildlife, Ms. Wright has the most obviously colorful career, and her work is the easiest to understand. But when the film goes to the laboratory to observe more complex and theoretical projects, the information it imparts is so sketchy we are reminded of how difficult it is to translate science into lay language.

Despite its ultimate lack of intellectual substance, "Me and Isaac Newton" is still inspiring. All seven of its subjects are fascinating, and most are extremely likable. Mr. Apted has done them all a huge favor.

MAKING**CONNECTIONS**

> **Try This.** Talk to scientists and see if you can identify a television show, a film, a video game or any number of other non-print media productions that in their view distort current scientific understandings or the reality of science. Find out what they object to specifically, and either review the work for a campus publication or write a short feature conveying the scientists' views.

Selection 8.3

This review by Jeannette Catsoulis lacerates a documentary that attacks evolutionary theory from the intelligent design perspective. The review is included for its brevity (350 words) and for the intensity with which the writer makes her case. No waffling here!

Movie Review
Resentment Over Darwin Evolves Into a Documentary
By JEANNETTE CATSOULIS

One of the sleaziest documentaries to arrive in a very long time, "Expelled: No Intelligence Allowed" is a conspiracy-theory rant masquerading as investigative inquiry.

Positing the theory of intelligent design as a valid scientific hypothesis, the film frames the refusal of "big science" to agree as nothing less than an assault on free speech. Interviewees, including the scientist Richard Sternberg, claim that questioning Darwinism led to their expulsion from the scientific fold (the film relies extensively on the post hoc, ergo propter hoc fallacy—after this, therefore because of this), while our genial audience surrogate, the actor and

Published: April 18, 2008.

multihyphenate Ben Stein, nods sympathetically. (Mr. Stein is also a freelance columnist who writes Everybody's Business for The New York Times.)

Prominent evolutionary biologists, like the author and Oxford professor Richard Dawkins—accurately identified on screen as an "atheist"—are provided solely to construct, in cleverly edited slices, an inevitable connection between Darwinism and godlessness. Blithely ignoring the vital distinction between social and scientific Darwinism, the film links evolution theory to fascism (as well as abortion, euthanasia and eugenics), shamelessly invoking the Holocaust with black-and-white film of Nazi gas chambers and mass graves.

Every few minutes familiar—and ideologically unrelated—images interrupt the talking heads: a fist-shaking Nikita S. Khrushchev; Charlton Heston being subdued by a water hose in "Planet of the Apes." This is not argument, it's circus, a distraction from the film's contempt for precision and intellectual rigor. This goes further than a willful misunderstanding of the scientific method. The film suggests, for example, that Dr. Sternberg lost his job at the Smithsonian's National Museum of Natural History because of intellectual discrimination but neglects to inform us that he was actually not an employee but rather an unpaid research associate who had completed his three-year term.

Mixing physical apples and metaphysical oranges at every turn "Expelled" is an unprincipled propaganda piece that insults believers and nonbelievers alike. In its fudging, eliding and refusal to define terms, the movie proves that the only expulsion here is of reason itself.

"Expelled" is rated PG (Parental guidance suggested). It has smoking guns and drunken logic.

MAKING**CONNECTIONS**

1

Try This. Editing is a skill that all writers need. Editing involves many things, but sometimes it means shortening a piece. Edit one of the first two reviews in this chapter to 350 words. Does your editing make the reviewer's opinions more intense? How did you decide what to leave out?

essays

FOR WRITERS WHO ARE CONSUMED WITH CURIOSITY, who are driven to explore what moves, inspires and troubles them and to mark it publicly with words, the essay can be a most compatible form.

In the essay, a writer analyzes and reflects on a subject in an attempt to understand it in fresh ways and convey that understanding to others. Journalistic essays come in many forms, but the most personal are characterized by a sense of intimacy and the freedom to observe, question, wonder, doubt, play, recollect and speculate. Such essays are both timely and timeless—usually pegged to events or developments, but timeless in their search for meaning.

The elements of the journalistic essay are as diverse as the people who write them. An essay may contain observations, knowledge, anecdotes, scenes, quotes from experts, recollections, speculation, historical and literary allusions, research results, statistics—anything so long as it serves the essay's purpose as "a mode of inquiry, another way of getting at the truth."[1]

There are no set ways to organize these pieces, according to Phillip Lopate, editor of "The Art of the Personal Essay." The essayist simply "attempts to surround a something [sic]—a subject, a mood, a problematic irritation—by coming at it from all angles, wheeling and diving like a hawk, each seemingly digressive spiral actually taking us closer to the heart of the matter."[2]

If anything structures the many disparate elements of the form, it is the writer's reflections, opinions and often-intuitive grappling for understanding. Put another way, what moves a narrative is action; what moves an essay is the writer's mind.

At The Times, according to science editor Laura Chang, essays complement the paper's regular fare "by providing a personal, more reflective or analytical take on science and health developments." The Times doesn't reserve a regular space for essays, she says, "because it's best to let them bubble up as an inspiration strikes or as events demand." But readers, she notes, love them. Chang's main requirement for those who want to try the form is "that it has a point and that it is well expressed. Also, essays rarely work if they exceed 1,200 words; a far better length is 800–1,000."

The two essays in this chapter are by physics writer Dennis Overbye. Overbye says he enjoys essay writing for several reasons: The essay is more personal than other journalistic forms, it is less formulaic, and "it allows me to make connections that I wouldn't have space for otherwise."

The first essay is Overbye's eulogy to a science fiction writer who affected him deeply. The second contains his musings on a discovery so fantastic as to appear to be a work of fiction. As you read these essays, notice the many connections the writer makes, including those to literature, science and his own past.

Selection 9.1

This essay lingers. It does so in part because the subject, science fiction writer Arthur C. Clarke, was both an important catalyst in Dennis Overbye's life and a significant personage in the larger culture. The essay weaves these personal and cultural threads together, shuttling back and forth between Overbye's deeply felt personal experiences of the science fiction writer and the more impersonal details about the man. The result is a moving piece that only someone with a special personal connection to the deceased, and the ability to convey that connection with evocative particulars, could have written. Interestingly, the essay does not use standard Times style. Times style would have been to refer to Clarke as "Mr." on second reference, but as an editorial note explains, an exception was made for Clarke because he was one of those people who "belong to the ages." The piece came in at just 1,200 words. Online, it was accompanied by a list of Overbye's best picks of Clarke's work and a link to Clarke's obituary in The Times.

ESSAY
A Boy's Life, Guided by the Voice of Cosmic Wonder
By DENNIS OVERBYE

On the night last week after Arthur C. Clarke, the science fiction writer and space visionary, died at the ripe age of 90, it was cloudy and threatening rain in New York. I was frustrated because I wanted to go outside to see if the stars were still there.

In his short story "The Nine Billion Names of God," published in 1953, Clarke wrote of a pair of computer programmers sent to a remote monastery in Tibet to help the monks there use a computer to compile a list of all the names of God. Once the list was complete, the monks believed, human and cosmic destiny would be fulfilled and the world would end.

The programmers are fleeing the mountain, hoping to escape the monks' wrath when the program finishes and the world is still there, when one of them looks up.

"Overhead, without any fuss, the stars were going out."

Published: March 25, 2008.

That was a typical Clarke ending, and it seemed only natural upon his death that nature might want to reciprocate.

Last week, lacking the chance of my own sign from heaven, I went home and dug out one of my most prized mementos, a letter Clarke had written to me in 1991 about a book I had written, "Lonely Hearts of the Cosmos." He liked the book, which featured sketches of astronomers he had known long ago in California, but hated the title, which he described as "cute" and "off-putting."

No matter. For me, with the receipt of that letter, a circle had been closed. Now it has opened again, and I have lost a distant grandfather of sorts.

To the world at large Arthur C. Clarke was probably best known as the co-creator with Stanley Kubrick of the classic 1968 movie "2001: A Space Odyssey," a visual tone poem featuring a malevolent computer named Hal and a pair of astronauts in search of a mysterious monolith that seems to be the key to the origin and evolution of humanity.

But Clarke* was much more than a science fiction writer. A genuine rocket scientist, he predicted in 1945 in the journal Wireless World that satellites in geosynchronous orbits would be used as "extra-terrestrial relays" for broadcasting to the Earth below. The concept he had been pushing for the last few decades, of an elevator to space, might yet become a reality. As he said last fall on the 50th anniversary of Sputnik, people stopped laughing at it a long time ago.

To space fans and perpetual adolescents everywhere he was simply the deceptively dry voice of cosmic wonder. Few writers have seemed to inhabit the cosmos, its grandeur, mystery and, yes, its ultimate coldness, with such aplomb, from the balletic spaceships and the mysterious fetus of "2001" to the Jesuit astronaut in the mischievous short story "The Star." The astronaut finds his faith sorely challenged when the expedition he is on discovers the remains of a great civilization that was torched when its sun exploded in a supernova 2000 years ago. It was that catastrophe, of course, that blazed forth in Earth's skies as the star of Bethlehem.

Destiny was Clarke's leitmotif, his own literary monolith. His earliest novel, "Against the Fall of Night," later reprised as "The City and the Stars," was about a city so traumatized by space and history that it had walled off the sky. In "Childhood's End," aliens known as Overlords come to Earth to enforce peace and help prepare for the next stage of human evolution, and then are left behind, like disappointed bridesmaids, as the new race, drunk with new powers, blows up its old planet and swoops off into the cosmos to merge with the Overmind.

---

* By the normal conventions of this paper, by the way, I should be calling him Mr. Clarke or Sir Arthur, on second reference. But there has always been an exception for people who "belong to the ages," and Arthur C. Clarke has always belonged to the ages.

I've lived in Clarke's universe ever since I was in eighth grade and a classmate slipped me a paperback edition of Clarke's "Reach for Tomorrow," a collection of short stories. Until that point my biggest ambition was to play second base for the New York Yankees.

Clarke yanked my sights quite a bit higher—a lot higher. In the triumphalism of postwar American middle-class life, it was a revelation to be reminded of the wonder of what I like to call cosmic ignorance.

I went from reading science fiction to reading books by George Gamow and pop-science explications of the debate then raging between the Big Bang and Steady State theories of the universe. The next thing I knew I was at M.I.T.

Now it's my own job to explicate those and even more abstruse debates. And it's a little embarrassing to admit now, as an alleged grown-up, an M.I.T. graduate, a father and a journalist, just how much of my metaphysical foundation comes from Clarke. I might sum it up as: the universe is a strange place, we are children here at best, ignorant of our origins, our future or even the right questions to ask.

I haven't lost my taste for cosmic mystery, for the curiosity about what might lie around the curve of the cosmos that Clarke first instilled in me. Clarke's gravestone says that he never grew up, and you could say that I haven't either. Like one of Peter Pan's Lost Boys, or the Who, I hope I never do.

Like one of the old horror masters, Clarke knew that imagination and suggestion always trumped explanation. In "The Sentinel," one of the most haunting science fiction stories ever written, and the seed from which "2001" later sprang, a pair of astronauts mountain-climbing on the Moon come across a pyramidal structure. Trying to open it, they realize they have set off a cosmic alarm. Somebody, somewhere, now knows we are here.

"I can never look now at the Milky Way without wondering from which of those banked clouds of stars the emissaries are coming," Clarke's narrator says at the end. "If you will pardon so commonplace a simile, we have set off the fire-alarm and have nothing to do but to wait. I do not think we will have to wait for long."

When Clarke died, one of his few disappointments was that we had not yet heard from any extraterrestrial intelligence, although anybody within 50 light-years sufficiently advanced could easily tell we are here.

As it turned out, though, there was something to be seen in the sky that night. In the kind of coincidence that would have delighted Clarke and set his fictive powers going, a new star appeared briefly on Wednesday morning, visible to the naked eye, in the constellation Boötes. It was the remains of a cataclysmic explosion, a gamma-ray burst, that must have torched a galaxy seven billion light-years away, around the curve of the cosmos, as Clarke might have put it.

Nobody knows if there could have been somebody or something living there, when the universe was half its present age. When I heard about it I couldn't help thinking about Clarke's Jesuit and the star of Bethlehem. Whoever or whatever was there now belongs to the ages.

Darkness has now reclaimed that spot in the sky.

MAKING**CONNECTIONS**

> **Try This.** Identify someone who strongly influenced your relationship to science. Write an essay about how that person affected you (and, possibly, others). Avoid chronological structure. Structure your piece around what you want to reveal about the person and his or her influence, instead. (Hint: Ask yourself: When I talk to others about this person, what do I usually talk about?) Infuse the essay with evocative details that support what you want to convey about the individual and his or her impact (the focus). You may or may not want to imagine this person's passing, but use as inspiration Overbye's musings on a figure important to him.

Selection 9.2

This essay was prompted by Japanese scientists' announcement that they had discovered a way to store messages on the DNA of a bacterium. The report precipitated a cascade of recollections in the writer—of a science fiction story, of a decade-old proposal to encode part of The Times in the junk DNA of a cockroach, even of staying up all night as a kid to play an album backwards to hear a hoped-for secret message. The recollections in turn prompted speculations—about the feasibility of storing secret messages in the DNA of cockroaches and humans, as well as interviews with scientists to check out these musings. And both sparked retrieval of the writer's stored knowledge of biology and the physical universe. Anyone could have been swept up by the implications of this news item, but Overbye surrounded the topic, creating layers of memory, speculation, information and knowledge that in the end offer arresting insights, not only into the topic but into his own fertile mind. The science fiction references at the start and finish are no accident, and they frame the essay beautifully.

Essay
Human DNA, the Ultimate Spot for Secret Messages (Are Some There Now?)
By DENNIS OVERBYE

In Douglas Adams's science fiction classic, "The Hitchhiker's Guide to the Galaxy," there is a character by the name of Slartibartfast, who designed the fjords of Norway and left his signature in a glacier.

I was reminded of Slartibartfast recently as I was trying to grasp the implications of the feat of a team of Japanese geneticists who announced that they had taught relativity to a bacterium, sort of.

Using the same code that computer keyboards use, the Japanese group, led by Masaru Tomita of Keio University, wrote four copies of Albert Einstein's famous formula, $E=mc^2$, along with "1905," the date that the young Einstein derived it, into the bacterium's genome, the 4.2-million-long string of A's, G's, T's and C's that determine everything the little bug is and everything it's ever going to be.

The point was not to celebrate Einstein. The feat, they said in a paper published in the journal Biotechnology Progress, was a demonstration of DNA as the ultimate information storage material, able to withstand floods, terrorism, time and the changing fashions in technology, not to mention the ability to be imprinted with little unobtrusive trademark labels—little "Made by Monsanto" tags, say.

In so doing they have accomplished at least a part of the dream that Jaron Lanier, a computer scientist and musician, and David Sulzer, a biologist at Columbia, enunciated in 1999. To create the ultimate time capsule as part of the millennium festivities at this newspaper, they proposed to encode a year's worth of the New York Times magazine into the junk DNA of a cockroach. "The archival cockroach will be a robust repository," Mr. Lanier wrote, "able to survive almost all conceivable scenarios."

If cockroaches can be archives, why not us? The human genome, for example, consists of some 2.9 billion of those letters—the equivalent of about 750 megabytes of data—but only about 3 percent of it goes into composing the 22,000 or so genes that make us what we are.

The remaining 97 percent, so-called junk DNA, looks like gibberish. It's the dark matter of inner space. We don't know what it is

Published: June 26, 2007.

saying to or about us, but within that sea of megabytes there is plenty of room for the imagination to roam, for trademark labels and much more. The King James Bible, to pick one obvious example, only amounts to about five megabytes.

Inevitably, if you are me, you begin to wonder if there is already something written in the warm wet archive, whether or not some Slartibartfast has already been here and we ourselves are walking around with little trademark tags or more wriggling and squiggling and folded inside us. Gill Bejerano, a geneticist at the University of California, Santa Cruz, who mentioned Slartibartfast to me, pointed out that the problem with raising this question is that people who look will see messages in the genome even if they aren't there—the way people have claimed in recent years to have found secret codes in the Bible.

Nevertheless, no less a personage than Francis Crick, the co-discoverer of the double helix, writing with the chemist Leslie Orgel, now at the Salk Institute in San Diego, suggested in 1973 that the primitive Earth was infected with DNA broadcast through space by an alien species.

As a result, it has been suggested that the search for extraterrestrial intelligence, or SETI, should look inward as well as outward. In an article in New Scientist, Paul Davies, a cosmologist at Arizona State University, wrote, "So might ET have inserted a message into the genomes of terrestrial organism, perhaps by delivering carefully crafted viruses in tiny space probes to infect host cell with message-laden DNA?"

I should say right now that I am not talking about theology or the near theology known as intelligent design. The ability to stick a message in a cockroach does not make us the designers or creators of the cockroach—only evolution could be so kind or clever.

But I'm a sucker for secret messages. Once, long ago, I stayed up all night with my friends playing the Beatles' "White Album" backward hoping to hear the words "Turn me on dead man," referring to the rumored death of Paul McCartney. I'm ready to find Slartibartfast's signature and rediscover my cosmic heritage.

The sad truth is, as others will tell you, this is a bit like writing love letters in the sand. "I don't buy it," said Seth Shostak, an astronomer at the SETI Institute in Mountain View, Calif., pointing out that DNA is famously mutable. "Just ask Chuck Darwin," he added in an e-mail message.

It is the relentless shifting and mutating, the probing and testing of every possibility on the part of DNA, after all, that generates the raw material for evolution to act on and ensures the success of life on Earth (and perhaps beyond). Dr. Davies said that he had been encouraged by the discovery a few years ago that some sections of junk

DNA seem to be markedly resistant to change, and have remained identical in humans, rats, mice, chickens and dogs for at least 300 million years.

But Dr. Bejerano, one of the discoverers of these "ultraconserved" strings of the genome, said that many of them had turned out to be playing important command and control functions.

"Why they need to be so conserved remains a mystery," he said, noting that even regular genes that do something undergo more change over time. Most junk bits of DNA that neither help nor annoy an organism mutate even more rapidly.

The Japanese team proposed to sidestep the mutation problem by inserting redundant copies of their message into the genome. By comparing the readouts, they said, they would be able to recover Einstein's formula even when up to 15 percent of the original letters in the string had changed, or mutated. "This is the major point of our work," Nozomu Yachie said in an e-mail message. At the rate of one mutation per generation, Dr. Yachie estimated it could take at least millions of years for the bacteria's genome to change by 15 percent—a huge change. Only 1 percent separates us from chimps. But other experts say that a stretch of DNA that is at best useless, and perhaps annoying to the little bug could disappear much more rapidly.

Calling the idea of storing information in living DNA "a nifty idea," Dr. Bejerano said: "The bottom line is if you want something to perpetuate forever, you can't just come in and type what you want. It would get washed away."

That dream, he said, "is hopeless with our current knowledge."

If we want to leave a message that would last for eons, it seems, we have to be clever enough to make sure that the message would remain beneficial to its host pretty much forever.

The challenge for an erstwhile interstellar Johnny Appleseed is to make the message part of the basic nature of its host.

If that ever turns out to be us, if we find that we are the medium, to paraphrase the late Marshall McLuhan, then, in some sense, we are also the message. Never mind who or what are the intended readers.

But if we find, say, the digits of the number pi encoded in a cockroach, I want to have a talk with old Mr. Startibartfast.

MAKING**CONNECTIONS** 🤝

Try This. In the spirit of the word essay, which comes from the French word essai, meaning "to try," pick a discovery in science that attracts or repulses you. For 20 minutes, free-associate on its meaning for you, and perhaps for others. What does it remind you of—in memory, in history, in books or in the movies? What excites or worries you about it? When your imagination runs away with it, where does it go? Has this process given rise to any new thoughts? Do you have enough to write a good essay? After you have done this for a week, choose the idea that looks most promising and draft the first page of an essay.

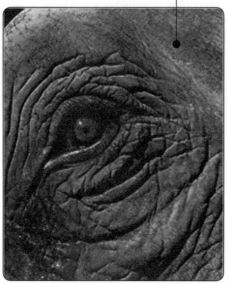

The New York Times

The New York Times

blogs and columns

REPORTERS WHO BLOG are the newspaper columnists of the 21st century. Like their print counterparts' corner of the media, their chunk of cyberspace is their own little soapbox—to provoke, reflect, harangue, inform, inspire.

But while traditional columnists labor over their pieces as if chiseling stone, few bloggers obsess over ledes, organization and word choice. Journalists who blog report on speed dial, and even if their copy must go through a layer of editors, as it must at The Times, they tend to post as soon as conscience and constraints allow. Should they leave a thread dangling in their haste, they know they can pick it up and begin again tomorrow.

Of course, some journalists who have taken up blogging do retain a sense of wordcraft. But most tend to write much more informally than they do for print—as if in conversation, which really, they are (though without the distracting *ums* and *urs*). Many blogs are running conversations with readers and sources, served up with links, video clips, podcasts, slideshows and other multimedia morsels that add nourishing breadth and depth and invite or provoke comment.

More and more readers rise to the challenge that blogging journalists pose, posting commentary, insight and knowledge drawn from their own reading and personal and professional experience. While not all the comments are constructive, journalists benefit from many of them, gleaning from the audience's diverse perspectives both new ideas for stories and posts and new ways of looking at familiar issues. Those who respond to journalists' blogs react to one another as well, creating entire communities of conversation. And many of these conversations go global.

As Andrew Revkin, whose blog on the environment, Dot Earth, explores planetary limits, says: "I have people commenting on my blog from the Amazon, from China, Japan, Eastern Europe, all over the world."

Revkin is passionate about the advantages of blogging for these reasons, and for others too:

• Blogging is a way to report changes, especially incremental environmental changes, that would never be dramatic enough, or new enough, to land on Page 1. As he told the Columbia Journalism Review in 2008, "One reason I started Dot Earth (my blog) is that it's hard to find space in the newspaper for . . . what I call 'slow drips,' or 'iffy' looming catastrophes. We don't do well with 'if' stories and we don't do well with dispersed stories. So the blog created a space to keep sustained focus on them."[1]

- The more informal conversations among journalists, expert sources and readers that blogging facilitates can also help audiences to grow comfortable with expert disagreement, Revkin says, and in the case of scientific issues, to understand science as an unfolding search for truth. (Revkin talks about this and related issues in the conversation at the end of this chapter.)

- Finally, bloggers often let readers in on their reporting process—how they stumble onto stories, how they find their sources and the kinds of answers they do and do not get from those they query. As Revkin once told a writer for PoynterOnline, the continuing education site for working journalists, blogging is "an important way to convey how I do my journalism as I'm doing it, helping create more transparency and credibility. . . ."[2]

The blog posts reproduced here are a little like fingerprints. You can identify the sensibilities of the writers by examining what they choose to write about, what they choose to say and how they choose to say it, the techniques they use to invite readers into conversation, and the links and other multimedia options they offer to enrich the experience.

The first post is by Revkin, who searches for understanding and insight with respect to the impacts of humans on this big blue marble we all call home. *Explore* is a key word for this thoughtful journalist: He likes to think of himself more as an explorer than a traditional commentator. Sometimes his readers and other bloggers get angry at him "for not spouting what I actually think about things. But . . . telling people what I think, or what I believe . . . is less and less relevant these days, given the complexities out there." For him, as for many essayists, inquiry and reflection are key.

The second post is by John Tierney. Tierney—who says he "always wanted to be a scientist but went into journalism because its peer-review process was a great deal easier to sneak through"—delights in recognizing both foolishness and oddball genius (including his own). In his blog, TierneyLab, Tierney pokes and prods, and he doesn't mind being an irritant if he can get people to think.

The third post is by London-based evolutionary biologist Olivia Judson. Judson uses her weekly blog, The Wild Side, to voice her wonder at new discoveries in the life sciences and let her audience in on some of the more enduring principles in the fields she covers. Hers is the sensibility of an educator.

In addition to these posts, the chapter contains a fourth, by Tierney, which is accompanied by a related column. On the science desk of The Times, a column can mean many things. It can mean Tuesday's "Vital Signs" or "Observatory" columns, which contain briefs about scientific discoveries. It can mean a news-you-can-use column about health and medicine. Or, like Tierney's biweekly column "Findings," it can mean an essay or feature story that has a personal voice and appears regularly in its own designated space. Though it's growing harder and harder to draw clear lines between columns and blogs in this new media age, in many parts of the media world there remain differences. This column and related blog post reveal some of them and show, too, some of the ways news organizations are encouraging readers to move back and forth among all kinds of media messages.

Anyone who reads the posts of these bloggers—or those of other Times bloggers[3]—will quickly realize how many different ways science writers can communicate when they blog.

What the future holds for journalism is anyone's guess. But for involving readers and for telling stories from multiple angles and communicating the value, complexities and occasional hubris of science, the possibilities offered by this technology and other new media are only as limited as the inventiveness of the journalists who use them.

Selection 10.1

In "About Dot Earth," journalist Andrew Revkin describes his blog's reason for being: "By 2050 or so, the world population is expected to reach nine billion, essentially adding two Chinas to the number of people alive today. Those billions will be seeking food, water and other resources on a planet where, scientists say, humans are already shaping climate and the web of life." Dot Earth "examines efforts to balance human affairs with the planet's limits. . . ." This particular post jumps off from research on the memory of elephants to consider the ability of humans to remember and learn from natural disasters. Revkin contacts experts on disaster preparedness to explore this idea, and reports on what some of them had to say. As you read this post, which was prompted by the findings of a new study, notice how it differs from conventional reporting on discoveries. In his final sentence, Revkin asks: "Is anybody listening?" When last checked, 81 readers indicated they were.

DOT EARTH
On Elephants' Memories, Human Forgetfulness and Disaster

By ANDREW C. REVKIN

Elephant families led by old females seem to survive drought better than those without the wisdom that comes with age, researchers say.

There's a certain gee-whiz aspect to research hinting that old elephant matriarchs, during severe drought, lead their kin to distant watering holes at locations that were evidently seared into memory from dry times in their youth decades earlier—even as elephant groups led by younger females stay behind and suffer.

Those were the findings of biologists from the Wildlife Conservation Society and Zoological Society of London studying elephant behavior in Tanzania's Tarangire National Park. The work was just published in Biology Letters, a journal of Britain's Royal Society. The scientists, led by Charles Foley of the conservation society, focused

Posted: August 12, 2008.

on a terrible drought in 1993 and the fates of three family groups, two of which—led by older females—left the park, found water, and had a higher survival rate for calves than a group whose older females were killed by poachers seeking their tusks. (*Here's a nice Times story on how this elephant study began*). [To link to this story, check the post on The Times Web site.]

You can almost hear the Internet chatter over the results: "So it's true; listen to your elders." . . ."Wow, so elephants really don't forget."

But to me, there may be some deeper significance to this observation (even with the caveats that attend analysis involving just a few groups of animals). Is it possible that intact elephant families have better disaster management skills than people? When you put together the findings of some of the scientists below, you do start to wonder.

The Tanzanian research immediately reminded me of a conversation I'd had about "disaster memory" with Herbert Maschner, an anthropologist at Idaho State University. We'd met at a meeting on Arctic science. For years he'd been studying the shifting patterns of settlement and activities of Aleutian islanders over many centuries by tracking changes in the positions and characteristics of ancient village sites.

One pattern: Villages tended to be situated on the coast, for the convenience of easy access to marine resources, until some year when the seismically active region was rocked by a big quake and tsunami. Then, for several generations afterward, villages would be set back from the sea. But time would pass and more recent ruins would be back by the water's edge again. The length of the "disaster memory" for the area—if my memory serves me right—was about 100 years (I'll adjust this if I hear back from Dr. Maschner; I sent him the elephant paper but he may be in the field). At that time and place, then, people were definitely listening to their elders.

But it may be that human disaster memory is getting shorter, despite the advent of written records, television, and the like. I sent the elephant finding Monday to about a dozen researchers focused on boosting humans' resilience to inevitable hard knocks like earthquakes and eruptions.

The Sunda Fault paralleling Indonesia's Indian Ocean coast is a ticking bomb.

It seems that just about everyone immersed in disaster preparedness and risk mitigation has an example of communities quickly forgetting wrenching lessons from past disasters. Most jarring, perhaps, was an e-mail I got from Costas Synolakis, an earthquake expert at the University of Southern California who I've interviewed many times on past—and future—calamities in communities along the sutures where great plates of Earth's crust are in perpetual collision. His main take-home line, which essentially says we are not listening to our elders, is here:

Communal memory of rare disasters is worse in more developed societies because knowledge now is passed on in schools, movies or the Internet leaving no time for oral history or reliance on the elders to learn about the world.

I'll be posting more experts' reactions to the elephant paper as time allows. More of Dr. Synolakis's thoughts on disaster, memory and resilience are here:

Preserving community memory is a vexing issue with human settlements, not only because of loss of community memory as survivors die, but also because survivors move following a disaster and people with no first hand experience move in. Here are some points. Use them as you wish.

In 1992, a devastating tsunami hit the coastal resort of El Transito on the Pacific coast of Nicaragua. More than 100 died; the downtown was reminiscent of Banda Aceh. The government relocated the population up coast and inland. When I visited again in 1995, I was astounded to see the town rebuilt, with new bars and canteens where we counted bodies 3 years earlier. I couldn't find a single eyewitness from those interviewed in 1992, the town was now inhabited with newcomers from Managua, who grabbed the opportunity of cheap coastal real estate—none of the new locals or the tourists remembered or knew that their resort had been severely hit.

I was reminded how community memory helps save lives only last week searching for eyewitnesses of the 1956 tsunami, the largest to hit the Mediterranean in the past 100 years. I have interviewed more than 80 survivors from this event from fifteen different Aegean islands. Only in the island of Karpathos did the people know to evacuate when the harbinger withdrawal of the [sea] appeared in 1956, even though they didn't feel any earthquake shaking. As it turned out, they had experienced another local tsunami a few years earlier, in 1948, and knew what was to follow. Interestingly, none of the survivors had discussed their experiences with their children and grandchildren until post Boxing Day 2004, when they suddenly realized that they had lived through a similar disaster, but at smaller scale. Communal memory of rare disasters is worse in more developed societies because knowledge now is passed on in schools, movies or the internet leaving no time for oral history or reliance on the elders to learn about the world.

As I've said here before, it now seems in some ways that scientists are like society's elders, with awareness of past disasters absorbed from years of studying mega-droughts recorded in tree rings, or coastal destruction etched in layers of sediment, or great earthquakes recorded in displaced stream beds.

They warn of inevitable hard knocks to come, even as ever more people crowd into harm's way, whether in the instant pop-up shanty towns of cities sitting on unstable faults or the spreading sprawl of the Southwest, where megadrought may have been the norm, and 20th-century moisture the anomaly.

The question remains: Is anybody listening?

Selected Comments From Readers

August 13, 2008

There is no question that elephants are far wiser than human beings. We think we are clever with rockets and computers, but which of these two species will be responsible for the extinction of us all?

August 12, 2008

Mankind is slow to make changes using past history as a guide, but eventually we do make the changes. Surviving a changing world simply comes down to two simple choices . . . Adapt or die!

August 13, 2008

Are scientists "like society's elders"? Is anybody listening?

Sadly, Andy, the answer to both questions is "no." Society's elders are now the political leaders and the media celebrities. The significance of local, community elders has declined in Western society with the rise of mass media. The sound-bites and, um, "eye-bites" are easier to digest. "Truthiness," a la Stephen Colbert, is winning out over Truth.

Human tendency to listen to advice is not based on rationality. We follow the advice of those who appear wise and charismatic—father figures, if you will.

That is why scientists can, at best, be advisors to the figures who really lead society. Their studies alone, though they be accurate and predictive and verifiable as much as you wish, will never sway public opinion.

Not a USA resident, I haven't seen the Alliance for Climate Protection's "we" campaign ads, but that sounds like the way to go, as long as you recruit influential-enough figures.

If you want people to listen, you should face the sad truth: Advertisers, politicians and celebs are today's "society's elders."

Selection 10.2

Staff writer and resident contrarian John Tierney uses his blog to "check out new research and rethink conventional wisdom about science and society." TierneyLab, he writes, is "guided by two founding principles: 1. Just because an idea appeals to a lot of people doesn't mean it's wrong. 2. But that's a good working theory." With a writing style that can be as cheeky as much of his thinking, Tierney invites readers to put ideas in science "to the test"—to participate in online research projects that scientists bring to his attention, to take tests and solve puzzles, and when they feel the need, to take him on. It is not uncommon for his posts to net more than 200 comments. Nor is it unusual for his work to be criticized by journalistic peers.[4] In this particular post, Tierney invites reader comment on his support for a scientist's proposal to resurrect Neanderthals. At last count, 463 readers had commented, many with disapproval if not outright indignation.

TIERNEYLAB
Why Not Bring a Neanderthal to Life?
By JOHN TIERNEY

Now that the Neanderthal genome has been reconstructed, as my colleague Nicholas Wade reports, a leading genome researcher at Harvard says that a Neanderthal could be brought to life with present technology for about $30 million.

So why not do it? Why not give Harvard's George Church the money he says could be used to resurrect a Neanderthal from DNA?

I'm bracing for a long list of objections from the world's self-appointed keepers of bioethics, who must see this new Neanderthal issue as a research bonanza. Think of the conferences to plan, the books to publish, the donors to alarm! I can imagine an anti-Neanderthal alliance between the religious right and the religious left, like James Dobson and Jeremy Rifkin—what I like to call the holier-than-thou coalition opposed to new biological technologies.

But I'm afraid I can't see the problem. If we discovered a small band of Neanderthals hidden somewhere, we'd do everything to keep them alive, just as we try to keep alive so many other endangered populations of humans and animals—including man-biting mosquitoes and man-eating polar bears. We've also spent lots of money reintroducing animals into ecosystems from which they had vanished. Shouldn't we be at least as solicitous to our fellow hominids?

Granted, it would be disorienting and lonely for the first few Neanderthals, but it would be pretty interesting for them as well as us. (What would a Neanderthal make of Disneyland, or of World of Warcraft?) If our species disappeared and a smarter species took over the planet, I'd take the offer to be resurrected just on the theory that being alive beats being dead.

What do you think? Should we try to resurrect a Neanderthal? And if so, what kind of precautions should we take, and what kind of lives should we help them lead? I welcome all answers, but I hope that we won't be distracted by talk of genocide or slavery. Yes, previous encounters between advanced and primitive civilizations did end badly for the primitives, but I think it's a stretch to imagine today's humans trying to exterminate or enslave Neanderthals. Let's assume we'd do our best to treat them well. How much would they enjoy living today? How much would we learn from one another?

Posted: February 13, 2009.

Selected Comments From Readers

February 13, 2009

Easy for you to say. You're not the one being coerced into a lonely existence to satisfy idle scientific curiosity. Let them rest in peace.

February 13, 2009

Please stop describing this as if you were bringing a species back to earth in a time-machine. What do you mean by "treat them well?" Would you confine them? What if you found their IQs to be 50? Would there be half-way houses? Would you help them find work as grocery baggers? What purpose would it serve, really? Bring back a mammoth. The science is the same, and the ethics a lot less complicated.

February 13, 2009

Pleaseohpleaseohpleaseohplease bring a Neanderthal back to life! This is seriously the best idea I've heard of since Jurassic Park. In fact, I'll start a fundraiser "Walk for Harry" where each mile I walk will bring us a few cents closer to meeting our stocky, big-brained cousin face to face. Here's the newly-created home for the Walk for Harry—http://walkforharry.blogspot.com/.

Honestly, I can't see anything at all wrong with this scenario. I've got all my fingers and toes crossed. This will be awesome!

Selection 10.3

Scientist Olivia Judson writes on contract for The Times. Normally her posts cover evolutionary biology, everything from paleontology and the evolution of species to sex. But this particular post is drawn from psychology and concerns humans' inability to assess themselves as well as they assess others. With characteristic references to history and literature, it reflects the writer's wide-ranging education. The notes at the end of all her blogs, including this one, offer annotated references for those who want additional reading. At last count, this post had provoked 165 responses from a growing following. A favorite: "I am an alien. I wish to study your kind and take a sample back with me. Please meet my saucer on the roof at 5 pm. Bring as many friends as you can. Oh, and some potatoes. —josh"

THE WILD SIDE
Wanted: Intelligent Aliens, for a Research Project
By OLIVIA JUDSON

If there is anything living on Mars, it's going to be weird bacteria or the like, not little green men. Which is a pity. Because what we humans really need is a group of friendly, intelligent aliens to study us, and give us a report on what they find.

The problem is, in many respects it's difficult for us to study ourselves.

First, there are practical problems. It's easier, for example, to study organisms with much shorter lives than our own: when organisms have short lives, we can accumulate lots of knowledge about them in a single human lifetime. Hence, we know far more about bacteria, fruit flies and mice than we do about elephants, giant tortoises or sequoia trees.

Another difficulty: it's hard to do certain sorts of experiments. Many of the experiments we can do on fruit flies would be impractical or unethical to do on people.

But there's a deeper problem as well: it's hard for us to see ourselves in an objective way.

The literature from psychology shows that, as individuals, we are good at seeing other people clearly, but poor at seeing ourselves. Most people, for example, describe themselves as being better drivers than average, and consider themselves better looking than other people consider them. (The fictional 18th century heroine, Moll Flanders, recognized that a high self-regard can be dangerous, arguing that women who believe themselves beautiful are easier to seduce: "If a young woman once thinks herself handsome, she never doubts the truth of any man that tells her he is in love with her; for she believes herself charming enough to captivate him, 'tis natural to expect the effects of it.")

In general, for "good" traits, such as generosity, friendliness, and sense of humor, most people rate themselves as above average; for "bad" traits like snobbishness and dishonesty people typically describe themselves as below average (less snobbish, less dishonest). Most of us thus believe we are less biased than other people, less racist, less prone to conform, and less prone to be influenced by advertising. Yet, while good at spotting bias and prejudice in others, we are routinely blind to it in ourselves.

These happy illusions extend to those we identify with. People expect that members of their own ethnic groups are more likely to smile (even in situations where a smile is inane, such as being alone

Posted: September 30, 2008.

in a room waiting for a computer to start up). Asked to pick out photographs of people likely to support the same political party as themselves, they pick more beautiful people than they do for supporters of an opposing party. In general, people tend to hold more favorable views of their "in-group," to exaggerate differences with a perceived out-group, and to treat members of their in-group more generously.

When it comes to studying ourselves—to trying to understand how we compare to other animals on the planet—we run into similar problems. We consistently overestimate human uniqueness and underestimate the abilities of other animals.

On the overestimation side, we only need to look at history to see that humans tend to have any number of self-aggrandizing beliefs—we have a long tradition of believing ourselves to be the center of the universe, for example, or to think the planet was created especially for us. We often forget that for the first two billion years of its existence, the planet was home only to bacteria, and that bacteria make all other life forms possible: we are as dependent on the bacteria in our guts as a termite or cow. And when the chimpanzee genome was published, there was a big disappointment. The genes that have been evolving fastest between our lineage and theirs turned out not to be those involved in head size or intelligence, but those involved in reproduction and the immune system—the same pattern you see between any other pair of closely related species of mammal.

Moreover, in our assessments of other animals, we are consistently surprised. My favorite example of this comes from a headline in Nature a few years ago that announced that "sheep are not so stupid after all." The reason for the re-evaluation of ovine intelligence was a series of elegant experiments that showed that sheep can recognize and remember other sheep. But sheep are social animals: they live in flocks. It would be astonishing if they could not do this. (A sheep newspaper would no doubt have run the headline, "Humans Amazed Again!")

The idea that we need outside help in assessing ourselves isn't new. The great 19th century scientist Thomas Huxley, in his classic text about the evolution of humans and their similarities to chimpanzees and gorillas, wrote:

Let us endeavor for a moment to disconnect our thinking selves from the mask of humanity; let us imagine ourselves scientific Saturnians, if you will, fairly acquainted with such animals as now inhabit the Earth, and employed in discussing the relations they bear to a new and singular "erect and featherless biped," which some enterprising traveler, overcoming the difficulties of space and gravitation, has brought from that distant planet for our inspection, well preserved, may be, in a cask of rum.

Huxley goes on to argue that only a human could deny the extraordinary resemblances between humans and their primate cousins.

Since then, the genuine difficulty in disconnecting the "mask of humanity" has grown more apparent. As we continue to learn about the inherent human tendencies towards bias, and the flattering illusions we like to maintain, it may get easier to guard against the problem, and to assess ourselves more clearly. Yet perhaps—probably—there are some biases that our brains have that we simply can't see at all, blind spots that we, as a species, can never discover we have.

If any aliens are reading this, please make yourselves known.

Notes:

[Judson's trademark endnotes.]

For a fascinating review of biases in how individuals see themselves and others, and of our blindspots, see Pronin, E. 2008. "How we see ourselves and how we see others." Science 320: 1177–1180. For people overestimating their driving ability, see Sundström, A. 2008. "Self-assessment of driving skill—a review from a measurement perspective." Transportation Research Part F 11: 1–9. For people considering themselves better looking than they are, see Epley, N. and Whitchurch, E. 2008. "Mirror, mirror on the wall: enhancement in self-recognition." Personality and Social Psychology Bulletin 34: 1159–1170. For the quotation from Moll Flanders, see Daniel Defoe's novel of the same name; the text is available from Project Gutenberg.

For people expecting members of their own ethnic groups to smile more, see Beaupré, M. G. and Hess, U. 2003. "In my mind, we all smile: a case of in-group favoritism." Journal of Experimental Social Psychology 39: 371–377. The political party membership experiment is cited here, too. General attitudes towards ingroups and outgroups are reviewed in Robbins, J. M. and Krueger, J. I. 2005. "Social projection to ingroups and outgroups: a review and meta-analysis." Personality and Social Psychology Review 9: 32–47 and Krueger, J. I. 2007. "From social projection to social behaviour." European Review of Social Psychology 18: 1–35.

For fast-evolving differences in humans and chimpanzees being genes involved in reproduction and the immune system, see the Chimpanzee Sequencing and Analysis Consortium 2005, "Initial sequence of the chimpanzee genome and comparison with the human genome." Nature 437: 69–87. For sheep being less stupid than we thought, see Kendrick, K. M. et al 2001. "Sheep don't forget a face." Nature 414: 165–166. (This paper had a minor correction in 2007: see Nature 447: 346.)

For the quotation from Thomas Huxley, see page 71 of the 2001 reprint of his classic text, "Man's Place in Nature"; this was edited by Stephen Jay Gould, and published by the Modern Library.

MAKING**CONNECTIONS** 🤝

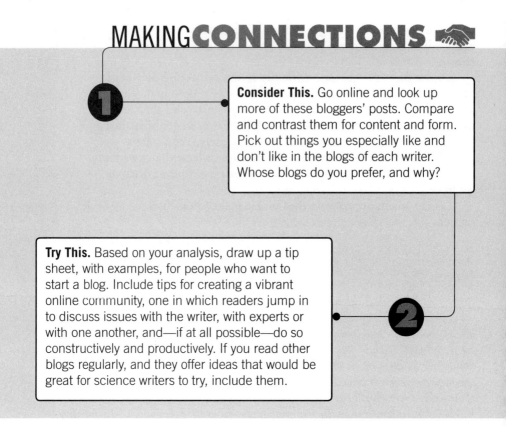

1

Consider This. Go online and look up more of these bloggers' posts. Compare and contrast them for content and form. Pick out things you especially like and don't like in the blogs of each writer. Whose blogs do you prefer, and why?

Try This. Based on your analysis, draw up a tip sheet, with examples, for people who want to start a blog. Include tips for creating a vibrant online community, one in which readers jump in to discuss issues with the writer, with experts or with one another, and—if at all possible—do so constructively and productively. If you read other blogs regularly, and they offer ideas that would be great for science writers to try, include them.

2

Selection 10.4

John Tierney writes both a blog for The Times and a column, "Findings," which runs every other week in Tuesday's Science Times. Often the topics of his columns and blogs overlap, as the following column and blog post demonstrate. Notice how Tierney uses the column to direct readers to his blog. And when you get to the blog, notice how he refers back to the column. This kind of "intertextuality" is increasingly common in media.

FINDINGS
Message in What We Buy, but Nobody's Listening
By JOHN TIERNEY

Why does a diploma from Harvard cost $100,000 more than a similar piece of paper from City College? Why might a BMW cost $25,000 more than a Subaru WRX with equally fast acceleration? Why

Published: May 19, 2009.

do "sophisticated" consumers demand 16-gigabyte iPhones and "fair trade" coffee from Starbucks?

If you ask market researchers or advertising executives, you might hear about the difference between "rational" and "emotional" buying decisions, or about products falling into categories like "hedonic" or "utilitarian" or "positional." But Geoffrey Miller, an evolutionary psychologist at the University of New Mexico, says that even the slickest minds on Madison Avenue are still in the prescientific dark ages.

Instead of running focus groups and spinning theories, he says, marketers could learn more by administering scientifically calibrated tests of intelligence and personality traits. If marketers (or their customers) understood biologists' new calculations about animals' "costly signaling," Dr. Miller says, they'd see that Harvard diplomas and iPhones send the same kind of signal as the ornate tail of a peacock.

Sometimes the message is as simple as "I've got resources to burn," the classic conspicuous waste demonstrated by the energy expended to lift a peacock's tail or the fuel guzzled by a Hummer. But brand-name products aren't just about flaunting transient wealth. The audience for our signals—prospective mates, friends, rivals—care more about the permanent traits measured in tests of intelligence and personality, as Dr. Miller explains in his new book, "Spent: Sex, Evolution and Consumer Behavior."

Suppose, during a date, you casually say, "The sugar maples in Harvard Yard were so beautiful every fall term." Here's what you're signaling, as translated by Dr. Miller:

"My S.A.T. scores were sufficiently high (roughly 720 out of 800) that I could get admitted, so my I.Q. is above 135, and I had sufficient conscientiousness, emotional stability and intellectual openness to pass my classes. Plus, I can recognize a tree."

Or suppose a young man, after listening to the specifications of the newest iPhone or hearing about a BMW's "Servotronic variable-ratio power steering," says to himself, "Those features sound awesome." Here's Dr. Miller's translation:

"Those features can be talked about in ways that will display my general intelligence to potential mates and friends, who will bow down before my godlike technopowers, which rival those of Iron Man himself."

Most of us will insist there are other reasons for going to Harvard or buying a BMW or an iPhone—and there are, of course. The education and the products can yield many kinds of rewards. But Dr. Miller says that much of the pleasure we derive from products stems from the unconscious instinct that they will either enhance or signal our fitness by demonstrating intelligence or some of the Big Five personality traits: openness, conscientiousness, agreeableness, stability and extraversion.

In a series of experiments, Dr. Miller and other researchers found that people were more likely to expend money and effort on products and activities if they were first primed with photographs of the opposite sex or stories about dating.

After this priming, men were more willing to splurge on designer sunglasses, expensive watches and European vacations. Women became more willing to do volunteer work and perform other acts of conspicuous charity—a signal of high conscientiousness and agreeableness, like demonstrating your concern for third world farmers by spending extra for Starbucks's "fair trade" coffee.

These signals can be finely nuanced, as Dr. Miller parses them in his book. The "conspicuous precision" of a BMW or a Lexus helps signal the intelligence of all the owners, but the BMW's "conspicuous reputation" also marks its owner as more extraverted and less agreeable (i.e., more aggressive). Owners of Toyotas and Hondas are signaling high conscientiousness by driving reliable and economical cars.

But once you've spent the money, once you've got the personality-appropriate appliance or watch or handbag, how much good are these signals actually doing you? Not much, Dr. Miller says. The fundamental consumerist delusion, as he calls it, is that purchases affect the way we're treated.

The grand edifice of brand-name consumerism rests on the narcissistic fantasy that everyone else cares about what we buy. (It's no accident that narcissistic teenagers are the most brand-obsessed consumers.) But who else even notices? Can you remember what your partner or your best friend was wearing the day before yesterday? Or what kind of watch your boss has?

A Harvard diploma might help get you a date or a job interview, but what you say during the date or conversation will make the difference. An elegantly thin Skagen watch might send a signal to a stranger at a cocktail party or in an airport lounge, but even if it were noticed, anyone who talked to you for just a few minutes would get a much better gauge of your intelligence and personality.

To get over your consuming obsessions, Dr. Miller suggests exercises like comparing the relative costs and pleasures of the stuff you've bought. (You can try the exercise at nytimes.com/tierneylab.) It may seem odd that we need these exercises—why would natural selection leave us with such unproductive fetishes?—but Dr. Miller says it's not surprising.

"Evolution is good at getting us to avoid death, desperation and celibacy, but it's not that good at getting us to feel happy," he says, calling our desire to impress strangers a quirky evolutionary byproduct of a smaller social world.

"We evolved as social primates who hardly ever encountered strangers in prehistory," Dr. Miller says. "So we instinctively treat all strangers as if they're potential mates or friends or enemies. But your happiness and survival today don't depend on your relationships with strangers. It doesn't matter whether you get a nanosecond of deference from a shopkeeper or a stranger in an airport."

Selection 10.5

In this blog post, Tierney does not duplicate what's in his print column on the same topic, but he provides readers with "added value." He gives readers an exercise to try at home and urges them, if they have suggestions or questions for the researcher, to make them. When this book went to press, 210 readers had responded to the post, many with the lists the exercise demanded, others with questions for the scientist who designed the exercise, still others with what they thought of the test—not much in many cases.

TierneyLab
Stop Us Before We Shop Again
By JOHN TIERNEY

Why we do compulsively shop—and how can we stop? Geoffrey Miller, the subject of my *Findings* column, has offered to answer questions from Lab readers about our obsessions for brand names and about what he calls the fundamental consumerist delusion: that people will treat us differently if we buy the right stuff.

Dr. Miller has some ideas (and an exercise I'll get to shortly) to tame the passions of brand-obsessed consumers, but he's not a dour ascetic. He doesn't denounce evil corporations for seducing customers, or denounce the vapidity of people who buy things he can't afford himself on a professor's salary. Dr. Miller, an evolutionary psychologist at the University of New Mexico, sees much of our consuming as the result of the impulse (often unconscious) to send "costly signals" to others of our intelligence and of the other Big Five personality traits—the signs of fitness that will make us more appealing to prospective mates and allies. People have always displayed fitness by one means or another, and Dr. Miller says that, by historical standards, splurging on iPhones or Viking ranges or BMWs isn't so bad.

"Consumerist capitalism is the least oppressive system of mass trait display ever developed," Dr. Miller told me. "It's much better than a militaristic dominance-based society or a theocracy or lots of other ways in which you basically display your intelligence and conscientiousness and disagreeableness by how efficiently you can oppress slaves or minority groups. But I think we can still do better."

Dr. Miller discusses some strategies for improvement in his new book, "Spent: Sex, Evolution and Consumer Behavior." He argues that people displaying stuff isn't an effective signal of fitness because it doesn't persuade (or fool) the people who matter in your life—the people who talk to you, thereby getting a far better gauge of your personality and intelligence than anything that could be signaled by your

Posted: May 18, 2009.

possessions. He urges you to put shopping in perspective by performing the following exercise:

List the ten most expensive things (products, services or experiences) that you have ever paid for (including houses, cars, university degrees, marriage ceremonies, divorce settlements and taxes). Then, list the ten items that you have ever bought that gave you the most happiness. Count how many items appear on both lists.

You're welcome to post the results of your exercise as a comment here, or to offer any other thoughts on how why we consume and what we get out of our possessions. You can also pose questions for Dr. Miller to answer in a future post here. (Here's Dr. Miller's page with some of his publications.)

Selected Comments From Readers

May 19, 2009

$
kids
divorce
house #2
house #1
Harvard
:)
guitar #1
guitar #2
kids
Harvard
many computers
Lesson—buy more guitars.

May 19, 2009

I have a major problem with this column: the use of the words "we" and "our." Compulsive shopping may be common, but it's hardly universal.

I'm one of those who've escaped the affliction: on my list of least favorite activities, the physical act of shopping falls somewhere between scrubbing the toilet and having a colonoscopy. It's not, or at least not just, a reluctance to spend money. Though I like what I do buy to show a return in the use or pleasure each item gives me, I'm no more fond of shopping for minor items like clothes than I am for more expensive ones.

That might be a good question for Dr. Miller: what creates the difference between the shopaholic and the shopping averse?

May 19, 2009

As others have said, there're too many apples & oranges. I've spent the most on health care & dentistry (which I typify as real masochism—paying someone to inflict pain on me) but I realize I'd be miserable w/o having done that. A better exercise would be listing the 10 things that give you greatest pleasure & looking at how many of them didn't cost much at all.

MAKING**CONNECTIONS**

Consider This. Compare this blog post to the related column. Based on this comparison (and any other comparisons you have time to make between related blogs and columns), what tips would you give to a Times staffer who has just been assigned to produce both a column for the print edition of the newspaper and a blog? What should a blog post do that a column doesn't, and vice-versa? Consider content, style, length and anything else that comes to mind.

Try This. Tierney's column alternates with a column by Natalie Angier called "Basics." Angier, unlike Tierney, is strictly a print columnist. She doesn't blog. But she could. Go online and find one of Angier's columns that with a little effort could invite reader participation. Using Tierney's column and blog post as inspiration, do any additional reporting you need and draft a 400-word post that could link to the column. The post should not repeat the column, but add to it in a way that will engage readers and initiate comment. If you want to "play," as Angier does in her writing, by all means do so. Sometimes imitating another writer's style stretches your own.

A Conversation with . . . **Andrew C. Revkin**

BLOGGER AND ENVIRONMENTAL WRITER

© The New York Times

As a college student, Andrew Revkin immersed himself in courses about the natural world. He aspired to be a marine biologist, but in his words, he was "too a.d.D. for a PhD," and while traveling the world on a postgraduation research fellowship, he grew fascinated by wider issues. "The interplay between people and the planet's natural wonders" particularly enthralled him, a story that in his mind was "just too good . . . to resist telling."[5]

Needing the skills to tell this story, he studied for a master's degree in journalism. He then honed his skills as a writer for Science Digest and the Los Angeles Times, as a freelancer, and as a senior editor for Discover Magazine. He also began to write books about environmental issues. Finally, in 1995, he landed a position as environment reporter for The Times, where he has covered a range of environmental issues, including Hurricane Katrina, the Arctic melt, the Asian tsunami and environmental policy and politics.

With a background in photography and an interest in art and graphics, Revkin has quickly moved to the forefront of multimedia storytelling at The Times. In 2003 he recorded video and audio while camping on the floating sea ice at the North Pole. He returned to the Arctic twice, visiting Greenland and Alaska's north slope and producing a pioneering blog, "Postcards from the Arctic." While there, he helped conceive and produce an award-winning Discovery-Times documentary, "Arctic Rush," and a companion print series, "The Big Melt."[6]

In January 2009, Revkin moved from The Times science desk to the newly created environment desk,[7] where he worked full-time until he took a buyout in December of the same year.[8] His continuing blog, "Dot Earth," which he launched in 2007, covers science and public policy issues related to population growth, diminishing resources, climate change, the loss of habitat and biodiversity and other subjects that fall under the broader issue of sustainability or "how we manage our infinite aspirations on a finite planet."

Revkin lives with his wife and two sons in the Hudson River Valley. When he is not tethered to his computer or cell phone, he writes songs and plays in a "retro-rootsy" band called Uncle Wade.

He was interviewed by telephone in the summer of 2009. It has been edited for length and flow.

I wonder if you could talk a little about the origin and evolution of your blog, Dot Earth?

Well, when I came to The Times in the mid-1990s, I had a background in photography. I had just loved photography always. So even in the '90s I focused on the pictures as well as the words. But then in 2003, I spent a couple months getting ready to go to the North Pole for the paper, and I thought: "This is a one-time opportunity, it's a very hard place to get to. It's harder than Antarctica, the South Pole, because it's sea ice floating in the ocean, not like a continent with a base and everything. If I'm going to go there, I'd better bring every possible means of collecting, of doing journalism, not just a pad and pencil." So I brought TV-quality video cameras and sound recording equipment and a satellite phone so I could send images and stories back in real time, from the ice.

One thing we did as an experiment while I was there was a reader forum on the Web. An editor put up a note saying something like, "Andy Revkin is at the North Pole. He's going to answer reader questions, so e-mail your questions and we'll post responses," and while I was out there floating on sea ice with scientists and 90 degrees north, I started answering reader questions, and that struck me as really cool. That was one of our first efforts to really do interactive journalism from the field, and I really got hooked on it.

Then when we came back, we developed a bunch of multimedia stuff on the North Pole and my experiences there. The following year, I went to Greenland, and working with a couple editors from the online side of the paper, we decided I would try to do what today you would call a blog. At that point we didn't really know what to call it yet, so we called it "Postcards from the Arctic." The most I did in a day were three or four little dispatches about what I was seeing while I was out there reporting the longer, bigger feature story that I went to work on, so I sent back photos and these little sort of mini-reports. Readers couldn't comment. I didn't have that function, so it really wasn't like a real blog yet, but it was sort of like messages from the field: Here I am to report on the reduction of the ice of this great ice sheets in Greenland, but guess what? I just bumped into a guy who is studying peregrine falcons, and this is what he had to say, and here's a picture of them tagging falcons. It had nothing to do with the bigger story, but this is the kind of thing you see as a journalist in the field, you just want to tell people about.

So I got hooked on that whole process, and from then on it's just been a progression from wanting to tell the story of our changing Earth in every possible way, not just in printed stories in a paper, made of paper, but online, using audio, video, photography, graphics and animation when possible.

So what are the biggest challenges you face in trying to tell this story of our changing Earth?

I've actually written a book chapter on this subject,[10] and the journalistic thirst for what I call the front-page thought . . . that's actually a phrase in our newsroom—the front-page thought.

Can you say more about this?

Sure. "So, you've got this story idea, Mr. Reporter." (This is the editor speaking.) "Here's this story you're pitching to me on the risk of earthquakes in Sumatra. We already know they had a big earthquake there, they had a tsunami, where is the front-page thought in that? There's more risk?"

Well, to me, if you overstate the risk, in order to serve that need to have the dramatic point that fits on the front page, that's a problem. If you are true to the science, we really don't know when this next great earthquake is going to happen along the coast of Sumatra. We know it's coming, and we know that millions of people are vulnerable, in ways that weren't that way 50 years ago. But you have to find a way to tell the story that is true to the story and doesn't artificially pump it up.

There has been a lot of pumping up in recent years, particularly on climate. There may be drama in a new study of drowning polar bears off of Alaska, but we don't really know routinely how many polar bears drown each year just as a normal matter of course. Just because a scientist saw it happen doesn't mean it's a new thing caused by global warming.

The Web process allows me to explore those questions in an open-ended way and not to sort of artificially say this new study of polar bears is the new truth. I think it is a better reflection of how science works, to say this is a journey. We're learning about polar bears. There are things we learn every day. Sometimes we unlearn things. We think we knew something and we kind of go in a new direction when new findings come out.

But how do you determine this? Because, as you know, scientists can get extremely enthusiastic about their claims, and even when findings are published in respectable peer-reviewed journals, their own thinking about their work can obscure the very uncertainties that you are talking about.

For sure, and not only just individual scientists, but you do end up sometimes with a kind of a body of thought in a field. In a field concerned with sea ice as it relates to global warming, or with a mountain species that might go extinct in a warming world, or what's happening with hurricanes through climate change, those are really small universes. Each one of them probably has 20 or 30 people deeply engaged in that question, so you end up often reviewing each other's papers, and that can lead to groupthink. And it makes it very challenging as a reporter.

So, after more than 20 years of writing about global warming, I have a list of people I've come to trust as someone I could show a paper that's coming out and get their reactions, and of course, that too is just one person's reaction. It's always imperfect, this process of determining what is a real advance in this field and what isn't. But to me it's vitally important if you have the time, and that's harder and harder these days, and if you have the background to know where there are experts you can draw on, which is getting harder and harder too. Then you do the little double-checking, the little extra due diligence, to make sure you're at least getting it relatively right in how you're casting it.

You say it's harder and harder to get the time to do these things. Why is that?
We have less time and less space than ever to convey pretty complicated ideas. I call it the tyranny of time and space. Climate and energy are not like writing about the Yankees, where everyone kind of knows the basics. We all know sort of how baseball works, for the most part, but writing about climate, you have to fit in a certain amount of explanation in any story, because you can't assume readers understand even the basics, so it's like you reinvent the wheel every time. But we don't get extra space in a newspaper because we're writing about climate. In fact, it works the other way.

But don't you get more space online?
Yeah, but then we've learned from studying about how people read online, people don't push that button that says "More." Online, we tend to read for headlines and summaries, but not read in depth, and so even though I always thought when I first started working online, "This is great, we can fit in the longer version of the story that didn't make it into print," and I do sometimes put that all in there, I have to recognize most people won't see it. The good news is it's there for those of us who want it.

You said finding sources is more and more difficult too . . .
In areas, it's easier. If you're artful at Googling, for example, I think it's pretty easy, if you know generally how to look for things. I think it's possible, although that has its perils as well. There is a huge amount of disingenuous content online, and if you don't have at least some sense of how to determine what's real and what's not real, or who is a serious professor doing serious peer-reviewed work in a field versus someone who has just got a blog, that can be a problem. That can lead you in wrong directions.

Have you developed any rules of thumb to handle this issue?
The key is to know what you're writing about. If it's a news study on amphibians and climate change, what you want to do is quickly find people who have worked in that field, so then when you're searching online, you put in key words that relate to that. When I'm searching for a professor's home page, I include "fax," because that implies they are going to go to a page that has the person's contact information, and "edu," which will direct you to university sites more than others, so if you have "edu," "fax" and "amphibian, and climate, and tropical" if its tropics, I guarantee that will lead you to some serious people right away.

Sometimes I will collect four or five such people, and I'll e-mail them all, in a cc, a question. I'll say I write for Publication X. I'm doing an article about whether amphibians are dying from a fungus or from climate change, and here's a new paper, and what do you think? That way they see each other's names and they can respond to each other, and you start a little conversation sometimes, which I think has been very valuable. I did a blog post where I actually included some of those exchanges, that people could see. This was on this newly revealed pattern of droughts in Africa, and it was fascinating to show readers kind of the raw input that I get, and show them the tensions that can arise from scientists working in fields that relate to global warming.[11]

How has blogging changed the whole journalism process for you?

Well, it's harder work. One thing I try hard to do, and I think blogging helps to do it, is to remind readers that disagreement is the norm, that the growth of a scientific understanding emerges from dispute and debate and this sort of piranha-style nibbling that happens, where someone has an idea that pushes the envelope in a new direction, and others test that idea really strongly. That's normal. Just because scientists are disagreeing with each other doesn't mean we don't know anything! I'm desperate to break that pattern.

So have you developed guidelines for when experts disagree?

In the end, it all really should come down to data. As everyone who understands science knows, it's not a belief system. It's not about believing in global warming or believing a species will go extinct. It's about understanding and knowing the levels of clarity, the levels of uncertainty, and so if I see scientists who are speaking definitively, that immediately for me raises little warning signs. Because except for the basic forcing you get in the atmosphere from a molecule of carbon dioxide, there is nothing, particularly in climate, that isn't uncertain because of all the things that are required for you to get a lot of warming out of a buildup of greenhouse gases. Clouds can work in different directions, you get more clouds, on and on.

So as soon as you get away from that basic fundamental question of how much carbon dioxide is being added, and how much is that going to warm the world, it gets very complicated. So, if people are speaking in definitive terms, and there have been some very popular people out there in the last few years who really did this, you've got to really dig in and say, how do we know that? Which thing is this? When you are talking definitively, are you talking about the basic question, if we add greenhouse gases to the atmosphere, is that going to warm the planet? Or are you talking about hurricanes in a warming world? Entirely different question, with much more uncertainty.

So, that is an important thing, just to be sure you understand what is the question that we're all addressing here. And then to ask what do you know? What do you do? Find out if a scientist works in that field. One of the great challenges of global warming science now is that it is about the most multi-disciplinary issue you can imagine. It relates to everything from atmospheric chemistry and physics to biology, oceanography, computer science, statistics, and glaciology. It's all intertwined. The level of sea level rise has so many components that it's sort of dizzying.

So if someone is out there making loud, dramatic claims about sea level, one way or the other, it's well, what aspect of this do you work on yourself? What is your level of knowledge of what we're talking about? That is important. It doesn't mean a really smart person who isn't deeply immersed in every aspect of that doesn't have a role to play in discourse on it; it just means you have to be a little more careful.

What about the politics of environmental science, or the politics of global climate change science? How do you deal with that?

One of the harsh realities about global warming is that the heart of how we make money in this country still relies mainly on fossil fuels and how we live our comfortable lives. If it were something that didn't have that import, well, we wouldn't be writing about it as much, but also it would be easier to write about. But because it challenges 250-year-old norms, or 150-year-old norms for energy and for how we run our economy and how we think about our choices in our lives, it comes with an extra level of needing to be sure you understand who is speaking to you and why.

As a journalist, you're responsible for a couple of things. One is, again, knowing what the story is. If it's about trends on sea ice on the Arctic Ocean, then I talk to scientists, and maybe to people who are thinking about expanding oil exploration in the Arctic or the Inuit communities who are worried about limited ability to travel on the ice to hunt seals, but I don't necessarily take it beyond that. If the story is about the climate legislation, then everybody has a voice in the story, including Exxon/Mobile, including Peabody Energy (the giant coal company) because when you're in the policy arena, it is suddenly a much broader question. The science essentially provides the framework for how we examine the choices society has, but it's not just about science anymore. And that means also, in a story about the climate bill, you would talk to Greenpeace and you would talk to Environmental Defense Fund and you would talk to the National Association of Manufacturers.

While we're on politics, journalism no less than science is subject to those political pressures, no?

Well, on my blog, we get lots of complaints. One guy in particular posts comments every day about our accepting ads from Exxon/Mobile, as we cover these issues. But I have never yet seen what I would say is a cause-and-effect relationship between our imperative to attract advertising and to also cover the news.

If you had one piece of advice for aspiring environmental reporters, what would it be?

We're living in an amazing moment, where humans, everything about us is cresting in a way that has never happened before, and probably will never happen again. It is this great pulse of humanity going from one billion to nine billion between 1800 and 2050, and we're right at the crest. Plenty of species have come and gone and become planetary forces. Plants in general, they oxygenated the atmosphere. They didn't know it, though. Dinosaurs ruled the world. They didn't appreciate that. They didn't have an awareness of it. We have this unique moment where we have become a planetary force, we have a growing recognition of that and we're stuck in our own tension between our instincts and our intellect, and that is a fabulous story that needs to be explored and revealed and how that plays out is the story of our time. We are the story of our time.

So it's a great time to be immersed in this field, but it has to be thought of in a way that is very much outside the traditional framing of environment, which is "there is some pollution coming from some very bad person doing something over there, and we need to fix that." This is very different than that.

How so?

The real story is we've grown up as a society with norms that don't look like they can be sustained without really disrupting things on this planet in ways that will probably be unpleasant, and where does that leave us? What do we need to push through this transition in a smoother way? And that innovation is part of the environment story to me for that reason too. So that's why I keep swinging back to that as well.

We as journalists have to be caustically honest about our own perceptions and what the story is here. What is the real problem? And what are the real solutions? We have to worry less about traditional framing: It is a pollution problem, we need a regulation and it will go away, that kind of thing. That's less and less relevant, I think. At least in developed countries. It's like what can the rich world do to facilitate a smoother transition for the poorer countries, that without help will simply replicate our history of heavy pollution and social disruption before they get to be rich and clean?

So your one piece of advice for aspiring environmental writers is . . . ?

It's a great time to be a communicator on the intersection of humans and their habitat. I think of communication more than journalism. Journalism is a part of this thing called communication, and whatever comes in these next two decades will have components of that. It is a great time to be communicating about humans and their habitat.

TIMES WRITERS ON SCIENCE, SCIENCE NEWS AND PUBLIC PERCEPTIONS OF SCIENCE

Altman, Lawrence K., M.D. "The Doctor's World: For Science's Gatekeepers, a Credibility Gap." The New York Times, May 2, 2006.

The Times' resident physician examines the merits of the peer-review system in science and medicine. The system has its problems: "If peer review were a drug," say its critics, "it would never be marketed."

Goleman, Daniel. "Hidden Rules Often Distort Ideas of Risk." The New York Times, Feb. 1, 1994. (With chart: "Ranking Risks: Reality and Perceptions.")

Scientists have identified a variety of "outrage" factors that skew public perceptions of risk. Former New York Times reporter Daniel Goleman reports on these factors and how they often lead to a mismatch between actual and perceived risks. Goleman doesn't fall into the trap of portraying experts' risk estimates as right and public perceptions of risk as wrong. The implications of scientists' research on this topic are as true today as they were when Goleman wrote this story: The reality is that experts and lay people can have different perceptions of risks based on values, and both perceptions can have validity.

Kaufman, Joanne. "Need Press? Repeat: 'Green,' 'Sex,' 'Cancer,' 'Secret,' 'Fat': The Unsubtle Art of Composing a News Release." The New York Times, June 30, 2008.

According to one PR consultant, "If you say something is first, most, fastest, tallest—that's likely to get attention. If you can use the words like 'money,' 'fat,' 'cancer' or 'sex,' you're likely to get some ink in the general audience media." This story—which begins with the case of the toxic shower curtain—catalogues the many ways research is hyped to get media attention.

Kolata, Gina. "Experts Strive to Put Diseases in Proper Perspective." The New York Times, July 2, 2002. (With chart: "Assigning Numbers to Health Risks.")

How a risk estimate is presented can have a significant effect on people's perceptions of the dangers to themselves. In this piece, medical writer Gina Kolata reveals some of the ways advocacy groups have manipulated public perceptions and concerns, leading people to exaggerate the risks of getting and dying from dreaded diseases. The experts Kolata interviews advocate presenting estimates in context and moving away from statistics to put risks in terms of individual people.

_____. "Searching for Clarity: A Primer on Studies." The New York Times, Sept. 30, 2008.

Appearing in a special Science Times section, "Decoding Your Health," this article discusses the difference between observational studies and randomized clinical trials, using beta-carotene as an example. The article was accompanied by an informative graphic—"How to Read a Medical Study (Skeptical)"— which walked readers through three articles on beta-carotene, beginning with a review article in 1981. That article concluded that the more beta-carotene in people's blood the lower their risk of cancer. The final article, in 1996, was based on a randomized clinical trial and concluded that beta-carotene had no effect on cancer rates, after all.

Revkin, Andrew C. "In Debate on Climate Change, Exaggeration Is a Common Pitfall." The New York Times, Feb. 25, 2009.

In this news analysis, environment reporter Andrew C. Revkin discusses how easily climate change science gets hyped by figures on both the left and the right, confusing the public and polarizing debate on this important issue.

_____. "News Analysis: Climate Experts Tussle Over Details. Public Gets Whiplash." The New York Times, July 29, 2008.

In another news analysis, Revkin discusses the cognitive whiplash that the public can experience when contradictory findings are reported one right after the other, as they historically have been in medical science, and as they often are now in the science of global climate change. His reporting uncovers some potential remedies.

Wade, Nicholas. "Crumpled Papers: Lowering Expectations at Science's Frontier." The New York Times, Jan. 15, 2006.

Writer Nicholas Wade explains the difference between emerging (or "frontier") science and "textbook" science.

DISCUSSIONS BETWEEN TIMES JOURNALISTS AND THEIR READERS

Periodically, Times editors, reporters, columnists and executives respond to readers' e-mailed questions in an online feature called "Talk to The Times." Several of the journalists who have contributed to this Reader had done so when this book went to press, including Laura Chang, science editor; Henry Fountain, science writer; Amy Harmon, national correspondent; and Dennis Overbye, physics writer. Deputy science editor Barbara Strauch has also responded to readers' questions, along with The Times' graphics director, the editor of the Web newsroom and members of The Times' Interactive News Collaborative. Go to: www.nytimes.com/ref/business/media/asktheeditors.html/.

OTHER COLLECTIONS OF SCIENCE WRITING

"The Best American Science Writing" (New York: HarperCollins, annual) and
"The Best American Science and Nature Writing" (New York: Houghton
Mifflin and Houghton Mifflin Harcourt, annual).

*These annual collections of science and nature writing aren't "readers" that
explicitly show how to read—and learn—from others' work, as this Reader does.
But the newspaper and magazine articles they contain comprise some of the best
science writing of the year in the judgment of the scientists and science writers
who have selected them. Great for bedside reading.*

Zivkovic, Bora, series ed. "The Open Laboratory: The Best Writing on Science
Blogs." Lulu.com, annual.

*You are not likely to find these collections in your neighborhood bookstore, but
if you have an interest in science blogging, you can download copies from the
publisher for a small fee. The posts are by a variety of science bloggers—from
award-winning science writer Carl Zimmer, whose work is also featured in this
Reader, to blogs by graduate students in the sciences. Top posts are selected with
the assistance of the science-blogging community, and the collection is released in
conjunction with ScienceOnline, an annual meeting about science on the Web:
www.scienceonline2010.com/index.php/wiki/.*

PROFESSIONAL ASSOCIATIONS FOR SCIENCE WRITERS

National Association of Science Writers (NASW): www.nasw.org

*NASW is the premier professional association for science writers who work to
convey science to the public through the news media. Membership includes
writers for magazines, newspapers, broadcast media, Web sites and blogs, as well
as public information officers, educators and students. The association produces
a quarterly newsletter and holds an annual meeting in conjunction with science
briefings organized by the Council for the Advancement of Science Writing.
It also gives several awards for outstanding science writing. In 2009 NASW's
award for excellence in medical writing went to The Times' Denise Grady,
whose work appears in this collection and whose insights on science writing
appear in the Q&A at the end of Chapter 1.*

Society for Environmental Journalists (SEJ): www.sej.org

*The Society for Environmental Journalists aims to advance the public's
understanding of environmental issues. The SEJ publishes a newsletter, supports
an active discussion list and mentoring program for members and holds
an annual meeting that brings together scientists, policymakers, journalists
and others for workshops and panel discussions. To maintain journalistic
independence, the organization restricts voting membership to working
journalists and refuses financial support from industry and environmental
organizations. Full-time students of accredited institutions are eligible for
academic membership.*

University Research Magazine Association (URMA): www.urma.org

This professional organization is for editors, writers, designers and others who produce magazines about research and scholarship conducted at universities, nonprofit research centers or institutes. The magazines cover faculty work in both the sciences and the humanities and are targeted to lay audiences, usually these organizations' constituents. URMA holds an annual conference on rotating campuses.

BOOKS AND ESSAYS ABOUT SCIENCE WRITING

Blum, Deborah, and Mary Knudson, eds. "A Field Guide for Science Writers." New York: Oxford University Press, 2005.

Produced by members of the National Association of Science Writers, this collection of essays by outstanding science writers discusses the many opportunities and challenges of a career in science writing. Despite significant changes in media and in science since its publication, much of the information and advice remains up to date. The Guide includes an essay by The Times' Andrew Revkin, who is featured in this Reader.

Bubela, Tania, Matthew C. Nisbet, Rick Borchelt, Fern Brunger, Cristine Critchley, Edna Einsiedel, Gail Geller, Anil Gupta, Jurgen Hampel, Robyn Hyde-Lay, Eric W. Jandciu, Ashley Jones, Pam Kolopack, Summer Lane, Tim Lougheed, Brigitte Nerlich, Ubaka Ogbogu, Kathleen O'Riordan, Collin Ouellette, Mike Spear, Stephen Strauss, Thushaanthini Thavaratnam, Lisa Willemse and Timothy Caulfield. "Science Communication Reconsidered." Nature Biotechnology 27 (2009): 514–518.

For the more academically minded, this commentary in Nature Biotechnology reviews what academics have learned about the public communication of science, considers many of the challenges for scientists and science writers in this age of new media and growing private financing of academic research and offers recommendations to enhance the communication of science to the public. The commentary grew out of a workshop on science communication involving experts from the United States, the United Kingdom, Canada, Germany and Australia.

Friedman, Sharon M., Sharon Dunwoody and Carol Rogers, eds. "Communicating Uncertainty: Media Coverage of New and Controversial Science." Mahwah, N.J.: Lawrence Erlbaum Associates, 1999.

A readable introduction by science communication scholars, science writers and others to the timeless challenges that the unknowns and uncertainties of emerging science present for science journalists. (Disclosure: One of the chapters is by the first author of this Reader.)

Mooney, Chris. "Blinded by Science: How 'Balanced' Coverage Lets the Scientific Fringe Hijack Reality." Columbia Journalism Review (Nov./Dec. 2004).

In this essay, author and science blogger Chris Mooney makes a forceful argument against the kind of journalistic balance that gives equal weight to unequally weighted scientific evidence.

notes

preface

1. Sylvia Nasar, ed., "The Best American Science Writing" (New York: Harper Perennial, 2008), viii–ix.
2. These elements are ordered from most to least important. Students who examine elements of writing in this order will come to see that editing and writing problems often go back to organizational issues, and organizational problems to reporting issues, and reporting problems to matters of story focus. So the first thing to check for, when evaluating one's own work or that of others, is a strong, fresh focus, then the reporting, then organization, then the writing and finally the editing.
3. In my own classes, I have sometimes brought in a scientist who is willing to discuss his or her discovery with the entire class; other times I have simply sent students out to find and write up their own discovery stories. The first approach tends to offer more opportunity for learning, as students will make mistakes that are instructive for everyone. But the second approach gets students writing what they want to write about from the get-go. I've done both, and both ways can work.
4. Claudia Dreifus, who writes most of the Q&As for Science Times, has written about the process in a collection of her work, "Scientific Conversations: Interviews on Science from The New York Times" (New York: Times Books, 2002).
5. In my own teaching, I've often chosen a book for the class to read in common. If you let the students know about the book assignment early enough (and even read a few chapters together at the start), students can be reading the book the entire term. Usually I have asked the students to write their reviews for a newsletter for science writers, so they can read to learn more about reporting and writing techniques of the author and not duplicate what reviewers have written for other audiences. It's also possible, of course, for the students to choose their own books (or films) to review—and if the books are new enough, to even sell the reviews to college or university alumni magazines or to newspaper book review editors hungry for material. Each approach has its advantages.

introduction

1. One such site, begun in 2009, is Futurity (http://futurity.org).
2. Jane Harrigan, a former journalist who taught at the University of New Hampshire for years, came up with this clever mnemonic.
3. A number of the pieces in "The New York Times Reader" appeared with corrections online. For all but one of the pieces (an op-ed piece by a scientist), those corrections have been made in the text.

part I

1. Talk to the Newsroom: Dennis Overbye, Science Reporter, The New York Times, July 7, 2008.

chapter 1 • discoveries

1. See, for example, Fiona Clark and Deborah L. Illman, "A Longitudinal Study of the New York Times Science Times Section," Science Communication 27 (June 2006): 496.
2. This number comes from search of peer-reviewed, scientific journals in English-speaking countries conducted by reference librarians at Indiana University–Bloomington in the fall of 2009. It is a rough estimate obtained by averaging the results of searches that used multiple search tools.
3. Nicholas Wade, "Crumpled Papers: Lowering Expectations at Science's Frontier," The New York Times, Jan. 15, 2006. In this article Wade explains the difference between "frontier" (or emerging) science and "textbook" science.
4. For several articles that report on or illustrate the changing nature of emerging science, see Jane Brody, "Analysis of 23 Studies Suggests Abortion Can Slightly Raise the Risk of Breast Cancer," The New York Times, Oct. 12, 1996; Jane Brody, "Big Study Finds No Link in Abortion and Cancer," The New York Times, Jan. 9, 1997; and Gina Kolata, "Study Dismisses Protein's Role in Heart Disease," The New York Times, June 30, 2009.
5. Eliot Marshall, "Embargoes: Good, Bad, or 'Necessary Evil'?" Science 282, no. 5930 (Oct. 30, 1998): 860—867.
6. Denise Grady, "Deadly Invaders: Marburg Virus, Bird Flu, And Other Emerging Viruses" (Boston: Kingfisher Publications, 2006).
7. Jane E. Brody and reporters of The New York Times, "The New York Times Book of Women's Health," ed. Denise Grady (New York: Lebhar-Friedman Books, 2000), and Jane E. Brody, Denise Grady and reporters of The New York Times, "The New York Times Guide to Alternative Health" (New York: Times Books, Henry Holt and Company, 2001).
8. Gina Kolata, "Studies Find Beta Carotene, Used by Millions, Doesn't Forestall Cancer or Heart Disease," The New York Times, Jan. 19, 1996.
9. Denise Grady, "Doctors Put Hope in Thin Wires To Ease the Clutches of Epilepsy," The New York Times, May 24, 2004.

chapter 2 • meetings

1. See, for example, Andrew C. Revkin, "The Daily Planet: Why the Media Stumble Over the Environment," in Deborah Blum, Mary Knudson and Robin Marantz Henig, eds., "A Field Guide for Science Writers," 2nd ed. (New York: Oxford University Press, 2005): www.onthemedia.org/episodes/2006/12/08/chapter.html.

chapter 3 • explanatory features

1. Marcela Valdes, "Angier Dives in Again," Publisher's Weekly, March 5, 2007, on Natalie Angier's personal Web site: www.natalieangier.com
2. Angier's first book was "Natural Obsessions: Striving to Unlock the Deepest Secrets of the Cancer Cell" (New York: Houghton Mifflin Company, 1988), a work she calls "an inside look at the high-throttle world of cancer research."

In addition, she has written "Woman: An Intimate Geography" (New York: Houghton Mifflin Company, 1999), what she calls "a celebration of the female body and biology," and "The Canon: A Whirligig Tour of the Beautiful Basics of Science" (New York: Houghton Mifflin Company, 2007), what one critic called a "romp" through the basic principles of science. She also has edited a collection of her Times pieces on invertebrates, "The Beauty of the Beastly" (New York: Mariner Books, 1996), and "The Best American Science and Nature Writing" (Houghton Mifflin Company, 2002 and Ecco: Harper Collins Publisher, 2009.)

3. For a story that made me laugh out loud, see Natalie Angier, "Why Babies Are Born Facing Backward, Helpless and Chubby," The New York Times, July 23, 1996. (But then, I've given birth twice.)

4. Natalie Angier, "Basics: Taxing, a Ritual to Save the Species," The New York Times, April 13, 2009.

5. Natalie Angier, "The Canon: A Whirligig Tour of the Beautiful Basics of Science" (Boston: Houghton Mifflin Harcourt, 2007), 190.

6. Natalie Angier, "Many Women Buy Foot Trouble With Fashionable High Heels," The New York Times, March 7, 1991.

7. Natalie Angier, "Busy as a Bee? Then Who's Doing the Work?" The New York Times, July 30, 1991.

chapter 4 • stories about scientists

1. Christopher Frayling, "Mad, Bad and Dangerous?: The Scientist and the Cinema" (London: Reaktion, 2005).

2. To find more profiles, go to "Scientists at Work" on The Times Web site, or check out this book: Laura Chang, ed., "Scientists at Work: Profiles of Today's Groundbreaking Scientists from Science Times" (New York: McGraw Hill, 2000).

3. For more of this writer's Q&As, and a discussion of how she does these interviews, see Claudia Dreifus, "Scientific Conversations: Interviews on Science from The New York Times" (New York: Times Books, 2002).

4. Nicholas Wade, "Taking a Cue from Ants on Evolution of Humans," The New York Times, July 15, 2008.

chapter 5 • trends, issues and other stories

1. William E. Blundell, "The Art and Craft of Feature Writing" (New York: Plume, 1988), 70–76. Blundell explains these elements more completely in his book. Decades of students have found his advice extremely helpful, especially if you want to learn to write compelling trend stories and profiles.

2. Alison Gopnick, "Cells That Read Minds? What the Myth of Mirror Neurons Gets Wrong about the Human Brain," Slate, April 26, 2007.

chapter 6 • extended narratives

1. Roy Peter Clark, "Writing Tools: From Telegraph to Twitter: The Language of the Short Form," posted on PoynterOnline, Sept. 4, 2009.

2. Sylvia Nasar, ed., "The Best American Science Writing 2008" (New York: Harper Perennial, 2008).

3. Jon Franklin, "Writing for Story: Craft Secrets of Dramatic Nonfiction" (New York: Atheneum, 1986).

chapter 9 • essays

1. Phillip Lopate, ed., "The Art of the Personal Essay: An Anthology from the Classical Era to the Present" (New York: Anchor Books, Doubleday, 1994), xxxviii.
2. Ibid., xlv.

chapter 10 • blogs and columns

1. Curtis Brainard, "Q&A: Andrew Revkin, NYT Reporter Discusses Climate, Sustainability, and Long-haul Reporting," Columbia Journalism Review, Dec. 16, 2008.
2. Pat Walter, "Beat Talk: Using New Media Tools to Beef up Environmental Reporting," PoynterOnline, Oct. 23, 2006.
3. Consider the immensely popular David Pogue whose amusing reviews of new communication technologies often pull out all the technological stops. Pogue's wide-ranging use of online media can be observed by going to: http://pogue .blogs.nytimes.com.
4. Zachary Roth, "The Problem with John Tierney," Columbia Journalism Review, Dec. 1, 2004.
5. Q&A with Andrew Revkin: www.journalism.columbia.edu.
6. Andrew Revkin, "The Big Melt" series, Oct. 10, 20 and 25, 2005.
7. Curtis Brainard, "Environmental S.W.A.T. Team: New York Times's New 'Pod' Gathers Talent from Multiple Beats," Columbia Journalism Review, Jan. 13, 2009.
8. Cristine Russell, "The Observatory—Revkin Taking NYT Buyout: Veteran Climate Reporter to Leave Paper after Copenhagen Summit," Columbia Journalism Review, Dec. 14, 2009.
9. Andrew C. Revkin, "The Daily Planet: Why the Media Stumble Over the Environment," in Deborah Blum, Mary Knudson and Robin Marantz Henig, eds., "A Field Guide for Science Writers," 2nd ed. (New York: Oxford University Press, 2005).
10. Andrew Revkin, "Dot Earth blog. Debate Over Climate Risks—Natural or Not," The New York Times, April 16, 2009.